Peter Blazey graduated from Melbourne University in Political Science. He joined the *Australian* newspaper in 1967 before publishing his first book, a biography of Henry Bolte, in 1972. He became press secretary to Moss Cass in the Whitlam Government and co-authored *The Political Dicemen* in 1975.

He stood as the Gay Liberation candidate during a NSW state by-election in 1978, before returning to journalism, writing for the *National Times*, the *Nation Review*, the *Weekend Australian*, the *Financial Review* and as a columnist on the *Bulletin*.

In 1993 he published the satirical work *The Secret Diary of Jeffrey Kennett* and in 1995 was co-editor of the Australian fiction anthology *Love Cries*. A columnist on the gay magazine *OutRage* for over five years, Peter Blazey died of an AIDS-related illness in 1997.

ACKNOWLEDGEMENTS

My thanks to the many people who helped me in the writing of this book, especially to editor Virginia Fraser for her lavishly lateral approach to my manuscript; Picador editor Virginia Lloyd for her logic and patience; Con Anemogiannis for his witty boutades and cutting computer skills; Lyn Tranter, whose stalwart advice kept the show on the road; Rhyll Nance and the Australian Centre of the University of Melbourne; Jim Hillman, an adept researcher; Dick Briggs at Scotch College; Robin Gerster and Jon Basset for their book *Seizures of Youth: The Sixties and Australia* (Melbourne: Hyland House, 1991); William Yang, Julia Perry, Beatrice Faust, Judith Hall, Dr Michael Keating, Danny Aboud, Christopher Pearl, David Wilson, Kristin Williamson, Phillip Knightley, Clive Blazey, Sasha Soldatow, Alex Kaufman, Shar Adams, Joanne Burns, Philip Sargeant, Jonathan King, Tim Cooper, Crusader and Rowland at Hares and Hyenas. I am grateful to Hilary McPhee, whose idea it was; and to Tim Herbert for his support throughout the project and who inspired me to finish it.

The names of some figures in this book have been changed.

Screw Loose

Screw Loose

Peter Blazey

GAZEBO BOOKS
ELIZABETH BAY
2018

Gazebo Books
PO Box 752
Potts Point
New South Wales 1335
Australia
gazebobooks.com.au

First published 1997 in Picador by Pan Macmillan Australia Pty Limited

Acknowledgements are due to the following authors and publishers for permission to quote from: Hal Porter, *The Watcher on the Cast Iron Balcony* (UQP, 1993); Thomas Szasz, *The Therapeutic State* (Prometheus Press, 1984)

National Library of Australia
Cataloguing-in-Publication Entry
Blazey, Peter, 1939–1997.
Screw Loose
Second edition
ISBN 978 0 9876191 0 5 (paperback)

Cover and interior design by Mountains Brown Press
Printed and bound by Ligare Book Printers, Australia

Photograph on pages 336-337 by William Yang

CONTENTS

FOREWORD

The Hon. Michael Kirby AC CMG*

Peter Blazey and I were both born in the same year, 1939. Though we hated to admit it, we were both pre-war babies. We both discovered our sexual orientation at an early age and tried to keep it a secret for a very long time. We both enjoyed a sound, traditional education in famous schools – his private, mine public. We were both active in student politics and interested in changing the world. With the advent of the Boeing 707, we both explored the world and saw more than a few flesh pots. And yet, after more adventures than I ever dreamed of, he became infected with HIV and died 20 years ago. I did not. I have been asked to introduce this second edition of his biography, first published in the year of his death, 1997. I do so with enthusiasm.

In a wild and exuberant life Peter Blazey went through many lovers and partners. For the last six years Tim Herbert accompanied him on the journey to the end of his life. Tim's beautiful epilogue republished in this book is a piece of poetry. He, not I, should be writing this reflection on Peter Blazey's

---

* Former Justice of the High Court of Australia (1996-2009).

life and book. The fact that I was chosen suggests that a different perspective was desired. However, our hero's life was not one that can be easily reduced to dispassion and clinical analysis.

Scattered throughout this book are the names of countless contemporaries whom Peter Blazey and I knew at roughly the same times. So far as I know, we never met. Whereas he confronted and defied the conventional sexual mores of the fifties and sixties, I basically conformed to the unnatural demands that were placed upon him and me by Australian society in those years. Whereas for him, the Anglican Church brought childhood sexual experiences, for me the ecstasy was ethereal and confined to the local church choir and the beauty of the Book of Common Prayer. Whereas for him school delivered moments of sexual bliss, for me good grades and loneliness were all I won. Whereas he used his adventures in university student engagements to secure insider jobs for Ministers, Coalition and Labor, at a time of great changes in Australia, I kept my head down. I saved up my reforming zeal for later: as very many LGBTIQ Australians did at that time. Peter Blazey bucked the system. He stood up for himself. I cannot but admire him.

As this book shows, he had real courage and fearlessness that sometimes bordered on the reckless. He refused to be intimidated or bullied; and this helped shape his life. He had a strong commitment to his family. This resulted in a struggle for acceptance. It led him to some bizarre engagements, striving against all the odds to prove that he was at least bisexual and maybe able to turn straight or nearly so. A last minute cancellation of his black-tie wedding saw guests flying from far and wide who doubtless cursed him for going too far this time. He tagged himself 'a political bisexual'. But basically he was a radical gay man and a reformist.

Peter Blazey eventually came clean with his family about his sexuality. Despite his mother's warning, it did not kill his father, who had known for years. He took his university student activism seriously. He became a paid-up member of the radical anti-Vietnam War generation. He was there when the first Mardi Gras Parade occurred in Sydney ('our own Stonewall'). He took part in the resistance to police and the political oppression of gay men. As time went on, he became ever bolder. From his family and friends he rejected *toleration*. By then, nothing less than *acceptance* would do. He rejoiced in countless sexual experiences. Not for him the quiet respectability of straight-like relationships in the Australian suburbs. He confronted those homosexuals who were searching for respectability with the demand, when standing for election to the NSW Parliament, "Put a Poofter into Parliament".

Peter Blazey rejected rational persuasion as the only means to secure the repeal of the old gay crimes. Instead he set out to shame our timid politicians into belatedly enacting the necessary reforms. Truly, in his political and journalistic lives, as his sexual and drug infused energies reached their zenith, he was bold, experimental and determined to taste most of life's experiences to the full. His confrontational, helter-skelter life doubtless upset a lot of those around him.

And yet, looking back, we can now see that Peter Blazey was right in much that he did. For too long, too many (myself included) hoped, in the face of all the evidence, that science, rationality, patience and politeness would secure gay equality and reform. Peter Blazey knew that noise and outrage were required to win traction from the apathetic, indifferent and timid political process in Australia. He was a change agent. Not all of what he did was helpful. But he was correct in his belief that confronting prejudice and slapping its venomous face was sometimes an essential step to advance change.

The last part of Peter Blazey's story concerns his struggle with HIV and ultimate death from AIDS. He later pinpointed exactly the transient sexual encounter in Manhattan that had exposed him to HIV and set him on the journey to his death. He wrote that he never regretted the sublime sexual experience of that event. Yet in those early days, like my partner Johan and me, he knew many friends who died for want of an effective therapy. This was a fearsome time for gay men in Australia. It is still a time of dread in many places in our world. The advent of antiretroviral drugs came just too late to save Peter Blazey's life. This was the ultimate challenge that he was forced to address. He had not believed that an effective therapy would come quickly. But that it would come yet not save his life was a hard discovery. He was sustained during that time of turmoil by the love of Tim Herbert.

Peter Blazey's life had been rich and eventful. Although unexpectedly cut short, he had made it his business to challenge convention and ideology. He had done so with exuberance and wit. He cherished some words that Patrick White had written. They exemplified, contrary to White's disdain, his own outlook precisely. He sought to experience "a life so lived as to outstrip all discretion". In this, substantially, he succeeded.

Yet, the closing chapters of this book reveal a different side to Peter Blazey as he journeyed to a conclusion that finally began to tame even his wild spirit. He reached a point where he declared himself ready to die. He embraced a kind of stoicism. He seemed to attribute this to a late encounter with Buddhism. However, when he launched the first edition of his book, the writer Frank Moorhouse declared a feeling of sadness about this stoicism. It was so alien to the values Peter Blazey had lived to the full: *"I think Peter wanted, figuratively, to cry about his life and, in part, he did not deserve to be allowed to cry about his life. Instead, both in the book and in life, he gave such a superb example of bravado. For me he exemplified bravado. Bravado in the face of the inexplicable, in the face of angst and in the face of the petty, and not so petty, injustices of the world. That's how I will remember him."*

None of us can ever entirely shake off the influences of our early years. In Peter Blazey's case, they were the deep enduring memories of his wealthy, privileged family; of his school with fife and drum that celebrated endurance; and of his final illness that made it so difficult to be joyful, even for a man who had made joy into a new and passionate art form.

Peter Blazey's life still carries lessons for the very different world of today. If he had lived on to old age, he would still be saying many of the same things as are recorded in this book. Necessary reforms to secure full equality for gays and other minorities should be delayed no longer. Leadership is necessary. If only leadership had been there, Australia's contemptible delay over gay marriage would have evaporated overnight. "The whole thing was over in a week. There was no backlash; a courageous [leader] would have done it years earlier" (p. 329). Peter Blazey declared "every act of gay visibility is good in itself… Gay liberation is about personal resistance and public affirmation. It is one of the only ways we can beat the many forces that still want to keep us isolated, fearful and silent".

There are still isolated fearful silent people around. And these include frightened, ashamed, suicidal LGBTIQ school children, denied knowledge of their normality and assurance about their grand potential. To them Peter Blazey still speaks with clarity. Be bold. Enjoy life. And be yourself, he is saying. Stand up for others and against the enemies of justice and equality. He is right. So we still need the voice of Peter Blazey. And that is why this second edition of his life story is timely and important.

11 February 2018

Earth and Water

Looking back I wonder if I didn't do it a tiny bit to spite my mother.
Christopher Isherwood

A five-year-old boy is watching a swarthy, nuggety man bending over his vegetable patch. The old man is digging up onions, tugging and cursing and sweating. They are both naked.

'Get out of that ground there, you bloody little bugger.'

He is addressing a big Spanish onion, bashing the dirt off it on the back of his spade. He tells his grandson to wipe the onion clean before putting it in a bucket.

This old man was my maternal grandfather, Bradford Smith, or as I called him then, 'Poppop'. He usually worked in his vegetable garden alone, but occasionally he invited me to his patch. As an ardent nudist, he was lucky to have this private sun-soaked island in the middle of Balwyn. Surrounded by a cypress hedge where the Outer Circle railway used to run, and a high, knothole-free paling fence that went the length of Barnsbury Road, secure on all sides, it was the perfect cubbyhole of my childhood. Silver-haired Brad had turned this secluded occupied triangle into his own nudist paradise, while paying the Victorian Railways a peppercorn rent. Such a deal was typical of his go-getting capitalist spirit. My father, who disliked Brad, used to say he operated on the principle of what's mine is mine and what's yours is mine too.

In those early days of World War II, my father Alan was away serving with the Ordnance Corps in New Guinea and later in Whitehall, London, where he once shared an elevator with Prime Minister Churchill. When he returned from the war in 1946 bearing presents, I was six years old. He was a stranger. I thought Brad had stayed at home especially to look after me: he was my 'real' dad.

Brad was a nuggety nimbus of sexual energy. In those days I loved him dearly. To my young eyes he seemed like an old, old man with his white hair, yet he was not much older than I am now, in his late fifties. He had a trim, tanned body, flinty brown eyes, flappy ears and a huge, pitted 'strawberry nose'. He also had a large circumcised dick and a protuberant old man's scrotum, the first I'd ever seen. He bent low, while tending the carrots, the broad beans and the Grosse Lisse tomatoes, and gave me a powerful eyeful. He must have been aware of my interest. My stiffening little cock could not be hidden.

Poppop and I pottered on for hours, both naked, hoeing, digging and fertilising with armfuls of straw and buckets of manure from the horses that pulled the Jellis Bakery carts from Kew Junction. Each morning when Brad heard the clop, clop, clopping, the horse whinnying and snorting, he dropped everything. Showing a tidiness even then labelled 'anal', Brad would stealthily follow the van in a stalking ecstasy, armed with a bucket and shovel, dressed in starchy white shirt and cricket creams. For a businessman who had already made a huge pile, this activity was one of the ecstasies of his retirement. No opera devotee tailed a diva from city to city in Europe with greater dedication. Brad had only vaguely heard about Maria Callas, but he was passionate about the horses of Mr Jellis: they offered something for nothing.

Sooner or later, maybe in Palm Grove, maybe in Highton Grove next to Camberwell Grammar

School, the horse, quietly observing the baker running from house to house with a basket of Viennas, osloaves and crusty rolls under his arm, would raise its bushy tail, distend its black rubber sphincter and slowly extrude a string of moist, steaming, mustard-coloured nuggets onto the road. Returning, bucket in hand and crying, 'Look at what I've got!', Brad looked as if he'd just made his first million.

It was Poppop who said to me on mornings in the vegetable garden, 'Have you done your business yet?' which was meant to be more grown-up than the 'jobs' of my mother's parlance. Yet they were related: jobs, business, labouring and money. Nowadays it may sound more like an economics forecast, but in the forties it was more basic. Where there was muck there was money, and both my father and grandfather were in it up to their necks.

After Brad had finished gardening we would dress and he'd go into the house, while I would undress again, lie down on the ground and wildly masturbate. From my earliest days, I found my grandfather's house, Millbra, an exciting and sexually charged landscape. Always after I'd been with the naked Brad among the vegetables, if I thought there was nobody around, I'd pull up my Aertex shirt, pull down my shorts and start frotting on pillows and cushions or the living room carpet. But most exciting was the manure-strewn, straw-bedecked vegetable patch. My adored Grandma Millie sometimes discovered me at these onanities, but far from reproving me, she would make no reference to them. It was a secret between us. I always felt I was her favourite, a common enough delusion of childhood.

*

I am writing these words at my family's holiday house at Portsea, sixty miles from Melbourne. Named 'Whimsy' by my literary mother, Lorna Josephine ('Doone') Blazey after Lord Peter Whimsy, a hero of Dorothy L. Sayers' detective novels, the house sits in three acres of tea-tree near the crashing breakers of Bass Strait. It has become the central site of our family history.

When Doone bought Whimsy with her own money in the mid-sixties, she hoped to marry off her three sons to suitable girls whom they would meet in this posh seaside town; but this only happened with one, my youngest brother Clive. Both my middle brother Antony and I have disappointed Doone in matrimony. Antony's first marriage ended in a messy divorce and I, after a spectacular broken engagement announced in Whimsy, proclaimed myself gay on national television in 1978, an act which Doone thought was uncalled for, to say the least.

It is now May 1996 and I am staying here with writer Tim Herbert, my partner of five years. There was a time when Doone would have disapproved of such a liaison in her beachhouse but she, like the rest of the world, has mellowed. She even became fond of my ex, Philip Juster, in the final years of our relationship. But in her late seventies she slipped off into Alzheimer's land and now she can barely recognise anyone. I am back here trying to understand why I have turned out to be the sort of person I am – rebellious, stubborn, and often in trouble – and why I have fought with my mother so often during my life.

It is a difficult task and there may not be too much time. I discovered I was HIV-positive in 1983, having caught the virus in New York, probably in 1980. Fourteen years later I was diagnosed as having

AIDS (Category Four: Kaposi's sarcoma). This is not so unusual. There are now 20,000 people (mostly gay men) who are HIV-positive in Australia and already 4000 have died. Everyone, even the straightest person, now knows of someone who has died, or will die, of this disease after fifteen years.

Although I totally distrust efforts by Western medicine to combat the disease with cytotoxic drugs, I acknowledge that I have a life-threatening illness. My immune system is definitely below par. Several deep purple Kaposi's lesions have already appeared on my wrist, shoulders and back. If they break out on my face, I shall regard that as a cosmetic emergency and remove them with liquid nitrogen, but for the moment I am avoiding doctors like the plague! I am treating this disease myself with the help of naturopathy.

In the meantime, waves are breaking on the back beach, long, reverberating boomers which, strangely enough, remind me of the weeklong storms that occurred before Harold Holt foolishly stepped into a rockpool. Is this my life starting to pass before my ears and eyes? I am not being melodramatic. I have inherited a strong constitution and will to live, and staunchly reject the theory that the virus is inevitably fatal. I am lucky to have Tim, because I know he will stay with me whatever happens.

It is three in the morning. If I look out the window to the north, I can see the lights of Melbourne's CBD glowing platinum above the black waters of Port Phillip Bay. Who would have thought the old wen could look so unearthly at night? Tim is sleeping upstairs, the glass door open to the stars and the thumping of the breakers. At this time of year he always recognises the constellation of Scorpio, my astrological ascendant.

I wonder how I'll react if things get worse. I know scores of others who died in their twenties and thirties. Many were stoic and serene, others panicked. I can understand them panicking but hope that I won't. As Thomas Nashe wrote in 'Time of Pestilence' in 1593:

Beauty is but a flowre
Which wrinckles will devour,
Brightnesse falls from the ayre,
Queens have died young and faire.

Roaring Forties

In love there are two things – bodies and words.
Joyce Carol Oates

My parents were mad about each other during the war, and absence prospered their passion. They married in 1938 when she was twenty-four and he was twenty-eight, and had me on November 24, 1939, on the cusp of two decades and, as it turned out, two worlds. Already Hitler's war had been going on for two and a half months.

My father Alan had a good war, as they used to say. He volunteered in 1941 and served first in New Guinea, then, via America, he finished up with the Australian Army in Whitehall. He wrote many very revealing letters to Doone, sometimes one a day. I came across them a few years ago.

In one dated November 1944 from Hawaii, he says that their ship, the M.V. *Lurline*, was overloaded with thousands of US troops returning from action and was taking three weeks to get across the Pacific:

Our little party of Australians has been split up, I and a Major George sharing a cabin with four Americans (three army and one navy). The navy bloke asked one of his army compatriots how long he had been in Australia and got this reply: 'Boy, I was there so long I was wishing the goddam Yanks would go home!'

We get on very well together and are fairly comfortable. Two chows only a day, but a bellyful of fruit silences midday gastronomical whingeing. It's been vilely hot all day, a fact which makes the conversion of the two large swimming pools fore and aft into latrines a rather poor show.

We get bucketfuls of fresh water every day for the six of us, which of course means we wash ourselves cursorily but not our clothes. However we've solved the laundry problem by wearing nothing in the cabins, and shorts, sandshoes, meal tickets and life preservers on deck.

We are not alone in this, the whole ship being a series of nudist colonies. Day and night, inside the cabins, you can see naked men tossing and turning in their sleep.

The few females on board have enough good judgement to look neither to the left nor the right when walking down the corridors. Should any luckless spinster desire a cheap thrill she can study 1000 nude men within two minutes, as all the cabin doors are kept open, firstly for air and secondly so they will not jam in the shut position in the event of a torpedo attack. Unluckily, I have not had an eyeful of any WAC (Women's Army Corps) in déshabille. (Everyone else has.) But then I always miss the best things in life.

When my father got to London he was a Major in the Australian Ordnance Corps seconded to the British War Office. Although English girls from an armed forces hospitality section took him out to dances and to teas, and several broke down and told him they were in love with him, Alan was always home by midnight, writing an air letter to his Doone. A bit of a tease, in one of his letters he asks, 'Can I have a picture of you in a bathing gown? All the men have them, though I hope that the picture shall be taken by a woman friend and not a man.'

From London in January 1945, he sent me an air letter saying how sorry he was that he hadn't written before. *Dear Peter*, it said, *Here it is very cold and I am often thinking of you playing in the street with a hose. The little boys here cannot play with the taps because the water in the pipes has all turned into ice and the taps won't run. I saw the ducks and swans in the water and it looked so funny for birds to be walking on the lake.*

He ends by saying: *I want you to give Mummy a kiss. I am too far away, will you give her one for me please? One of those really long kisses that you remember I used to give Mummy and hold her very tightly while you do it just like I would. It would be very nice if you would give Mummy an extra kiss every night as you go to bed and say, 'That's for Daddy, Mummy.'*

*

Armed with sepia photos, I can see myself at this time with Franz, my best friend who lived nearby. We were in swimsuits gambolling under a sprinkler, its four arms flailing round and round like metal spaghetti. We were dancing, practically naked, on one of those appalling Melbourne summer scorchers when the sun rises early in the morning like a porthole in hell, then clangs out of a stainless steel sky and bushfires explode all over the state. It was only six years after the worst-ever recorded fires of 1939, which devastated much of Victoria.

Franz and I went up to Mont Albert Road to

watch long cars powered by wood-burning furnaces shower sparks over the bitumen. These 'gas producers' were a response to the strict rationing of petrol for private cars. We returned to View Street, which, like others all over Melbourne, bore a yellow-painted sign in tin on a lamp post announcing: This Is A War Savings Street.

I can still see Franz's mother, a German-Jewish refugee with 'internee' status, a large and compassionate woman with her hair in a bun. She emerges from her weatherboard house carrying a plate of Brockhoff biscuits and two glasses of Stone's ginger beer, announcing that one or another batsman had reached a century in the cricket she was listening to on the radio.

'Here you are, boyss,' she says. 'My, how hot it iss. Vot an amazing country ve are in. Yess?' She shakes the sweat from her face and wipes her hands on her brown skirt. 'To think, after Tchermany and Britain, we should live in a place so hot. Yess, boys. The bar iss now over one hundret degrees.' She said 'bar', not trusting herself with a word like 'thermometer'.

We gulped down the ginger beer and ran off. 'Franz!' she calls. 'Vhere, vhere are you going, boyss?'

We left the sprinkler and ran towards Canterbury Road. It was the first of several elopements in my life. We tore through lanes and leapt fences to get to our bosky hideaway. This was the mysterious turret at the back of Terrill's house. Terrill was a tomboy friend of ours. Her parents' tower was a classic Victorian folly built around the turn of the century, a viewing platform of iron and wood surveying Canterbury, Surrey Hills and other suburbs spreading north and south from the Ferntree Gully railway line.

Franz and I went there often. It was an isolated cubby, hidden by Virginia creeper, wisteria, and quince and walnut trees. It was our place. Franz had dark, curly hair and a strange accent. I loved him; he was my first friend. There would be many more, but he would always be the first. We took our pants down and started feeling each other up, our excitement mounting. Afterwards, in this shady, secret place, we started talking about Santa Claus; in this dementing heat, it would soon be Christmas.

'I wonder if Santa has a weese,' Franz asked me with the trace of an appealing German accent. 'I don't know,' I said. And Michael, who was more than usually inquisitive for a six-year-old, said: 'If Santa has a weese, I would like to stick a pin in it.' This was a wild thought for a young boy. I giggled at Franz's speculation.

Later I heard that Franz tried to do a 'rub' with his older brother Joachim, but Joachim dobbed him in to his father who gave Franz such a brutal beating that I didn't see him for weeks. After this hiding, Franz and I would never go to our cubbyhole again. He'd been scared by this thrashing, and now feared his father. 'I can't do it again, Peter,' he said. 'My father will find out, and bash me up.'

Useless for me to say that his father wouldn't, couldn't find out, or that I would never, ever betray my most intimate friend. Franz had now lost his childish insouciance and had been traumatised. It was my first alarming experience of the violence that surrounded many sexual taboos. Soon after, his father got a job in South Australia and Franz passed out of my life.

ure of Bearer

Daddy Comes Home

But what talk we of fathers when there is such a man as Orlando?
SHAKESPEARE, *AS YOU LIKE IT*, III, iv

At the age of thirty, my mother gave birth to her third son, Clive. It was a year before the end of the war. After me and my middle brother Antony, who was two years younger, Doone had been hoping for a girl. Indeed, before Clive, she had miscarried a daughter who was forever after called Meredith. Perhaps Doone would always regret this female absence in a monstrously male household. But as fate would have it, her firstborn son, myself, turned out to be her maiden daughter: perhaps not maiden in the Victorian sense, but determinedly unmarried – to a woman, anyway.

Vivacious and principled with a large, generous heart, Doone worked in the Women's Land Army during the war. She was faithful to Alan, although driving trucks with soldiers for long distances gave her plenty of opportunity to be otherwise. To appease her loneliness, she wrote radio plays for the ABC and short stories for little magazines such as *New Signatures*. They are well-observed stories, very naturalistic in the wartime style. Twice dux of Fintona Presbyterian College in Balwyn, she had a brilliant passage through Melbourne University, at a time when women students were rare. She was an exceptional sportswoman, got an MA in English with her thesis on Shakespeare's comedies, and could have won a Rhodes Scholarship had they been available to women then.

My father had it all in many ways. With straight black hair and blue eyes, Alan Clements Blazey was sometimes compared to Clark Gable. He even sported a moustache during the war. He always claimed he was a virgin when he married Doone, remaining faithful to her for the rest of his life.

While both our parents were away, we were looked after by a sweet-natured mothercraft nurse called Ray Owen, whom we adored, and by Brad and Millie, of course. A striking pair, my grandfather was a swarthy, ballsy little man with a mane of wavy, silvered hair that he kept until his eighties, while Millie was tall, long-limbed and elegant. I recall her flapper's hats, feather boas and fur coats. Her glamour suggested the elegance of the twenties, the decade of Scott and Zelda.

Many Sundays, Brad and I would climb into his swanky Daimler and we would ride off to investigate the far-flung reaches of his domain. An imperious twosome on royal progress, we motored down Barkers Road, through the Kew cutting over the Yarra, and onto the Richmond river flat, clattering along the tramlines past Charles Ruwolt's engineering firm and the Skipping Girl Vinegar sign with her neon rope flying up and down, turning left at Hoddle Street to visit the first jewel in Brad's commercial crown, the Boomerang Cigarette Paper factory. Turning out billions of 'rollies' each year, exported to Australian and US servicemen all over the Pacific, this was one of Brad's smartest investments. We toured the factory inspecting the chrome presses, the cutters and the huge rolls of rice paper, I got a kick when Les, the old Sunday watchman, referred to us as 'Mr Brad and his son'.

The next stop was a gloomy bluestone warehouse in Queen Street, the site for J. E. Hunt and Son, distributors of W. D. and H. O. Wills products.

Pushing around trolleys in this old cavern and banging cartons of State Express 333s and Craven As into voluminous stacks was an absorbing occupation for a small boy. I was deputised to pick up stray pieces of string and place them in a huge bag by the creaking old lifts. 'Get him, there's one over there, son!' Brad would say to me, pointing out bits of errant twine. He talked to the watchman and picked up his mail and then we would get into the Daimler and motor back to Millbra, where Millie would make us afternoon tea.

*

Daddy was demobbed and came home in 1946. He immediately resumed his horticultural business which was to become, twenty years later, the market leader in the Garden State. He became a chartered accountant through night school and distrusted university education as totally impractical, especially his wife's MA. He had come up the hard way through the 'school of life', working as an accountant for years at Gadsens, the packaging firm, before buying Avery's Insecticides the same year that he married Doone.

Later on he bought the small firm of Horticultural Industries in Burnley Street, Richmond, about five streets away from one which was to be named Blazey Street in honour of the historic length of his father's tenure (forty years as Town Clerk) on the Richmond Council.

Showing the luck that accompanies great success, Alan picked the industry that was ready for exponential growth. Fertilisers, seeds and horticultural products were a perfect trio in the garden-mad city of Melbourne, which was about to enter a thirty-year period of unbroken prosperity after the war.

Alan's advertising agency came up with an agreeable new name and look for the company. The old title HIPLE (an acronym made up from Horticultural Industries Pty Ltd) was abandoned in favour of Hortico, and the firm devised flashy colour packaging, strategies to penetrate the home garden market and adopted the sassy catchphrase: 'Hortico, Our Business is Growing'.

It was brilliant advice. Over the years, the firm's market share increased to over seventy per cent. By good management, inspired marketing and an excellent product range, Hortico dominated all competition. The company employed about a hundred people, mostly migrant male labourers, at various plants around Melbourne. The main works was a large factory at Plummer Street, Port Melbourne, serviced by a fleet of twenty cars and several boiling-down works to create the blood and bone which was the company's mainstay.

With a temperate climate, endless Liberal governments, good soil and a mania for homes and gardens, the expansion of Hortico couldn't have happened in any other Australian city. In the early sixties, after Hortico had taken over a small family-owned business called Yates Seeds, the firm was virtually unstoppable.

*

Despite my father's business, in the houses I visited in my childhood there always seemed to be some dark, deep and mysterious vegetation I was scared of. At the neighbouring Spicers' it was a stand of bamboo by their veranda which seemed dank and mephitic to me, full of spiders and centipedes. John and Serena had a mother called Audrey whose only words I recall were, 'It's always best to go to the toilet in your own home.'

My mother, like many Melbourne matrons, was unrelentingly upwardly mobile. As three growing boys placed increasing demands on space, we moved a mile from a brick bungalow in treeless View Street, Canterbury, to a double-storeyed, four-bedroom house in leafy Salisbury Street, Balwyn. The wide streets and Anglo-ambience of Balwyn off Mont Albert Road may not have been Toorak, but it was certainly a move in the right direction. But for me, now eleven years old, it seemed a backward move.

Across View Street lived tomboy Terrill of the tower. One day while my parents were over at the Granville-Smiths' on Balwyn Road playing tennis, I invited Terrill and Jane Granville-Smith over and I rubbed my dick on the horsehair bed in front of them until it got hard. I rubbed and rubbed till I had an orgasm for the first time. I was stunned with wonder at it. This was the start of a lifelong interest. I wanted to share it with the girls and demonstrated, saying, 'If you rub on the bed like this, you'll get a nice feeling from nowhere. Come and try it.' But it didn't work for them; they must not have been doing it the right way. Despite our ages, we vaguely knew we were doing something wrong.

We had left the street life of the demotic, febrile forties for the sedated, claustrophobic fifties. This was a conventional, leaden, middle-brow time, weirdly re-enacting the Cold War in practically every aspect of personal life, and blazoning forth the age's grisly triple goddesses: Debbie Reynolds, Doris Day and Queen Elizabeth II. The decade opened ominously. Dressing up as a paper boy for a photograph, I was supposed to be delivering the news of Menzies' election win in 1949 on my bike with a Melbourne *Herald*. Standing outside his home in Reid Street, Balwyn, the new Prime Minister patted me on the head, thanked me for the news and called me 'a nice young fellow'.

After that, things improved little. The fifties were really about fighting world communism in order to make lots of bread – and babies – at home. There were many problems, many phobias: getting over the Depression, the War, Communist expansionism, new diseases – and, overhanging it all, the dread of the A-Bomb, which in 1953 became the H-Bomb. Interspersed with these dreads were a few circuses

– like visits from the Queen and the 1956 Olympic Games. When HRH visited in 1953, I stood for hours in the sweltering sun with thousands of other schoolboys waiting for her to motor along Mt Alexander Road in her Rolls Royce. Waving my small Australian flag, I guess I thought she was radiant, but nobody is worth a three-hour wait.

Melbourne's bourgeoisie competed for tickets to the latest musicals and an LP record bought from America of, say, *South Pacific* was one of the greatest trophies of the decade. Other musical hits included *Brigadoon*, *Annie Get Your Gun*, *Oklahoma!* and *My Fair Lady*. Our houses in Canterbury and later Balwyn flaunted such utilitarian books as *Life Begins at Forty*, *Playing Golf with Von Nida*, *An Ideal Marriage* by Van der Veldt with a sprinkling of American bestsellers, while my mother preferred more off-beat fiction by the likes of Daphne du Maurier, Lin Yutang and Pearl Buck. As Dux of Fintona, Doone's first prize was the complete novels of Charles Dickens, and in her second year, the complete novels of George Meredith (no Modernist, she).

Yet the fifties was also a nice family sort of a decade. We always went away on holidays together in the Holden station wagon, usually staying in a rented house at Torquay. I remember sitting on the front beach there with my brothers. It is about 1954. My mother is wearing a white one-piece bathing suit with red stars which we all hated. As she is a good swimmer, she goes out to the first breakers, but unwittingly is carried out to sea. She puts up her arm for help. Bells ring, reels are unrolled, lifesavers start swimming towards her. The whole beach is watching. Finally, Mother is rescued and brought ashore, where she lies on the beach and is resuscitated. We three boys are ashamed and embarrassed by the attention so we don't go to see her. She lies there, unclaimed, as it were. Finally she gets up and comes over to where we are sitting in the sand. 'Why didn't you come and help me?' she asks. We cannot answer her.

Torquay was handy to Geelong Grammar, where Antony and Clive were studying. The reason they went there while I stayed at Scotch College is because Antony was so mediocre academically that he had failed the Scotch senior school examinations, a failure which prompted his lifelong resentment towards academics and his determination to win by any means. My dear mother, unable to accept that a son of hers could be hopeless scholastically, immediately visited Geelong Grammar's Dr J. R. Darling, the legendary headmaster who was receptive to boys 'who were good with their hands'. Antony was enrolled at Geelong and Clive soon followed him.

My father bitterly objected to the removal of his two younger sons away from 'his' school – he didn't think Geelong was 'tough enough'. But mother's private income allowed her to pay the school fees by herself, so she did. This was the source of their most acrimonious fights, fights which went on for years and came closer than anything else to wrecking their marriage. Sometimes they didn't speak for weeks: silent breakfasts, silent dinners. I couldn't stand it. I wished I were at Geelong (I had earlier foolishly declined to go), or a boarder at Scotch, or anywhere but here. Naturally, Doone got her way. She was unbelievably stubborn. After Clive went to Geelong it got worse for me at Balwyn. Longer silences, more tension and now no Clive. In a later generation, Doone and Alan would have split up, but my parents' generation didn't get divorced. I loathed living there with a passion, coming home to this morgue as a day boy at Scotch. Of course my father's *amour propre* had been wounded at the thought that his wife was paying the school fees for two of his sons. But he shouldn't have worried too much. After all, he knew he was marrying an heiress and he wouldn't have got Hortico going without her father's money. This was the price he had to pay.

*

Both my father and grandfather were making money, but they seemed to be somewhat hostile. Since he was so successful, you would have thought my father could have been more generous to his father-in-law. But he wasn't. Of course he owed Brad money, both at the start of Hortico and later when he went national in the mid-sixties, and that didn't help. Their competitiveness as entrepreneurs added to the friction. While Alan's business was growing, Brad's operation was static with a steady turnover and a minuscule staff. According to Father, Brad's company was a joke: 'It's just a warehouse and a few trucks. He doesn't make anything,' he told me.

Since Brad was distributor of Wills products, there were always cartons of cigarettes lying all over the View Street house: Players, Capstan, Craven A, Turf, Ardath, as well as non-Wills brands such as du Maurier and the exotic de Reske. Brad belonged to the pre-war days when smoking was sold as a mark of continental sophistication.

Much later, Alan contracted emphysema and used this as a reason to hate his father-in-law while he was coming to terms with a long and painful attempt to give up smoking. 'I was given my first cigarette at school, and I wish to hell I'd said no,' he'd say. He later graduated to an old cherry wood pipe with an air-cooled aluminium stem which he constantly cleaned with Star pipe cleaners. His struggle with nicotine went on for years, and he only beat the weed in his fifties, by which time it was probably too late.

'Your grandfather is penny wise and pound foolish,' Alan would say to me. 'He will spend hours cutting pieces of string from parcels and collecting them but waste thousands of pounds on idiotic advertising that affects nobody.' It was more or less true. On another occasion, while denicotining himself, he said darkly, 'You know, Brad should be put in gaol.' This was at Christmas and his sons were amused by his sharp and sardonic vision. When we asked delightedly, 'Why?'

Father replied: 'Because he's a legal criminal selling dangerous and addictive substances to the public.' He then told us that every time ships carrying tobacco were lost during the First World War, Brad doubled and trebled his prices. 'That's how he made his money – he was a war profiteer,' said Alan, reaching for another brandy. What was worse, he said, was that Brad hadn't volunteered during the war. He had stayed at home to make a pile.

The issue of hottest contention came up in the sixties. It was a saga which went on for several years, and ended with Dad telling Brad he had to retire from the board of Hortico. By that time it was a legitimate request since Brad, now in his early seventies, was well over the then retiring age of sixty-five and had long ago outlived any usefulness to the board. For several years my mother nagged Alan, who was chairman, about this. She never let up: they fought at almost every meal. I remember it became particularly intense in the years leading up to 1956, exacerbated by school bills from Geelong Grammar and Doone's enthusiastic advocacy of Dr Darling, whose educational principles Alan thought a lot of neo-socialist hogwash. Doone was herself a member of the Hortico board and watched her father's performances with growing disbelief. But my father procrastinated, hoping to avoid a confrontation and knowing it would provoke stormy accusations of ingratitude and worse. After several years' pressure, he left written requests for Brad to call him, which the stubborn old man refused to answer. The issue became so explosive that the regular Sunday card nights were abandoned, to everyone's relief.

Finally, cowardly Alan was goaded into doing something. He sent Brad a note pointing out that he was over the retiring age and directing him to resign from the board (in agreement with the Victorian Companies Act) before the next meeting. Having done nothing for too long, Alan's eventual action was too sudden. Although he submitted his letter of resignation, Brad was livid and never forgave Alan or Doone.

*

But little really changed for the energetic Brad as he pounded around the tennis court with his cronies, all dressed in creams under a dark and forbidding Canary

Island palm. Brad flirted openly with an increasingly repellent string of housemaids (carefully chosen for their ugliness by Doone and her sister Nell). There were vegetarians, war widows, large ladies with aprons and buns, small Catholic bundles of energy with seven children; there were Rechabites and staunch nonsmokers and teetotallers, a moustachioed Jehovah's Witness called Ruth and one woman who was semi-paralysed. The more unattractive the better, according to Brad's daughters. He dismissed many when they didn't come across, but others were declared 'unsuitable' when, sizing up the situation, they came across all too willingly. Brad may have been a ram, but he wasn't a slut. These affairs were carried on with growing brazenness the more impatient he got with the inordinate time – about ten years – it took Millie to die. His cyprian energies were unstoppable.

Alan disapproved of the way Brad was treating Millie in the last years of her life. 'Listen, son,' he'd say to me, 'there's no fool like an old fool. I know your middle name is Brad. I just hope you don't end up like him.' But despite Alan's growing success and maturity and his often expressed scorn for Brad, he seemed strangely scared of him. 'For God's sake, woman, get off my back,' Alan would shout across the breakfast table at Doone, who would continually nag and rebuke him to 'do something' about Brad's neglect of Millie.

It became family lore to despise Brad for his dalliances. The worst was the outrage he provoked by marrying Rae, a Tasmanian widow, hand-picked as his housekeeper for her Wagnerian size, her huge family and her advanced age. This marriage occurred within six months of Millie's death and merely served to reinforce the black comedy of my family's failed attempt at guardianship: not only did this rebarbative woman from Burnie marry him with unforgivable haste; she was also (unfairly) blamed when Brad rewrote his will to exclude my mother, collecting several million dollars for herself.

With the precision of a fairy tale by the Brothers Grimm, the new will rewarded Doone's sister Nell with a half share of everything, for accepting Brad's new wife – a thing which my mother resolutely refused to do. Many droll family stories were told of the ageing Brad, now in his seventies, bending on creaking knees to propose to Rae in the huge picture window of Millbra, of his requiring a walking stick at the private wedding (attended almost exclusively by her relatives). There was one marital duty which we all knew Brad would perform with his customary energy. Their marriage lasted two years until Brad's death in 1962; sad for Rae, since she was now exposed to the full fury of Brad's 'real' family.

It could be said that Rae had won, game, set and match, over the manipulations of Brad's daughters. My mother's disinheritance – only revealed at a Dickensian reading of the will at Millbra on Brad's death – seemed to cast a permanent shadow over her sanity. Her stutter, for one thing, seemed to get worse. Doone in fact never recovered from this rejection, nor from the retrospective hatred she summoned within herself to make it bearable. 'Brad was such a bastard, such a little, little man,' she would intone, almost to herself, for years after, trying to make sense of what had happened. From that day in 1962 onwards, Doone never forgave her once-adored father.

*

At the age of seventeen, while completing my matriculation year at Scotch College, I used to visit my grandmother as she lay dying at Millbra. With her watery blue eyes, beaked nose, long strands of white hair and skinflaps on her arms, it was obvious that Millie didn't have long to go. Her chalky bones, constant pain from Parkinson's disease and intermittently broken hips pointed to an imminent end. I remember slipping into her huge double bed where we gave each other platonic comfort. There can be no doubt that she enjoyed these occasional bed-sharings with her oldest, 'artistic' grandson; for my part, they were expressions of love and a mute commentary on the bad behaviour of her husband, who had long ago abandoned this bedroom for his own palatial room overlooking his beloved tennis court. But she steadfastly refused to criticise Brad.

One conversation between us sticks in my mind. At school I was studying the abdication crisis of Edward VIII in 1936, for the then terribly relevant subject of British History. Befitting a semi-military academy run by Calvinistic royalists, we students naturally received an extremely hard line on this event. From the ageing, eccentric history teacher 'Fort' Clayton, then in his sixties and author of such Kiplingesque textbook classics as *From Colonies to*

Commonwealth and *Civics and Citizenship*, we heard that Edward, the Prince of Wales, was an idiot for having fallen in love with a divorcee from Baltimore named Simpson, and that he deserved to be forced off the throne.

Millie disagreed, surprisingly agitated. 'What happened was a terrible tragedy and shouldn't have happened at all,' I remember her telling me. 'He was the most wonderful man and would have been a great king – much better than his stuttering brother, Albert, who was totally unfit for the job.' Millie asserted that Mrs Simpson was a sweet and loving woman who absolutely adored the Prince of Wales, and that they were a marvellous couple whose love should have been honoured not reviled.

This was a remarkable revision of the received wisdom about a triply married American strumpet who'd ensnared a biddable fool and wrecked a dynasty. It was also, though I didn't realise it at the time, Millie's comment on the romance of her marriage to Brad, of the triumph of Venus over Mars.

By now Brad distrusted his sensitive, literary grandson, believing him to be in cahoots with Millie and Doone. Brad correctly picked me as a sook and a wimp, with no facility for sport and competent only at such suspect pursuits as debating, drama and long-distance running. He must have sensed I might be similar to his sensitive, literary brother Jim who lived in Stawell and hadn't married until he was fifty.

Once I tentatively raised the subject of Shakespeare's *Sonnets* with him. He was hardly helpful. 'I don't know what possible use that stuff can be to you,' he said to me. Ensconced in his favourite armchair, Brad was not even remotely affable. He was twiddling the knobs of his bakelite radio as he sought the seven o'clock ABC news, the program that meant his day was complete. 'When I was your age,' he said, 'I was playing football. And your mother, at least, was a champion tennis player.' His response signified the deepest disapproval. For though he had been disappointed by having two daughters, at least one of them had become a brilliant sport – both a Tennis Blue at Melbourne University and later a State Champion of the Ladies' Golf Union. As far as Brad was concerned, his eldest grandson seemed to be turning into something 'even worse' than a woman.

Relations between us soured permanently when,

at seventeen, I pointed out that the piano in his ballroom was never played and that I was having piano lessons myself (from a remarkable teacher at Scotch College). He said nothing, which I conveniently interpreted as permission to 'borrow' it, and one morning I quietly wheeled the piano out of the ballroom, along the footpath of Mont Albert Road, past Camberwell Grammar, and into the back room of our house in Myambert Avenue. Brad was furious when he found out. But it was a *fait accompli*, a fairly deliberate provocation and the first of many 'outrages' that seem to have peppered my life.

*

Brad may have been a boastful, boorish, bullish, pig-headed little philistine who was none too bright, but when I was a child, I idolised him and he aroused me in ways which my prudish father was never able to do. I may think I hate him now, but I can't deny that Bradford is my middle name. Nor can I deny the legacy of his energy and his rude health – especially since I should, by all medical prognoses, have been dead from this virus many years ago.

Scotch College I: First Blood

There are men in Church and State,
Men of influence, men of weight,
Who regard us with a keen but loving eye …
School Song

One of the finest functions a school can perform is to provide a person with a healthy object of hatred: few things can give a life more focus, and in this regard, Scotch College, Hawthorn, was perfect. In the fifties, it was philistine, militaristic and sports-obsessed; it was Calvinistic, male supremacist and even gerontophilic. Yes, in those days, there was no better place to prepare for a career in law, medicine or sport, or to toughen up a young sensitive.

There are Scotch Colleges in Adelaide and Perth and a Scots College in Sydney, but the one in Melbourne takes the haggis. For one thing it was the oldest, having been founded in 1851. For another, it had shared in Melbourne's amazing gold rush wealth and the fact that Victoria is the most Presbyterian state in Australia (think of Menzies and Fraser). Melbourne's Scotch College was a repulsive exemplar of the Scottish 'cold shower' theory of education, of that hearty, muscular Christianity that swept through the farthest reaches of the British Empire after the paranoia and fear induced by the Oscar Wilde trials of 1895. Bearing the motto *Deo Patriae Litteris* ('For God, Country and Learning'), the school seemed to be run by a menagerie of teachers who were either tragic, neurotic failures or tough, reactionary bullies – all acting out the school's unlatinate code which seemed to be 'Kill or be Killed'. Whether 'tough' or 'wet', most masters would have failed elementary personality testing, since many were Old Boys and were virtually unemployable outside of this Hobbesian zoo in Hawthorn Glen. Others had been brought out of retirement during World War II and were still discoursing on the Whig theory of history or the Ptolemaic Universe – a living mockery of the huge sums our innocent parents were spending on school fees.

At this Caledonian hellhole there was a geography teacher who burst into tears when told he would have to take vicious remedial classes, an algebra teacher who articulated v-e-r-y s-l-o-w-l-y and walked absent-mindedly into trees if addressed, a Latin teacher we called 'Slut' who loved slicing boys' bums with steel rulers, an art teacher who wept to discover his nickname was 'Creeping Jesus', a woodwork teacher who flung chisels at students and an English teacher with one testicle who raved about what a great poet Ernest Hemingway was. In this crazed, all-male locker room, the only female on the staff was an ill-favoured, middle-aged female biology teacher called (Auntie) Violet Wilcox who used to send boys into deliriums of delight with her calculated double entendres such as: 'Down tools and pay attention, boys!'

I had been sent there because my dutiful father went to that Presbyterian *école militaire* and naturally one's eldest son followed suit. Dad regarded going to Scotch as one of the defining experiences of his life, though the school conferred upon him nothing more than the Intermediate Certificate and the signifier Middle Class, Melbourne. Since he came from a Depression-blighted generation obsessed with frugality, denial and getting on, the little he got from Scotch was more than enough. But for his eldest son, a self-indulgent oddity in the heart of the me-generation, it was a disaster. With limited skills and no schoolmates who developed into friends, Scotch set me up as a lifelong clown and eccentric. I was always a rebellious and mediocre student who excelled only in English, geography and mutual masturbation.

The first report for boy number 1497, compiled in 1951 by my form master and scout leader Larry Cropper, shrewdly detects the first glimmerings of a fellow moonling: 'Works hard sometimes, but lacks diligence and is rather frivolous. No great ability, a very untidy worker,' it reads. Although we schoolboys regarded Larry as a clown and a totally laughable wet, I admit he was dead right about the 'frivolous'. By 1953 and the onset of puberty, the report was even less distinguished: 'No trouble as a boy but is v. weak in maths & seems to make little effort to remedy the defect. Well behaved but not v. diligent.'

Not recorded in reports were certain social lessons at which I was making brilliant progress. Since the school's real motto was 'Down with Wogs, Micks, Poofters, Scouts and Jews', it was essential that one never be seen as belonging to any of these contemptible categories. In these profoundly important exercises of school socialisation, I was showing great promise. The most exciting classroom game played in the early fifties was 'Spot the Jew'.

During my second year I became friendly with a gang leader called Bob Douglas. Douglas would divert attention from his crippled leg by sucking up to sportsmen and scapegoating social outsiders, notably a sensitive and lonely Jewish boy with pale skin and black curly locks called Joseph Kaufman. On one occasion, Douglas had recruited me along with eight other boys and we surrounded Kaufman in a dusty classroom near the old tuckshop. Douglas called Kaufman by the special nickname he kept for him – 'Cunty'. He implored us to call him by his Christian name, but Douglas said Joseph could not be a Christian name since Kaufman was a Jew. Therefore he could only be called 'Cunty'. Cheered on by Douglas, we milled around Kaufman, standing on a desk and chanting, 'CUNTY KAUFMAN IS NOT JOSEPH, CUNTY KAUFMAN IS A JEW!' Kaufman broke down and ran weeping from the classroom. Next term his parents took him away from school.

By pleading and being emotional, Kaufman had failed two of Scotch's most powerful commandments:

Keep Your Feelings to Yourself, and Always Go with the Crowd. Douglas was triumphant, but his hyper-conformity hardly prospered his career, since he finished up an advertising executive for a Melbourne radio station.

At the time I was unaware of Scotch's earlier liberalism, not to say aestheticism. At the end of the forties, there had been an artistic resurgence led by some idealistic young schoolteachers returning from the war. A troupe of gifted and creative schoolboys sprang up around this time including such gay blades as Don Smith, Philip Sargeant and John Worrall. Sargeant later became an architect, and in 1994 self-published a book of poetry called *Something in Between*, with a foreword written by his friend Barry Humphries. Now in his sixties, Sargeant has always been an unashamed homosexual man. 'The irony of Scotch,' he told me, 'was that while the captain of the school was fucking boys in the prefects' room, I was in my ivory tower writing Sitwellian love poetry.'

I knew nothing when I arrived there. Because I mixed with the lower, more philistine streams and was desperately anxious to integrate, I was unaware of any nascent culture that might be developing in the romantic and riverine grounds of this Gormenghast by the Yarra. Unsurprisingly, the atmosphere was highly homosocial. Perhaps it had something to do with the seething propinquity of the boarding house, the Cadet Corps and the school's unique cult of sacrifice. In the sixties and seventies, Scotch possibly produced more practising gay men than any other major private school. They formed a diaspora as they escaped to Canberra, Sydney, London, Europe – or just stayed in Malvern and East Melbourne, some opting for sham marriages as a cover. I have run into these old Scotch queens all over the world: a former school captain in an Earl's Court leather bar; a gifted architect who sired twins with a lesbian mother in West London; an academic in a tavern in the Plaka, Athens; solicitors in Melbourne's eastern suburbs; as well as many old boys in the former Australia Hotel in Collins Street.

*

In this college of 1500 boys, the Cadet Corps was – and still is – accorded semi-divine status. Its purpose in those days was to churn out Cold Warriors to fight the Third World War against the country's worst enemy yet: godless atheism. It was Scotch's duty to help by producing underofficers who might finish up in the Citizens Military Forces or at Royal Military College, Duntroon. But joining the cadet corps wasn't compulsory. Schoolboys had the option of doing sport, or joining the Scotch Scout Troop.

The very mention of the word 'scouts' made one's testicular schoolmates break out in a frenzy of derisive laughter, and even Scout Master Larry Cropper was greeted with Red Indian war whoops as he moved around the school's quadrangle from one classroom to another every Wednesday. The catch was that as hard as the Scouts strove to be competent and useful, their considerable bushcraft skills were tagged as frivolous. No matter how intensely they tried to appear 'manly' – the word is, curiously, one of Baden-Powell's favourites – they were regarded as effeminate misfits, unworthy of the serious task of killing. Only dills and poofs were scouts, which was probably why I allayed suspicion by joining the cadets.

The 'school spirit' at Scotch was based on a quasi-fascistic cult of sacrifice, but the experience of whipping it up became quite camp. Musically, the school year worked its way towards the furiously spirited pre-Head of the River sing-alongs in the gloomy Memorial Hall. On occasion, these 'musical events' were fifty per cent Boy Scout jamboree and fifty per cent happy hour with a version of SA Chief Ernst Rohm in deputy choirmaster Reg Sherriff:

Make me a captive, Lord,
And then I shall be free.
Force me to render up my soul
And I shall conqueror be.

Members of the Guard or Quarterguard, glamorous in their white webbing and tartan kilts, stood at the front of the hall, singing lustily. These 'boys' – some as old as nineteen – were prefects. They were the Praetorian guard, the elite, the SS if you like. With their swaying kilts, sporrans, hairy legs and black leather sash belts, they were the objects of desire among the younger boys. And good-looking school captains like 'Gus' Hawthorn, Bob Shillinglaw, Russ Frater or (vice-captain) Andrew Peacock gained that adoration reserved for Hollywood movie stars like Marilyn Monroe.

But the actual leader of the singing was a very bohemian fellow called Claude Monteith, the school's choirmaster. Baton in hand and bespectacled, his hair thinning and dishevelled, this crazed-looking creature started proceedings by conducting one of the great warm-ups in the repertoire:

We are Scotch Collegians all,
and we rally at the call,
as our fathers and our brothers used to do . . .

This was often followed with the Scotch boating song, a foot-stamping, throat-opening hymn which began with the primally powerful words:

Sometimes in your dreams you'll hear a deep'ning roar
Like the ocean surf that beats upon the shore,
Long forgotten voices will greet you,
Scenes long past will rise up to meet you . . .

The chorus built up into an orgasmic, hall-deafening, suburb-saturating, MCG-lifting roar, as a thousand boys stamped their feet and rhythmically chanted: 'Giving us the Victory. Long will we remember.' It was powerful, life-bonding stuff. Especially if you stayed at the emotional age of fifteen for the rest of your days. (Even as I write this now, my heart beats faster and I yearn to recapture this adolescent tribalism.)

Often, proceedings in the Memorial Hall finished with everyone shouting several war cries, the most bardic being:

Hi, hi hi, Generals Monash, Smith, MacKay,
We'll be with you, wet or dry,
Ready to do or die, Hoch hi!'

At the end of Monteith's practice-cum-rally, we burst out of the hall and went clattering down the bluestone steps, sexually charged, patriotically fired, yabbering to each other. The school, from long experience, knew how to inculcate us.

*

I was usually a member of a lunchtime gang of four, but often after these stirring sing-alongs I'd prefer to go down to the river with John Oliver, who seemed to be turning into a shirtlifter. We were excited with what we were about to do. Sometimes we would go to the grass below the line of Algerian pin oaks that stood between the main and rugby ovals and fellate each other in the grass. Sometimes we even made clumsy attempts at penetration. John was curly-haired and angelic-looking. We had both just sprouted our first pubes, and we were stunned and awed by our hormonal changes, best negotiated with endless torrents of nervous dirty talk about sheilas and spunk and giving girls a petting grade from one to ten.

Although my sexual antics with John Oliver were more on the par of a friendly feel, my attraction to Ian Dodswell was on another level entirely. I had met him through the Scotch Dramatic Society, in rehearsal for *Julius Caesar*, with myself in the title role and Ian playing a Roman centurion. With his long tanned legs and high cheekbones, he became my first love and our affair continued intermittently for the next five years. But Ian was ambivalent about the intensity of my affections.

Mentally he was somewhat clod-hopping and pedantic and held the view that 'B-F-ing' (his quaint abbreviation for bumfucking) was either immoral or immature. And yet we had discovered the joys of sodomy one sunny, pagan week in the school holidays on his father's Gippsland property. Meant to be clearing the scrub for cattle production, we lay on a double mattress in the December warmth using Johnson's baby oil to massage each other and facilitate a B-F. I enjoyed ordering my Roman foot soldier about. I loved his hairless balls and adored rimming him, while his slow, dopey voice thrilled me, especially when he said: 'Oh, Peter, I think it's time we tried to have another B-F.'

On the night of the full moon Ian and I reached a bestial low. We snuck up to the cattle yard through swirling mist intent on intercourse with a poddy calf. Although we found a docile specimen, the selected calf initially gagged on Ian's penis. I had come well prepared, however, and passed Ian a knob of butter to be used as a lubricant. He tried again with success as I bumfucked him from behind. We worked this trick on several other golden, fatted calves until the animals became so obstreperous that we feared the farm manager was coming with a torch to investigate. We disentangled and made our escape and then to bed – in separate bunks, naturally. While we may have been calf molesters, we weren't poofters, were we?

*

My major platonic friendship before the age of sixteen was with the school's champion sprinter, an ardent heterosexual called Jim Baxter. Jim was a dynamo of earthy sex appeal who tried hard to convert me to the straight and narrow. A non-academic athlete, he lived with his mother, a Plymouth Brethren widow, at Beaumaris. He had a younger brother who resented our friendship and later publicly abused me for being a poofter.

By fifteen and alone in our class, Jim had a sexual precocity which was breathtaking. He was having affairs with sheilas, as he called them, all over town. He had a large member which he personally addressed as Jake. Using a charming phrase I'd never heard before, he freely admitted he was 'cunt-struck'.

Like Albert Finney in *Saturday Night and Sunday Morning*, Jim was well built with fair hair and a buoyant manner which both girls and sheilas found irresistible. Girls were sheilas you might marry but sheilas were only roots. Jim didn't discriminate, he rooted them all. Since I was nothing if not confused, I was hoping some of his charisma might rub off on me.

He would give me little homilies about how to make it. 'Now, Perce,' as he called me affectionately, 'when you're with a sheila you never talk about books otherwise she'll think you're a big droob.' The way to win a goer was to talk about the footy, or clothes or cars or film stars. Jim was miles ahead in the fashion stakes. He brought a light grey woollen cardigan to school with silver buttons, called a Perry Como jacket. Along with shiny blue pants, he wore this groovy ensemble whenever he went dancing or winning hearts.

One week he took out a girl called Penny who lived near Ruyton Girls' School in Kew. After rooting Penny for a few weeks, he decided to try Penny's mother, Imogen. He spent Wednesday (sports) afternoon, when Penny was at school seducing Imogen. Soon he had his way with her in the matrimonial bed. He told me that she cried out, 'Oh, Jim, I know I shouldn't be doing this and I love my husband. But I do love youth,

youth, youth!' Jim was so thrilled by this conquest that he rooted mother and daughter, sometimes both in one day, until Penny got suspicious, confronted her mother, and immediately dumped Jim. Doing so much homework (in other people's homes), it's not surprising Jim's marks started to decline.

Academic results were not helped either by the school's annual cadet camp in May, which turned into a saturnalia in the mulga. These night journeys were the most thrilling trips of my fourteen-year-old life. Going to Mildura, three hundred miles from Melbourne, our train thundered through wimmera and mallee towns on its way to what seemed the dead heart of Australia. We slept on floors, seats, passageways and on luggage racks which we called WRAACs, from the Women's Royal Australian Army Corps whom we encountered at Mildura.

The highlight was standing by the door as the locomotive chugged past Birchip, Wachupga, Woomelang, Speed, Patchewollock and Ouyen. What weird names, and such strange, flat eerie country. So *this* was the source of the huge knobbly mallee roots we burned every winter. All you could see were the dark shapes of wheat silos and long lines of mallee trees on the horizon. Even more surreal were the lit-up railway stations with uniformed workers that flashed by like spinning stage sets. As we whooshed past the engine emitted long mournful whistles and then belched clouds of smuts that caught in your eyes if you put your head out the window.

Members of D-company to which I belonged were allotted rooms in the long rows of huts called lines, which at first we thought referred to the clothes lines stretched between them flapping with cadets' khakis and underwear. We were scornfully disabused by our underofficers who stalked around with officers' hats, swagger sticks and the prefix 'Mr'. By day we marched in platoon and company formation over hard, red sand; sat patiently under mulga trees learning how to assemble and disassemble Bren guns; and even did some shooting at firing ranges with our .303 rifles. Bromided tea or not, we testosterone-driven adolescents were immensely proud of our rifles and lovingly cleaned them each night before falling asleep to the haunting strains of a bugler playing the *Last Post*.

One afternoon the word went round that Jim Baxter was pulling himself off and this could be watched for a shilling. His room-mate collected the money. Soon scores of cadets from Scotch and Xavier College were lined up at the door of Baxter's hut. Jim sat on the bed slowly masturbating his large tool. (Since we were a mere ten years after the most mechanical war in history, it's hardly surprising that human parts were still called tools and boxes.) Jim's 'Jake' was a whopper, and being from a good Christian home, he was circumcised. He sat there wearing only a khaki singlet, pulling himself faster and faster as more cadets crowded into his room.

'Who are ye thinking of, Jim?' one Scotch cadet asked.

'Donna,' he replied.

We had all heard about Donna. The Xavier boys were thrilled at this evidence of Protestant debauchery. They were nearly swooning as they stared and sighed. Jim ignored his audience and started addressing his dick: 'Come on, Jake. I'm putting you into Donna's box and you're gonna go in and out, real slowly at first, then faster and faster. And Donna's gonna scream for all of you, Jake. You old devil man you!' This patter went on for minutes until he definitely had his audience, then he increased his pace and finally ejaculated all over the cane-ite wall, sighing 'Donna! Jake loves you!' It was quite a performance. He repeated this act a few times collecting more than five pounds, which was a quite good 'door' with no expenses except a jar of Vaseline. Jim should have gone into entertainment; instead, he married too early, had four kids and spent his life selling bricks and used cars.

On the train back I asked him if he ever thought of anyone else but Donna. Strangely, though I loved Jim I was not attracted to him, he was too blokey for me. I asked him if he could ever think of a boy while wanking? 'No, Perce. Only a poofter could ask that question. I couldn't think of sticking Jake up a dirty arsehole – though I bet you could!' He said this affectionately, since he was starting to worry about me. He was concerned for me and my half-hearted attempts at winning sheilas. 'Don't worry, Perce. When we get back home, I'll take you down to Lorne over Christmas. If you can't get a root there, then I'll go he.'

*

We drove down to Lorne in the Christmas of 1956 in his Vauxhall Victor GUF 431. Jim already knew of a girl called Charlotte staying in the Cumberland Hotel. Charlotte had a friend, Paula, from Geelong, who was to be my blind date. For a few days Jim and I slept on the beach under a few blankets and met the girls in the morning in the Arab coffee lounge.

Lorne, about a hundred miles south of Melbourne, was an old-fashioned resort like Biarritz with both surf and mountains. Whereas Portsea and Sorrento are for Melbourne's conformist eastern suburbs, Lorne was a sedate watering hole for the holidaying western suburbs, with a sprinkling of graziers' families and, increasingly, young people who abominated postwar suburbia. An interesting mix.

In the days before jumbo jets, anything continental was exotic and the Arab traded on Italian chic. It was part of the opening-up that happened to Melbourne that year: the Olympic Games, the advent of television and the filming of *On the Beach*. Even so, the Arab was unique. Run by a local family, the three inspired Smith brothers, it attracted beatniks, musos, bongo drummers, surfers and heiresses. At the front were cappuccino machines and marble bars, but out the back, in the 'snake pit' or the harem, was a huge blue and white striped tent under which people sat on cushions. When the sun was shining it was miraculous, like being on a yacht. And such beautiful people: Byronic young men without shirts, and waitresses dressed in bikinis.

The music ranged from Brubeck to Gershwin to Paul Anka, while the food was minimal – spaghetti, coffee, toasted sandwiches and sundaes – but because the dishes were described in beat poetry, they sounded more tantalising than they were. The Arab wasn't a coffee shop, it was a state of mind, a travelling circus, a seedbed of the future. Peter Tully, who went on to become the design genius behind the Sydney Gay and Lesbian Mardi Gras parade, grew up in Lorne and spent entire summers there.

Jim quite liked the Arab, especially the waitresses, but he had misgivings. He said he didn't like Dave Brubeck and jazz was boring. 'Why don't they play Bill Haley?' he asked, aggrieved. Though he was dismissive of the menus he did get a charge from the bikinis, but the waitresses here didn't respond to his lairy pick-up banter. He said they were stuck up. Since he and Charlotte were madly shagging in the

Cumberland Hotel and Paula and I had nothing in common, his last attempt to save me had failed.

But left to my own devices I became friendly with an arty-looking blonde girl who was sitting alone at a table. Her name was Anna Rubbo and we started hanging around together. Anna told me she was a descendant of a noted painter and teacher in Sydney. We got on well simply because there was no sexual expectation.

Part of the Arab's spontaneity were impromptu dances. One night a few local groovers started dancing to an excerpt from *Nights in The Gardens of Spain* by De Falla on the tape deck. The crowd grew, people clapped in time and cheered. Robin Smith, one of the owners, encouraged us by putting on a more feisty Spanish tape of flamenco guitar. Anna and I began gyrating and twirling in what we thought was flamenco. Our corybantics became wilder and more frenetic. It wasn't that we danced well, so much as we totally let go in delirious abandon. At the sweaty end of it we got a large round of applause. We were stars of the Arab. Even Jim was impressed, though he didn't like me falling in with such a high-brow crowd. He knew he'd lost me. He had already left school, while I was starting my matriculation year. We loved each other for a while, but I never saw him again.

Scotch Coll

...e boy edits Young Sun

TODAY'S Young Sun was edited **by Peter Blazey,** 16, of Scotch College.

Peter was chosen by his head master to be Editor for a Day in Young Sun's scheme to give readers the chance to see newspaper production in action.

On this page you can see the stories that Peter thought you would like to read.

On Friday night, after he had helped produce this page, Peter said:

"Newspaper work is intriguing and I have learned a lot by watching the whole process.

Scotch College II: First Sex

A handsome son keeps his parents in constant fear and misery; so rarely do modesty and good looks go together.
JUVENAL

One thing that Jim Baxter never knew about was my liaison with Brother James Murray. At the same time as I was learning to be a lair, I was having an affair with an Anglican priest-in-training who was thirteen years older than me and had seduced me when I was fifteen.

Brother James was a gifted teacher, a staunch High Anglican and an ardent pederast, the latter two characteristics often being complementary. He just adored pubescent and post-pubescent boys. Jovial and rotund with a warm reedy voice, he could have been a thirty-year-old Friar Tuck. He was the centre of an admiring circle of gay teachers, actors and fellow Anglicans, all of whom regarded him as brilliant.

It is now widely accepted that most fifteen-year-old boys are hormonally crazed young goats capable of fucking anything that moves. Mostly it's the palm of their hands. By teaching at schools such as Ivanhoe Grammar, Brother James had a constant supply of randy boys and youths 'on hand', as it were. He could lead them to 'Our Lord' by massaging their priapic little dicks. It was a novel proposition for a practising Christian in those days, and not so hard to pull off.

My schoolfriend Nicholas, who was Brother James's ward, introduced us. Brother James had adopted Nick after his English parents had abandoned him ten years earlier. Quickly working out that I was worried about my marks in English and History, he offered himself as a tutor. My father readily agreed.

Brother James lived with his mother, father, retarded brother and Nicholas in Melbourne's Kew. Since Kew was en route to Balwyn on the 42 or 44 tram, I visited Brother James for tuition several days a week. He had a large rambling wooden study attached to the house with a peppercorn tree in the courtyard. His study was lined with groaning bookcases full of Chester-Belloc, Dorothy L. Sayers, C. S. Lewis, Renaissance art books, histories of music and of the church. He was a fan of Wagner, but the gramophone also gently played Monteverdi and Gregorian chants (my favourite) and the percolator bubbled on a tin tray. Warm in winter with an attractive amber glow, this was no anchorite's cave, it was a sybarite's boudoir and I looked forward to going there.

Our lessons started and before you could say John the Baptist, my tutor had seduced me. It wasn't terribly difficult. While whispering about Jonathan and David, his pudgy hands sought my grey serge uniform exclusively tailored by Walker's of Glenferrie. With practised fingers, he undid my fly, extricated my tumescing dick from too-tight Jockeys and caressed it lovingly as if it were a holy relic. All the time he talked about the love of 'our Lord' who looked with a particularly benevolent eye when His servants loved each other as we were now doing.

This was a theological novelty for me. I was more used to the brimstone of the Old Testament, tales of asses jawbones and the ungodly ways of the Canaanite as taught by Scotch's ethnocentric, silver-haired chaplain, the Reverend Alec Fraser, who loved impeccable suits and expensive cars. Not for Brother James the brutal imprecations of Leviticus, no, no, no; he was a modern churchman bearing Christ's message of love to the world, especially love between males which, he said, greatly surpassed the love of women. Since Brother James was a fifties queen he disliked young females, believing they were flawed, accursed temptresses trying to ensnare wholesome young men.

*

While I was indulging in sodomitic lessons from my tutor, I was also being instructed heterosexually at the Hans J. Myer School of Movement and Languages in Lisson Grove, Hawthorn, learning how to dance from a smooth-talking, monocled Viennese mountebank who looked like Mandrake the Magician and made feeble jokes about protocol. I didn't much like the Tintern, Ruyton and PLC girls and I saw no point in learning how to samba, rumba and tango with them. One year, when the Myers had a dance at the Hawthorn Town Hall, my friend Hugh Paton and I crept up to the electrician's box and pulled the switch, throwing the entire building into darkness for twenty minutes. It was exactly the sort of scandal the Myers didn't want. In the silence, the only noise that could be heard was Alice shrieking to her husband, 'Hans, ze lights are out!' The couples stopped sambaing as Scotch boys began to feel up the Tintern girls, who started to scream; it was agreed next day that Ruyton girls screamed loudest. But some couples weren't screaming at all. Hans shouted, 'I zink I know who has done it!' He set his wolfhound onto us but we got away, and at later interrogations we denied everything.

I also disliked going to dances organised by my parents' generous friends, the Abbott-Smiths, who, like the Bennett family in *Pride and Prejudice*, had five daughters who had to be married off. Instead of learning the steps for the chacha, I churlishly played glaring chords on their piano and threaded toilet paper through the venetian blinds, or so I am reminded by one of their daughters, Jenny, who hated the dancing classes equally and wanted to rebel.

Looking back, it was obvious that I was furiously resisting the middle-class values into which my parents were trying to induct me. In such a bind, the appearance of someone like Brother James offered an exciting alternative. As a teacher he was acceptable to my mother and father. Though Doone adored his cultivated banter, Alan soon had doubts about Brother James. He offered cultural sustenance, and soon after my marks started improving.

I was confused about our relationship and less attracted to him than he was to me, but this affair was an escape from the footballers of Scotch. Further, Brother James led me in the direction of that love which, absurdly in the Judeo-Christian tradition, is both unspeakable and unthinkable. I started enjoying the world of books, music and theatre that Brother James was offering. The utterly clandestine nature of our pact was part of its attraction. There was no way I would tell Doone about this.

My tutor would lie under a print of Salvador Dali's *Christ over the World*, his thick dick as erect as a stovepipe, while I would frot on his great hairy Buddha-like belly. Having dropped my pants, I would then lower myself onto him like a fighter plane returning to an aircraft carrier. His taste for the Latinate extended to the anatomy: it was the first time I'd heard it referred to as an *erection*; previously, I'd called it a fat. In our acts of mutual frottage, it didn't take long for me to come, though Brother James, being a tyrannical queen, had his household well trained: they had to knock loudly at the study door, and even then he might imperiously refuse to open it.

The one person never denied entrance was Nicholas, who was bright, witty, and a clever mimic. He was also deeply ambivalent about Brother James, often calling him a hypocrite to his face. As a child, Nick had several roles in Australian films, but like all child stars had found growing up difficult. Being more mature than I, he was trying to extricate himself from Brother James. Resenting the attentions his legal guardian had shown him throughout his childhood, Nick was grateful that I had come onto the scene; it allowed him to concentrate on his true erotic interest, girls.

We made an odd trio. Brother James showed me the high churches in Melbourne and took me to amateur productions of plays in which his friends were acting, such as *The Glass Menagerie*, while making bitchy comments about their thespian ability. He told me how lucky I was to bear the name Peter, Christ's beloved disciple. Seduced by incense and vestments, I soon professed myself to be 'High' and started praying to our Lord, often holding hands with my instructor. This pleased Brother James immensely since he was after my soul as well as my body. In Brother James's green Morris panel van, the three of us drove to Sydney to visit Christ Church St Laurence in George Street. Then we drove west to visit St Michael's at Crafers in the Adelaide Hills. This Anglican monastery on a wind-tossed rocky ridge was so high it was nearly airborne. Spending a week there was a gothic experience for me since it was about as monastic as Brett's Boys. Instead of escorts, men in long black cassocks flitted from the refectory to the chapel, their garments blown open by the wind. The monastery was controlled by bells: there were bells for the plain refectory meals, bells to start the day – and to end it – bells endlessly summoning the devout to the chapel for services such as matins, nones and evensong.

At the heart of the community, which was run by a rector who had been wounded in the war, was the white-painted chapel with its old creaking pews and stained glass windows. In the back row, at every service, a septuagenarian monk with a huge nose called Father Gabriel would go down on his knees and loudly intone, 'Jee-eesus, Sweeeet, Sweet, Sweetest Loving Jees-us, my very own sweet Lord', in a high voice for several minutes at a time. Nobody paid any attention to him as he was a bit ga-ga and everyone was preoccupied with their own prayers. Charming though the monastery was, the frequency of the services, and the air of celibacy and senility, started to test my piety within a few days.

But it was not totally celibate. Males openly eyed each other off at mealtimes while some of the younger, more attractive novices leered at me as if they were in a Fellini movie. Obviously the word had got around that I was Brother James's latest acolyte. The raunchiest place seemed to be the library. A thin, bespectacled Brother Joachim, no more than twenty-five, invited me into the stacks and opened his cassock to reveal his hairy genitalia. He took my hand and pressed it to his dick, but I was so shocked I returned to Brother James who laughed and said Brother Joachim was 'famous'. He wasn't the only one; others made passes, but none made me desert Brother James, to whom I was absurdly loyal, I am ashamed to remember.

Though I am now ambivalent about Brother James, I do not for a minute think that he 'made me gay'. Seduction is always a two-way street. I might have been compliant, even flirtatious, but I enjoyed our transgenerational affair at the time. Later I resented Brother James, realising he had abused a position of trust and probably given me a lifelong feeling of unworthiness.

Much later still I 'outed' the now Father James in *OutRage* magazine (May 1994) because he attacked the Mardi Gras in two *Australian* newspaper articles, calling it a national disgrace and saying that the behaviour of participants warranted arrest. Discussing the ABC televising of the event, he furiously wrote that 'mannish women and limp-wristed men' were providing an appalling example to the young. Ignoring the gay community's obsession with safe sex, he accused the Mardi Gras of pseudo-concern for AIDS sufferers. What infuriated me most was that he pulled the paedophile slander, saying how outrageous it was that some gay 'activists' were pressing for adoption rights. This – from a preacher who had himself adopted a young heterosexual boy who in turn finished up with severe alcohol problems – was simply too hypocritical for me to ignore.

I wrote the explicit story of our affair in the fifties, and *OutRage* magazine supported me in a national press release, claiming it was justified since Father James had not disclosed his own sexuality in making these attacks. My article was fairly light-hearted since moral outrage is boring to read. I ended it thus: 'Come on Father James. Times have moved on. We want life on Oxford Street, not *Death in Venice.*' Father James was humiliated by this outing; he was carpeted by his Archbishop and lost a number of paying teaching jobs. Was my anger revenge? There must have been a strong element of it. Was I finally expressing a lifelong resentment of the way he had abused me? I might have had gay tendencies, but I didn't want to be knocked off by a fat, hairy, ugly Christian amid all that guilt and fear. The fact I am a resolute atheist, or rather Buddhist, must have something to do with him.

I was savagely condemned by some media people (especially Paddy McGuinness) who claimed I had victimised a person exercising free speech. In the gay community, it was considered a 'justified outing', though four closet queens in the NSW Parliament were terrified and talked about 'gay fascism'. Others in the gay community staunchly supported me. I received a number of letters from people (many of them Asian) claiming he had abused them shamelessly and they hated him for it.

A more sedate letter writer to the magazine wrote: 'Congratulations on your recent "outing". Father James could hardly be surprised if his continuous vociferous attacks on gay and lesbian culture should finally result in someone saying, enough!' The writer, the Reverend Peter W. Allen of Laidley, Queensland, praised gay men and lesbians for the work they put into the church, even though the church still treated them with contempt. He said the Anglican church should show more courage to avoid its members 'being arrested at beats, falling into unwise emotional entanglements with adolescents, and castigating other gay and lesbian people for grasping their God-given freedom'.

Father James never sued me for this outing. He knew there were up to thirty other boys he had seduced or abused from the many schools at which he had taught. But also he said a Christian should never sue another Christian. When the dust settled, Father James and I discussed the matter without chagrin. He said he forgave me and that his two anti-gay pieces were 'written under instructions', which to me suggested the then Editor-in-Chief, Paul 'Monsignor' Kelly. Father James was mortified when he discovered I was HIV-positive. He claims that he prays for me daily, and that I am at the top of his 'intercession list'. A rather mixed blessing when you think about it.

Adland

Loftiest stars of unascended heaven
Pinnacled dim in the intense inane –
SHELLEY, *PROMETHEUS UNBOUND*, III

My final matriculation was less brilliant than expected; indeed, a compensatory pass meant I had to do a few more subjects before going on to Melbourne University. But at least I had a Commonwealth scholarship. In the early months of 1958, feeling I deserved the post-exam rest, I would still be sleeping in when Dad would stride past shouting, 'No son of mine will lie in bed after I've paid to send him to the best school in the state for six years' – an assertion I totally rejected, but I didn't press the point.

Since in those days jobs fell out of trees, I was soon employed as a messenger boy at the small Nicholls-Cumming Agency in St Kilda Road. The exotic types in advertising, with their paisley waistcoats, sunflower ties and silver cigar piercers, suggested a bohemia-within-bounds which appealed, though many of the 'creative types' turned out to be closet queens. No matter, at least there was a premium on panache and tolerance – all preferable to the RSL/Presbyterian morgue that I had just come from.

I became ambitious. I got hold of a book of TV scriptwriting and quickly learned those invaluable terms ECU (extreme close-up), MCU (medium close-up), slow pan and hold (camera on face). I wrote a few mock-TV ads and presented them to Bryce Kinnear, head of George Patterson's prestigious TV department. Since it was only the second year of TV in Melbourne, the new medium was hot and many agencies were expanding into it. Bryce felt my scripts, replete with quotations from Christopher Marlowe and musical scores from Arnold Schoenberg, were a little *de trop* perhaps, but he still hired me. I was his youngest copywriter.

George Patterson's was Australia's leading agency. Situated in William Street its many accounts included General Motors Holden's, Cadbury's chocolate, Prestige stockings, Glo-Weave shirts, Wardrop's tailoring and Four and Twenty Pies. I worked with a lively group of women scriptwriters and schedulers, the only other male being Barry Hines, a droll, easy-going young man who had the important job of buying time on the channels and was forever chiacking on the phone. Most of the girls in the office were in love with him. As 'Junior' my first major task was to go to the Channel Nine studios in Richmond and paint glycerine on the tops of a tableful of dry Four and Twenty meat pies. This made them glisten temptingly as the camera panned above them while TV star Hal Todd read a voice-over praising their meatiness.

Eventually I wrote a commercial for Cadbury's Choc 'O' Drink which was well received and contained the immortal lines: 'You put the choc in, you stir it around around around until the bubbles spin.' Thinking of fresh or offbeat things to say about Glo-Weave shirts and Wardrop's annual summer suit event required a certain amount of creative effort, similar, I thought, to writing some of the poems in A. D. Hope's *The Wandering Islands*, my favourite volume at that time.

But the real delights of Adland were in investigating Melbourne's tiny Bohemian quarter. I became a minor dandy and wore mustard waistcoats with the mandatory black nylon socks. My *quartier* started at the Buttery at Scott's Hotel (now pulled down) and swooped up to Flinder's Lane, the capital of the rag trade, finishing at the top of Collins Street. In far-flung Exhibition Street were Greek and Italian restaurants that made cappuccino; and at the risqué Savoy Cinema, a Swedish film called *One Summer of Happiness* showed a naked couple romping through a field – the first nude scene on a Melbourne cinema screen. This film ran for months as Melburnians young and old – like cattle at the end of a drought – poured in to watch with thrilled disbelief.

In Flinders Lane, Gibbies Coffee Lounge offered a mean English fare of percolated coffee and toasted sandwiches. Opposite was the World Record Club, out of which poured thousands of records of lukewarm Slavonic Dances and tepid piano concerti by Greig and Tchaikovsky at amazingly cheap prices. But the real seismic shift occurred when Gibbies was replaced by Gaggia. Dank Flinders Lane gave way to the expansive places at the top of Bourke Street, and the Society Restaurant and Florentino's with its adjoining bistro became the height of chic. At the bistro one could get an excellent spaghetti bolognese for about three shillings and a cappuccino for about nine pence. We always felt amazingly continental ordering Camparis or vermouth and soda. And we certainly didn't smoke Turf; we preferred black Sobranies. Sometimes we visited Prompt Corner, a theatre coffee shop in Collins Street run by the actress Bunny Brooke. But the smartest place for me was the Cafe Caprice at the top of Collins Street, where flamboyant queens from the rag trade swapped gossip.

I remember once my mother waking me up in the morning and saying, 'You cannot keep living in coffee lounges with their *vitiated* atmospheres.' Here was a bright new word and for a few weeks everything became vitiated.

Around this time, in the gloomy despatch department of George Patterson's, I met Christopher Pearl, who is now my oldest friend. We were introduced by one of the agency's 'despatch boys', the late Lindsey Stockman, an elegant, foppish, red-haired young man whom Christopher's journalist and artist mother Irma tagged a 'Titian-haired anchovy'. Christopher inherited Irma's facility for metaphor.

I was utterly entranced with Christopher. I admired his flair, his looks, his ability to improvise in dance and speech. I liked the fame of his parents.

His father Cyril had just published his scandalous bestseller, *Wild Men of Sydney*. Most of all, I was impressed by the fact that he called them by their first names instead of the boringly suburban Mum and Dad which I used. Tall, blue-eyed, with a huge head and a mobile mouth, Christopher's talents seemed endless. He could paint and draw, play the piano, was a hilarious mimic and a promising photographer then working for Athol Shmith. He was the classic bookworm but also a stinging satirist. Several of his coinages went to the heart of Melbourne's snobbery: the 'dry sherry belt' and the 'sweet sherry belt', for example. But for all his enviable attributes, he was curiously restless.

'There's nothing more deadening than endlessly being told you are talented,' he once said to me. 'It's as if people are willing you to fail.' Having never had to endure this burden myself, I could only nod knowingly. He was eighteen, the same age as me, yet he wryly referred to himself as having a 'Randolph Churchill complex', being the failed son of a famous father. Wasn't he being a bit precocious, I asked him. Surely he was not a lost cause at eighteen? But he wouldn't hear of it. He was determined that being a low achiever would be his major role in life, and so it became until his mid-fifties when he finally met some success as a photographer.

Christopher's primary gift was acting and he was able to fascinate people for the next forty years with the never-ending saga of his own life as the neglected youngest son of brilliant parents who cared more about their careers than their children. Irma was volatile, demonstrative and witty while Cyril was impassive, sluggish and oververbal.

His gender stability was mercurial to say the least. Inasmuch as she wanted children at all, Irma wanted daughters. Chris and his older brother Tony were thrown into boarding schools at a young age and rarely visited. Both sons resented Cyril for his distance as a father; they never forgave him for marrying again after Irma's death in 1961. In a funny series she wrote during the war for the *ABC Weekly*, Tony was 'Taffy' while Chris was 'Penny'. For many years after their births, Irma nicknamed Tony and Christopher 'Maggie and Mona'. At rare moments Cyril would storm around the house roaring: 'I will not have my two sons referred to as Maggie and Mona!' before relapsing back into a book.

One anecdote about Cyril remains unforgettable. Christopher, then about eighteen, is sitting alone with his father in the living room of their restored Victorian villa in Caroline Street, South Yarra. (Both Irma and Cyril were obsessed with Victoriana and wrote several books about it.) Christopher is trying to do a crossword puzzle from the *Age* Literary Supplement which mentions John Knox as a 'dour zealot'. He asks his father, the only other person in the room, 'What does "dour" mean? Does it mean sour, or does it mean fanatical?' He asks his father this question three times, receiving no reply. Finally Christopher says angrily, 'Would you please put that fucking book down!' Without looking up, Cyril said mechanically, 'Christopher, don't speak to your mother like that.'

My adoration for Christopher was not matched and he teased me for my affection. At this time there was no erotic connection between us. We used to cruise together wearing white Levi's and lamb's wool jumpers, walking down Toorak Road. At other times we would visit the camp bar at the Australia Hotel where I flirted mischievously with craggy closeted farmers who'd come to Melbourne for the day.

Christopher strongly disapproved of my Scotch larrikinism, more so when I acted tough and he claimed, quite correctly, that I was trying to avert suspicion from my equivocal sexuality. When I deliberately knocked the underside of an Ernest Hillier chocolate boy's tray in Collins Street, sending his wares all over the place, he was deeply unimpressed, as he was when I smashed the plastic sign of the Wild Cherry Cafe farther up the road. He displayed greater disdain when I managed to get myself beaten up by three 'nashos' we struck on Princes Bridge over the Yarra. They were drunk, having come from Young and Jackson's pub after the six o'clock swill. They swaggered towards me loudly calling, 'Poofter!' The discreet thing would have been to move out of their way and let them pass. But, stung, I stupidly stood my ground. A fight ensued in which my nose was smashed and remodelled into a Cubist style. Incensed, I managed to inflict a bone-crunching blow on the nose of one of the nashos leaving us both covered in blood.

I had thought Christopher was at my side, the two of us like Patrocles and Achilles, but was astonished to find he had suddenly gone looking for a tobacconist.

Bloodied but unbowed, I expected praise when he returned. Instead, he was horrified at my messy face and even more furious that I'd brought it on myself. I accused him of pusillanimity and he said I was showing the self-destructive bravado of a lout. Thus began a forty-year dialogue between us which has still not been resolved.

When I reached home in a taxi, covered in blood, my parents responded hysterically. I believe that around this time they had been reading my diaries (which I made no effort to hide), in which I rhapsodised about Christopher. Soon after, my father anonymously rang Irma Pearl and accused her son of seducing me. My father's idea that Christopher had corrupted me could not have been more wrong, and it was an outrageous way for him to make that suggestion. Irma quite correctly said, 'I don't acknowledge anonymous calls.'

But my father had foreknowledge of my predilections. It was almost eerie how much he knew. Earlier in the year, while I had been hitchhiking up Mont Albert Road, I had been led astray by a pair of famous Melbourne queens, Ron Elms and his blond boyfriend Neil. Ron was a successful dress designer and he and Neil cruised all over Melbourne in their khaki jeep looking for trade, schoolboys, or sailors when the fleet was in. To add to the romance they represented themselves as 'forestry rangers' and spoke of their holiday house in the Dandenongs which I later discovered was groaning with Greco-Roman statuary and featured Ron's white grand piano.

We engaged in my first threesome in mid-afternoon in the park opposite the family home. I was the ham in the sandwich and, to develop the metaphor, not only was I able to cut the mustard, but I loved it. It was a significant awakening and I fell madly in love with both of them, though I preferred the younger Neil, who was then twenty-four. I even strove to imitate Ron's precise queeny diction whereby he would dismiss everything and everyone as 'utterly dreary'.

Ron and Neil got to know all the dance troupes visiting Melbourne and went through the Borovansky Ballet and Luisillo's Spanish Dancing Troupe. To attract younger fry Ron used Neil as bait in their constant cruisings around Melbourne's beats and beaches. They held orgies in his heavily barred house in East Melbourne. I later went to several of these and they were quite spectacular: on the ground floor were queens standing around being pisselegant, drinking cocktails among French mirrors, while upstairs it was mayhem. French sailors, ballet dancers, local rent boys and many others running from one bedroom to the other semi-clad and jumping in upon the pairs of guests who were screwing each other amid screams of delight. But these hotly awaited orgies were rare. Obviously the police had to be paid off in some way. One of Ron's tenants told me he had come across Ron in the middle of the night frantically crow-barring up the front floor to get enough cash to satisfy them. At one stage in the seventies it seemed as if Ron and Neil had sexually initiated most of the queens of Melbourne.

Soon after I left school, and just before entering the world of advertising, I went away one weekend to the Dandenongs where I watched Neil gently insert courgettes in several attendant young men's rectums, while Ron played a dreamy rendition of Debussy's *Prelude to the Afternoon of a Faun* on the piano. If this were sophistication and continental living, I thought, then I wanted more of it. When I returned from this musical soiree, my father wanted to know where

I had been. I spun him a story about job hunting, telling him how they were forestry officers who were trying me out to become an assistant. Foolishly, I told him that Ron was a good pianist, which seemed to give the game away.

Father was rather droll. He said, 'I suppose you were planting *pinus radiata* trees, were you?' Pronouncing the *pinus* as 'penis' instead of its customary pronunciation. I blushed all over and denied it, saying they were genuine Australian foresters who only planted eucalypts. He finally said, 'I don't like the sound of this "Ron". And I don't think these young men are foresters, son. They sound very much like a pair of homosexuals to me.' My heart knocked with shame and I immediately left the room. How did he know?

Poetry, Bhang and the Mountain

... look there, my brothers. Do you not see it: the rainbow and the bridges to the Superman?
NIETZSCHE, *THUS SPOKE ZARATHUSTRA*

On entering 'the Shop', as Melbourne University was called, in February 1959, I was the quietest Arts mouse. My first year was a delirium of joining. There was the Dramatic Society, the History Society, the Film Society. I sniffed around the student newspaper *Farrago*, and for a bit of rude health joined the daggy Mountaineering Club, going on trips to Wilsons Promontory and rock climbs across the Barry Mountains and into the head – waters of the Wonnangatta River. These excursions got me away from the dismal family house in Balwyn where I spent stifling weekends with Doone and Alan.

I was both a 'hearty' and a dandy. Initially I became an aesthete, despising my recent commercial past and revelling in the purity of the ivory tower. Charles Peguy wrote that everything begins in poetry and ends in politics. Well, that's what happened with me: I discovered, soon enough, that being a poet was lonely and I was gregarious. My first club was the Arts Association, an effete group of beleaguered Arts males (several of whom were obviously gay). We went on outings, read poetry and put out a quarterly poetry magazine called *Hashish*, co-edited by myself and Tim Oakley, a philosopher. One Dutch member of the Arts Association had travelled to Morocco and talked about a mind-altering substance which he had ingested there and suggested that this would make the perfect title for the magazine. We looked it up in the dictionary and found that hashish was also called bhang and that bandits took it before assassinating someone. Ten years later, to smoke or eat hashish had become almost compulsory on campus.

I'm not ashamed of a satirical squib I published in *Hashish*:

I sought this morning, morning's King Size stand-on-table
Sack of,
Munchy, crunchy all in dapple dearest, freshest, deep-down
Pack of
Wax-sealed flakes.
My heart-in-hiding soared, let fall itself a sob for

the achieve of, the mastery of
the crisp-turned corn off cob.
I for pack reached, did up pack pick and
Tilt,
In a flash, at a crumpet crash, came tumbling,
the heartiest, huskiest straight-from-an-oven poppe
Flakes of summertime zest
Down on my table,
Spilt.

It was gall, heartburn. God's harshest of evils
Bitter would have me taste.
My heart-of-grain lay clear shot through with weevils,
and seemed with ooze-of-oil laced.

Why must disappointment all that I endeavour end?
Please, Mr Kellogg, me some crisper cornflakes send.

Maybe this pastiche of Gerard Manley Hopkins expressed my dissatisfaction with Melbourne's English department which was moribund and arcane and housed in the ancient dusty corridors of the old Arts building. After a year, I realised I had erred in majoring in English and History. I was unable to get interested in the weird Icelandic sagas taught by Professor Ian Maxwell, or disquisitions on Lady Gregory and W. B. Yeats in the Celtic twilight given by Vincent Buckley.

I didn't care for the Hibernian subtext which spelled the politics of Irish kings and Roman Catholicism. Yet Buckley, who was a significant political activist on campus, had a nice dry wit. In one tutorial a student wearing corduroy pants, 'brothel creepers' and a jumper – the uniform for Arts males – read out a paper on Yeats's great poem 'Sailing to Byzantium': 'That is no country for old men, / The young men in one another's arms . . .' the student misquoted, adding a 'men' in the second line not present in the text. (Maybe he was hoping.) Buckley quietly riposted, 'No place for young men either.' He said this with a twinkle as a dry academic joke, and it got a laugh. But this disdain for homosexual love was true of the campus in 1959.

The only young men in each other's arms that I knew about were in Trinity College which housed a coterie of Anglican-educated homosexual aesthetes, several of whom later became judges. There was the Dramatic Society where openly gay actors like Paul

Eddy and Jon Finlayson later dominated and there was the Beaurepaire Sports Centre. Outside this gymnasium stood a bronze statue of a naked Zeus whose testicles were often Brasso'ed by engineering students, and once even hacksawed off.

It was at the Beaurepaire that I met Bob Soloman, who was to provide a major romantic interest through most of my university career. We were in the changing rooms after swimming, alone and naked. Staring at each other, we could not help but exhibit our erections. We searched for unused rooms in the Union to slake our lust, but ended up, on this occasion, in his car. Later on I rented a room for a few pounds a week in Swanston Street. By the age of nineteen, I was finally free to have adult liaisons.

Bob was a bright medical student and introduced me to all his friends and boisterous acquaintances, one of whom was the playwright Jack Hibberd. Bob and I went away on several hard-drinking, poker-playing beach holidays where we pretended to be straight, but had furtive sex in the tea-trees and sand dunes. He was short, stocky, jovial and witty. He was far too ambitious to do anything silly like 'come out'. And, to be accurate, such a political statement in those days would have been meaningless. Naturally enough, Bob had a girlfriend and expected to marry, ending up a university professor with numerous children.

While Bob and I were being super discreet about our sexuality, there were others on campus who were flaunting it. Germaine Greer was in her last year at Melbourne while I was in my first. She was finishing English Honours and sometimes gave talks for the English Literature Club. I recall one about the Metaphysical poets in which she used words I had never heard before, like 'expository' and 'vapid'. Germaine used to wear silk blouses plus mohair skirts hoisted high, with coloured stockings, often red or black, as part of her bohemian, gypsy look. Her hilarious skits in SRC revues with Anne Harvey had already made her a campus celebrity. Tall, loose-limbed and good-humoured, she strode around the campus aware she was much talked about. Wild rumour swirled behind her like a nimbus. She wore the smile of someone preparing to quit Melbourne forever. We male Arts virgins gossiped about her as nuns might giggle over the visit of Madonna Ciccone to their nunnery. Germaine was said to have had abortions and rich lovers. There were scandalous stories of parties where 'Germs' was alleged to have had seven men, one after another, at her invitation behind a brick barbecue. In 1959, she was a walking one-woman sexual revolution.

Around this time there occurred an infamous confrontation between Melbourne University's two most famous personalities, Germaine and the bulbous, mordant Frank Knopfelmacher, a psychology lecturer whose European war experiences had rendered him fairly unshockable.

It was summer. We were drinking coffee in the 'buff ' above the 'caf ' in the Union building. The cafeteria bustled with tin trays banging on laminex tables and students drinking dishwater coffee. The buffet was more upmarket; it had curtains and upholstered chairs made of wood. Sitting around a coffee table was a clutch of undergraduates including myself, the late student leader Bill Thomas, who was overcoming a Catholic education with great rapidity, and the knobbly Knopfelmacher in shorts – not a delectable sight.

Germaine approached our table. 'Ah, there's Franta!' she said standing in front of him provocatively, her arms akimbo, her bag swinging. She could have been Sophia Loren in a fifties movie, she was so tall and radiant. She eyed his shorts, then said: 'How would you like me to suck you off right here and now – in the middle of the buff?'

Some of us gasped. But it took more than this to discombobulate Knopfels. 'Ah, Miss Greer,' he said in his gravelly Sudatenland voice, 'you are so unconventional – in such a conventional way!' Germaine laughed at this elegant put-down. In those days she didn't mind being sent up.

IN WHICH OUR HEROES FIND MOTHER NATURE ALWAYS WINS

At the end of 1959, when I had just turned twenty, I went on a mountaineering trip to New Zealand with my new rock climbing friends: economics student, Michael Keating and Keith Brown, a scientist. This adventure was the most dangerous, exhilarating thing I had yet done. We immersed ourselves in New Zealand. We noted national differences – the wild lupins on the side of the highways, the love of weak beer, of royalty, and the visibility of the Maoris. In the south we did some magnificent 'tramping' through mountains and headwaters; we did the Rotoiti, the Waimakariri and many others. But generally we felt New Zealand had a surfeit of mean, conformist Scots and not enough mad Irish who give Australia its unique larrikinism. We noted the Kiwis despised Australian 'roughness' and our 'Americanisation'. They thought they were refined and British while we were the boorish vulgarians.

Michael, our inventive leader, had organised this bracing working holiday. Through his printer uncle we got vacation jobs in the Tasman paper mills at Kawerau. These huge mills, the largest in New Zealand, were set amid vast pine plantations. They exported newsprint to Australia and Europe and had been nationalised by a Labor government in the fifties. But they were plagued with industrial troubles. Maverick unionists threw spanners and bricks into the huge heated rollers which squeezed the wood pulp into newspaper. The saboteurs caused panic and 'wet end breaks', which immobilised the whole plant for days on end. Every time this happened endless sheets of paper had to be laboriously rethreaded through fifty or more heated rollers. The mill was crawling with security men and workers doing nothing on overtime. We loved it and earned triple time over Christmas and the New Year.

Soon, we Three Mountaineers had earned sufficient money to go climbing in the South. We started at Arthurs Pass, midway between Christchurch and the west coast and a good base for climbing the many peaks in the vicinity. Here we practised with our carabiners, belays, relays and pitons (spikes hammered into rocks to hold up the ropes). Arthur's Pass was the place where Sir Edmund Hillary had trained though, as we were later to discover, we were not quite up to Himalayan standards. Besides which, Australian climbers were not welcome in New Zealand – considered incompetent since we were used to hard, ancient basalt, while the softer New Zealand sedimentary shale, called 'rotten rock', was a totally different thing.

We stopped off in windy, romantic Wellington for a few days. I left my two straight companions and snuck off to visit a clandestine gay bar down by the docks called Tête à Tête. Here I met, took back to my hotel and fucked a Maori drag queen whose name I've forgotten but who gave me my first dose of the clap.

Naturally I didn't tell Michael or Keith about this dalliance. It was only when we were preparing to cross the Alps outside Weheka, near the Fox Glacier on the west coast, that they found out. My attempts to piss in the snow were painful and unsuccessful. I had to go north to Hokitika to visit a doctor who scripted me with penicillin. 'It's just like a common cold,' he grinned.

Abashed, I rejoined the boys, and was now able to turn the snow bright yellow. But the boys were curious, almost furious. 'How come you got gonorrhoea?' they challenged me. 'We didn't know you had a girlfriend. You never told us you'd had a woman in Wellington!' They were jealous. I told them about my drag queen escapade and their envy changed to astonishment. I had come out to them. They had *no idea*, with Michael adding that it was a passing phase and it wouldn't make any difference, ' 'cos we were all mates.'

We then made a dreadful mistake which nearly killed us. We were due to hike up to the headwaters of the Copeland River, climb over an alpine saddle and cross a dangerous glacier on the Mount Cook side. We had no experience with icepicks and had also heard that three people was too few – four being the minimum party for safety. Our lengthy wait for a fourth person ended when along came a happy-go-lucky Scot called Duncan. One of nature's clowns, he was hitchhiking around the world.

Claiming to have done rock climbing back home (which he later admitted was a lie), Duncan had no parka and no hood – essential in alpine squalls. He merely had a Woolworths plastic raincoat. While we had climbers' heavy boots, Duncan had no boots at all; he wore sandshoes (he called them plimsolls) and for an icepick he carried a toasting fork. It was ludicrous to take him, but we did.

We trudged for days up the valley of the Copeland River to the last and highest hut. Clouds from the west coast would make the saddle impassable at about 11.00 am so we set the alarm for 3.30 in the morning. After crossing the ridge, the next five hours would be spent cutting ice steps down the glacier before reaching the other side and Cook Hut, hopefully at about 5.00 pm. A fourteen-hour day, it was nearly our last.

The first stage gave us no problems but when we saw the glacier at midday, we all felt a tingling in our bowels. The ice field was vast and alarmingly steep, a one-in-three gradient, falling away sharply below us. Slashed across the ice halfway down – like a huge gash – was a crevasse hundreds of feet long and ten feet wide. It had a lip at its edge, but inside was an ice-blue infinity that filled me with terror. We joked that to drop into this meant one's corpse would appear near Lake Pukaki in ten years' time.

Michael descended first, third came Duncan and Keith was fourth. We were all roped together, ten feet apart, the rope running through carabiners on our belts. Michael started cutting the steps in the ice, a slow and tedious process. We then moved into each new step and waited five minutes, shivering with nerves and cold, and waited as Michael made another cutting up ahead. Although a wind was howling the sky remained clear.

After an hour, Duncan started getting jittery. He almost slipped and cried out: 'I canna do it. I canna do it. I'm skit!' Michael told him to shut up, but his lack of confidence was infectious. At the next step Duncan lost his footing completely. If he'd had boots on he might have been able to kick a footrest in the snow, but he skidded down the glacier and started tumbling, the rope snapping tight as the rest of us followed him, packs and all. First Keith went, then I. Michael boldly tried to dig in with his icepick; it held for a few seconds, then gave way under the weight of three of us spinning like yo-yos. He shouted, 'Jees-sus Chri-ist!' in frustration, as over and over and over we rolled, roped together, getting closer to the deep blue crevasse. I watched it approach and thought it was *finis*.

Instead, we got within six feet and stopped sharply, saved by the crevasse's raised lip. We lay there panting and stunned. Eerily, Keith's pack banged and bounced past us, pitched straight into the gap. There was no sound of it hitting the bottom. For a full five minutes not one of us moved an inch, or even said a word. Finally, I snuck along the lip and tentatively looked over. I justified this bravado claiming I was curious to see if the pack could be retrieved, but all I could see were sheer walls of ice falling away hundreds of feet below. I went pale and stealthily crawled back to safety. Of course the others thought I was quite mad.

Our near-disaster had actually reduced by half the number of ice steps we had to make. This time we were patient. This time Duncan did what he was told. We got to Cook Hut at about six that night, just as a blizzard started. We lit a fire, cooked up a meat soup, ate curry and rice and collapsed with relief. Michael radioed the Hermitage telling them what had nearly happened. Apparently two Australian nurses had died in a snowstorm a week previously and the New Zealand ranger exclaimed, 'Jeesus. Now there are four bloody Australians out on the mountain!' He also mentioned something about a rescue.

'No, no, no!' corrected Michael. 'It's OK. We're safe in the hut. And there's only three Australians here and one Scot.'

'A pity it's nae the other way round,' crackled the Ranger, who had a South Island accent. 'At least the Scots are good climbers. All you Aussies are hopeless amateurs.'

We had spent nearly three months in New Zealand. We came back to Melbourne University fit, tanned and confident. Nothing would be beyond us in 1960. Back at Myambert Avenue, Balwyn, my loving parents were not at all impressed by my heroic efforts in the Southern Alps. 'You could have killed yourself,' Doone said repeatedly, annoyed at my recklessness.

But after New Zealand I was determined to put safety behind me, suffering as I was from youth's eternal delusions of immortality.

Campus Politics

I'd ring out danger
I'd ring out a warning
I'd ring out love between my brothers and my sisters
All over this land
AMERICAN FOLK SONG

In the early sixties we were on the cusp. We thought we were missing *something* at those beatniky parties in Carlton terraces with sea grass matting, Chianti bottles with dried candlewax, Spanish travel posters and naked red light bulbs hinting at brothels in Barcelona or London or anywhere but dreary old Drummond, Lygon and Elgin Streets. In those days it was chic to be scungy (later, 'grotty' and later still, 'grungy'). The men I knew were scruffy and the girls had long hair and wore black. We were rejecting our parental values, but were not yet openly rebelling. Beyond the streets of Carlton, named after English Lords in the Crimean War, were the dreary steppes of Kew, Heidelberg, Brighton or the bush where our parents lived their woefully dull, materialistic, *Reader's Digest* lives.

Even more escapist were parties in the art colony

country of Eltham and Warrandyte. Long drives up the Yarra Valley in clapped-out vehicles to mud brick houses with slate or clay floors, lashings of claret or mead (for the History students) and tasty cheese, where the children of silversmiths and fresh-faced young women wore white (later muslin) dresses and played recorder or spinet under mandatory prints of Breughel and Bosch. Actually, the Breughel country with its capital, the magnificent Montsalvat, a bluestone cathedral erected to the glory of Art, has vastly expanded in area and influence since then.

The early sixties were a time of transition, of yearning for worlds yet unborn. Student numbers nearly quadrupled between 1947 and 1968. As students we may have been naive and idealistic, but we weren't impoverished. Postwar prosperity saw to that. Vacation jobs were plentiful and there were generous Commonwealth scholarships and new universities personally provided by our Prime Minister Mr Menzies. Clothes, books and booze were all cheaper while Marlboro cigarettes were a mere three shillings and threepence (later 33 cents) a packet. It was easy to buy singles and LPs, even Austin Healeys and MGBs (although it was always better if Daddy bought them!).

When I came back from my alpine adventure to do second year, I was determined that my life should have more Meaning. Having nearly died on a glacier, there seemed no point in only partly living. My father would never have bought me a car, so I purchased for myself an Italian motor scooter – not a trendy Lambretta but an ISO – for one hundred pounds that I'd saved up working in the New Zealand paper mills. I threw myself into my political science studies and the ALP club. This club had been founded in 1947 by Vincent Buckley to distinguish it from the pro-communist Labor Club which continued to operate on the campus.

Change was definitely in the air. On 25 March 1960 Roger Cook, SRC president, speculated on what the sixties might offer. *Farrago* records him as saying that students should play a role in the 'social as well as the academic community'. He suggested holding a national student referendum on the White Australia policy along with a revised and more inclusive national union of students which later became AUS – the training ground in the sixties and seventies for many politicians ranging from the ALP's Gareth

Evans to Liberal Peter Costello, who would become federal treasurer. Moralistic Melbourne has always been the home of activism and social conscience on both sides of politics.

Racism, censorship, and town and gown all became issues as students flexed their muscles against the gerontocratic inertia of the 'RSL generation'. In June 1962, *Farrago* editor Stuart McIntyre angrily rejected a professor's claim that students were speaking out of turn: '*Farrago* adamantly insists that students have the right to express their views on anything without fear of staff disapproval,' he argued.

This defiance sprang from Melbourne University's Student Action, a 'front' of the ALP Club which attracted hundreds of students keen to protest against racism, apartheid and US nuclear testing. The ALP Club was ferociously democratic socialist; it hated the authoritarian Victorian branch of the ALP, it ridiculed 'political dinosaurs' like Calwell and saw hope in Whitlam. Although there were five political clubs on campus, the ALP Club was the largest. At its height in 1962–63 it had 250 active members.

Student Action's best year was 1961. Led by the lanky, charismatic Bill Thomas, it performed wonders of activism, consciousness-raising and student takeover. In that year we gathered money for AbSchol (an Aboriginal scholarship scheme), we demonstrated at the US consulates against the Bomb, against South Yarra landladies who put up signs reading 'Whites Only' and, of course, against an electioneering Menzies himself. It was the seedbed for a radical generation which organised the anti-Vietnam demonstrations at the end of the decade.

IN WHICH MR MENZIES AND I HAVE AN ALTERCATION

On the night of 24 November 1961, the night of my twenty-second birthday, about fifty unkempt radicals from Student Action heckled Robert Menzies until he literally went red in the face. He'd been in power for twelve years – far too long, we thought – and was now contesting the 1961 elections. The normally mild-mannered Menzies stood angrily denouncing us right at the very omphalos of Austral kitsch, the stage of the Moonee Ponds Town Hall. We twenty-year-olds saw this sixty-seven-year-old as an ancient, useless old fraud who worshipped British royalty, cosseted the DLP and sucked up to US Imperialists (and this was long before Vietnam). Every time he paused in his routine speech, we shouted 'Fascist!', 'Pig Iron Bob!' or 'Get off the stage!'

With my friends – John Paterson, Bill Thomas, Peter Samuel, Jim Jupp, Michael Keating and Rosemary Hansen – we won roars of applause from the Labor voters around us at the back of the hall. It was not exactly a Socratic discourse; it was just a fiery old-fashioned election meeting, the sort of thing that can't happen these days with short grabs and heckler-free studio audiences.

After Menzies' speech and during question time, John Paterson asked, 'Why hadn't the Liberal Party endorsed any Roman Catholics or Jews for the upcoming election?' Menzies became rattled at such impertinence, for no one had ever dared ask such a question. He said to the chairman with an angry wave in our direction, 'I want to say, having regard to the disgraceful behaviour of these larrikins, that half of them would not be at the university but for me.'

We shrieked with delight. His words implied he'd personally fathered us. There were cries of 'Rapist! Monster! Bigamist!' and Bill Thomas started singing

'Lloyd George was my Father'. This soon became 'Bob Menzies was my Father' and was taken up by the rows of Labor supporters, singing derisively. This was followed by the Liberals who began to vilify us as 'Labor rabble' and 'Communists'. It was 'extremely rowdy', the Melbourne *Herald* later reported.

Flustered at such an outbreak of disrespect, Menzies called out to John Paterson to stand up. Paterson, whose rare bone condition meant that he was only four feet tall, shouted: 'I am standing up, you big bully!' The applause for this calculated provocation became thunderous when the audience realised that Paterson was indeed a dwarf. It was not the last time that he would use his stature to great effect.

The whole episode was a marvellous birthday present for me, but it was not a good night for Menzies, who was personally terrified, and who only just squeaked back a few weeks later with a majority of one seat, the Brisbane seat of Moreton, won on Communist preferences. It is one of the tragedies of Australian history that the roughly decadal change of government didn't occur after these twelve years. Had Calwell won that election, Australia would not have become involved in Vietnam. But Menzies introduced conscription on 10 November 1964, which changed Australian history and helped elect Whitlam in 1972.

*

The interesting thing is how a conventional nineteen-year-old advertising copywriter had turned, in the course of a few years, into a raving leftwing radical intent on publicly humiliating his own Prime Minister. The ALP Club was the answer. The lunchtime meetings and annual Student Weeks of Socialism with disparate speakers such as Rodney Allen, Barney Carroll and Ken Davidson convinced me to make a commitment; but perhaps more influential were the club excursions, especially to Carlton and the now demolished Mayfair Hotel (classy) and the Horsemarket (cosy), as well as nearby Naughton's (gloomy) that still survives in Parkville. We had ALP Club conferences at guesthouses in the Yarra Valley, where I learned songs from Helen Palmer's songbook like 'Kevin Barry', 'Joe Hill', 'The Four Insurgent Generals', 'The Wearing of the Green' and the classic

'There'll always be a Menzies/while there's a BHP/ for they've been paying dividends/since 1883.'

But the real inspiration for the flourishing of campus politics was Bill Thomas. Everyone saw Thomas as a future Labor Prime Minister. Because he was a secular Catholic he was able to appeal to the left and the right wings, who were both convinced he belonged to them. Atheists and believers, who make up most reformist movements, were also manoeuvred in this way.

With his grand *joie de vivre* and savage tongue, Bill was exhilarating company. He also possessed brilliant organisational and operational skills. Then again, by dying in a car accident at just twenty-two, Thomas did generate many neo-religious genius myths. In an obituary in *Farrago* Vincent Buckley called him the 'most amazing political phenomenon' he had seen in sixteen years at universities. 'He was a passionate believer in human decency, a passionate hater,' Buckley wrote. Dr Knopfelmacher added his view also. He wrote that Bill was a 'Leninist type', in that he combined theory and practice along with a 'profound understanding of society'.

After Thomas's death, the zing went out of the

ALP club and it soon descended into bitchy faction fighting between socialists and Catholics to become merely a student reflection of the great Labor split off-campus.

OF KNOPFELS AND PORNO-POLITICS

Britain's Profumo scandal of 1963 was one of the most crucial cultural events since World War II. This incredible sex and espionage romp was one of the harbingers of the postmodern era. It certainly ended the then Conservative government in the UK, ushered in 'Swinging London' and the sex, drugs and rock 'n' roll with which the sixties is associated. After Profumo came Beatlemania. They both encouraged sexual honesty, helped to end censorship and seriously damaged faith in authority. I first read explicit descriptions of multiple partners, two-way mirrors and the bisexual osteopath Stephen Ward with disbelief. As I learnt of the doings of prostitute Mandy Rice Davies and her friend Christine Keeler, who had sex with John Profumo, the Tory Minister for War, I determined to get to London as soon as I could. The Melbourne *Herald-Sun* had never published such exciting copy.

Frank ('Franta') Knopfelmacher was also affected. At one of his regular lunchtime lectures on Friday 13 June, he was at his most scintillating. In his grating *mitteleuropeen* accent, he outlined Britain's terminal decadence with typical hyperbole, saying: 'Sexual aberration and blackmail are now regular features of British public life', and, 'Soviet agents have now penetrated all aspects of British society' (as well as Profumo, one or both of the girls had been screwing a Soviet military attaché called Ivanov). He warned students not to go to Oxbridge because these places too had been 'penetrated'. He said the British government was now controlled by a whore and the Soviet Embassy in Canberra should be closed. As usual, he was abusive of elites and lewdly entertaining.

At the end of his talk, Knopfelmacher was asked if there was any chance of the English rising in revolution against their corrupt establishment. He replied – years before Marshall McLuhan – 'You cannot have a revolution in a country where most people want to watch it on television.'

I reported the talk to *Farrago* editors George

Rousseau and Paul Lawson, two ALP Club members whose anarchism belonged to the seventies. We decided on a flip, irreverent coverage and a humorous graphic. We got a picture of Christine Keeler, cropped her head and placed Knopfelmacher's froglike features atop her big-breasted body. This joke predated the famous Gerald Scarfe *Private Eye* cartoon of Macmillan's head on Keeler's body. As a courtesy, we showed this altered picture to Knopfelmacher who, incensed, forbade publication. Later the photo was circulated on campus and Franta went off his head. He screamed about fascism, nazism, political gangsters, murderers and the mortal insult to his ageing, crippled wife. He ranted that we were Stalinist scum and bourgeois bolsheviks on a vile mission for what he would later classify as 'porno-politics'. We had intended a student joke, but now we had Gone Too Far. He lobbied the vice-chancellor, the Union council and before long the SRC invited the *Farrago* editors to resign and an inquiry commenced. What had started as an innocent prank became a Major Incident due to his hysteria. But that was the way he worked. The political corruption of the few communists at university now became the moral corruption of a generation. It was an example of his 'Knopfelmachiavellianism'.

In July 1963 Jim Jupp moved a motion that Knopfelmacher be expelled from the ALP Club. Jupp's motion asserted that Knopfelmacher's association with the extreme right wing of the Liberal party and the DLP is 'a source of embarrassment to the club'. It was not voted upon. Instead, Knopfelmacher resigned a few days later.

For more than twenty years, Knopfelmacher was the most effective anti-communist in Australia, publicly enacting his hatred of all totalitarianism. He couldn't believe that the Soviet empire would collapse like a house of cards as it did under Gorbachev, a Soviet leader who utterly mystified him. 'What is this Gorbachev,' he said to a friend in the late eighties, 'is he a realist or is he a novelist?' He was actually a left-liberal, the sort of person Franta had fought all his life.

DOING MUM, *BEING GLADYS*

I hoped to take on the political spirit that was now thriving on campus when I became co-editor of the

Melbourne University Magazine (MUM) in 1962. In one notable issue I had solicited articles from Knopfelmacher on 'Social Democracy and Defence', from Jim Jupp on '80 Years of Student Action' and from seven students, including two professed Christians, who now disclosed their agnostic beliefs. John Paterson wrote an attack on Scotch College to which I gleefully contributed, pointing out to him Cyril Connolly's 'Theory of Permanent Adolescence', an effective polemic against the clannishness, mediocrity and arrested development encouraged by the English public school system.

My languid co-editor, Brian Davies, had an entirely different take on student types in the early sixties. A psychologist working as a market researcher and making arty films on the weekend, Davies' main contribution to *MUM* was a jaundiced interview with Patrick White, who he said was overrated and enigmatic. In the editors' preamble, Davies said he had divined a new group of apolitical students who were both 'cordial and satirical, sophisticated yet unacademic, for whom there is only one great virtue – Talent'. 'They place great emphasis on control, coolness, the ability to ride all frustrations,' he continued. 'This almost compulsive relaxation, combined with their intelligence and hedonism, has produced a group of student Jokers . . .' Brian was writing about his stylish friends Simon Reed and Ian ('Jet') Jelbart, the architects whose finest gift lay in spotting the talent of others; he was also writing about himself, the hyper-intelligent, sophisticated cool cat who adored Truffaut, Fellini, de Sica and Mastroianni. Davies' isolation of the Joker, hipster type in 1962 was a prophetic insight indeed.

*

About the same time as *MUM* I also became involved with the Melbourne University Dramatic Society and its annual revue. The SRC hired the flamboyant theatrical entrepreneur Jon Finlayson to produce it. Acting talents from previous years had included Germaine Greer, Anne Harvey and Barry Humphries, and Finlayson and his theatrical friends kept up the satirical tradition. I found their camp banter both alarming and thrilling. They said things like 'Heavens Betsy!', 'Legs in the air, she didn't care!', or 'Get you, saucebox!', 'Up you for the rent' and 'Get her!', derisively tagging other males as female. Heterosexuals were said to be as 'square as a butterbox' which referred to more than just sexual orientation. They called cops 'Lily law', they said 'Dreary', 'Upstage', and 'On the roof ', with arcane usages like, 'Stop sending me up', which meant, kindly desist from sexually exciting me.

This saucy language was a new world at the Shop. But it didn't really convert me, since I was maintaining my position as bisexual. Everyone had a drag name – even the straight actors like John Joyce. At school I was Perce – now I became Gladys.

One of our great cross-dressing efforts was a song which sent up advertising about brassieres. Four boys wearing suspenders, stockings and bras sang the following:

Have you tried the Berlei Gothic,
Twenty-two sizes from which to choose,
Only Gothic has the flying buttress support,
More transom, more cuppage than any other bra,
In fact it has a lot more room than the latest Holden car . . .

Inspired, I co-produced a lunchtime political revue called 'Move the Gag'. It was a hit and made lots of money for the ALP Club. A résumé of the skits gives an idea of what we considered amusing in those days. We had Christine Keeler in bed with the Archbishop of Canterbury, a chorus of groupies dressed up as nuns singing 'Ave Santamaria' (inciting Catholic students to throw pennies at the actors) and Arthur Calwell played by a jeans-clad Peter Wood, miming one of the Jets in *West Side Story*. Peter's subtle and un-Calwellian pelvic gyrations went down particularly well, predicting, perhaps, his ultimate vocation as the Catholic Church's most sensitive spokesman on AIDS.

The funniest sketches were non-political: Princess Anne singing a song of her own creation called 'Under our Great Keeper's Sporran' and a skit about the first Russian woman in space having a *rendezvous* with a US astronaut, in which their sexual encounter is televised inadvertently and shown to cheering millions on earth. James Jupp proved himself a genius at dashing off fast Gilbert and Sullivan parodies. 'Three little girls from PLC/slashing our wrists in the lavatory', performed by three hairy males in drag, got a big laugh; as did one scene-change quickie which had Ruth Holt and myself dressed up as a little old woman and a little old man out for a walk in the Black Forest, and finding an abandoned baby boy. 'What shall we call him?' I asked Ruth. In a crackly crone's voice, she replied: 'Let's call him Elvis Knopfelmacher!' The very mention of that name was enough to cause hilarity, as Melbourne University was in the grip of a bad case of Knopfelmania.

Ruth had already made a name for herself by getting a three-month good behaviour bond several months before for shouting, 'You bastard!' at a policeman during a rare visit by Premier Bolte to the Shop in 1962. She was not charged for writing 'Hangman Henry' in coral pink lipstick on the windscreen of his limousine.

The show stopper was Menzies as the keeper of the Royal Spittoon. This was brilliant because we discovered an actor called Norm Higgs who had the timing and the fruitiness to carry off the part. Tall and ecclesiastical, Higgs referred to everyone as 'My boy' or 'My dear boy', and when he made a 'mistake' by referring to the fair sex as the 'Fairfax', he gave the false impression the PM was having an affair with

Lady Fairfax, a widely believed ALP rumour of the period. All rather Goonish, but engagingly innocent at the same time.

Carlton Romances

Where Apollo reigns, Dionysus will follow.
CYRIL CONNOLLY

My first infatuation with a woman came when I met Judy Gardner, the clever daughter of a Methodist minister, in the Baillieu Library of Melbourne University. She was tall with a sombre continental dress sense that appealed to me. I also liked her first confession, which was that she 'ate like a horse'. She was honest, bright, funny and musical and instantly engaged me with her teasing games and light banter. Passion, however, was not on the cards and our relationship remained platonic apart from one fumbled attempt. After it failed she asked me what was wrong and I said, '*Il n'y a pas de mystère*', which was a fairly heavy trip to lay on someone, albeit true. My preference for male bodies had been gaining the ascendancy as I had recently discovered beats as well as a Turkish bath in Collins Street which queens called Betty Bucci's Bum Boutique.

But the lack of sexual intimacy between Judy and myself was not really an issue as these were still prudish times when campus sex was usually lied about and practised mainly by the fast set. There was immense affection between us and I was hoping for a French-style companionate marriage, but there wasn't much in it for her.

When Alison Tudor, a mutual friend, told Judy about my affair with Bob Solomon, Judy was mortified. I had deceived her and used her. She said it explained my smirking arrogance and the fact that I wasn't sexually keen on her. After a while she was relieved, and it was my turn to be mortified. It now seemed undeniable that I was permanently camp. Judy could marry someone else, but it looked as if I would never get married, since I would not find anyone as perfect as her.

Before the breach, Judy and I and her charmingly vague sister Rosemary became close. I introduced Romey to my rough political friend Michael Keating. Unlike me, Michael was attracted to girls: he was crazy about Romey. He delighted in chasing after her in the rooms of their East Malvern house on all fours, barking and yelping, and his mix of clownishness and intelligence soon won her over.

Michael dropped out of student politics quite early in order to finish his Economics Honours degree, which he did with great distinction. He and Romey married in 1962, moved to Canberra and had four children. I was best man at his wedding, a 'dry' Methodist one where everyone carried hipflasks.

My own romantic life remained as confused as ever. These days it would be regarded simply as queer. After Judy Gardner, I started going out with Teresa Maguire, a boisterous, clever girl from Canberra whom I had met at Michael Keating's place in Heidelberg. I was playing crashing chords from Tchaikovsky's piano concerto in B flat minor and Teresa could perceive that the performer contained a *pianissimo* among all that *fortissimo*. Teresa had a quick wit and a high, clear operatic laugh. Effervescent and a great beauty, she could also be mulish and hysterical. Teresa was the daughter of a public servant and had journalism in her blood.

I ran into her again at the Horsemarket Hotel and convinced her to lend me her history notes since I was scared of failing (though I did anyway). Later, we went to see Bergman's *Wild Strawberries* at the

Australia Cinema. We held hands and both felt a frisson in the theatre only a few feet from the camp bar of that hotel where I ventured when lust got the better of me. Our affair began that night in her flat in Morrah (which we renamed Gomorrah) Street. I felt immense relief that I might be able to have an affair with a woman as appealing as Teresa. Maybe I *was* bisexual after all.

We read Dostoevsky, Henry James and Eysenck. We visited the 'Bughouse' in Carlton for continental movies, and the Genevieve coffee lounge. After seeing Bergman's depressing *Seventh Seal* we realised there was no point in continuing to live, so we attempted a double suicide by both putting our heads in Teresa's Early Kooka oven. As laughter overcame us with the first hint of gas, we decided that drowning would be a more romantic option. The next day we drove on my motor scooter to the St Kilda pier. We made up weighted bags which we would tie round our waists. Since there were two people but only one motorcycle helmet, I gallantly gave Teresa mine and improvised one by inverting a bakelite fixture from her standard lamp. This soon attracted the interest of a cruising police car on Beaconsfield Parade. The patrolman pulled us over as we motored towards our joint death pact, took us to St Kilda station and charged us. We told the sergeant our sad mission and he hooted with mirth, said it was a good omen, and that he would drop the charge if I bought another helmet. Obviously Teresa and I were meant to live.

We moved into a group house in Palmerston Street where we lived together for a year. We thought we were madly in love and were regarded by others as a natural pair. My friends approved of Teresa in a way they would never approve of a man. She was no mouse, she could chiack with the drinkers in the ALP Club and debate with great eloquence. On every level we seemed to work – socially, intellectually, scholastically, even sexually, which was quite a surprise to me. Formerly regarded as a somewhat wimpish character, I gained a lot of kudos from having a girlfriend as accomplished, formidable and attractive as Teresa. I guess she was also the perfect cover for my homosexuality.

She wore loose, full-length dresses and we loved screwing to Sibelius' violin concerto or, more often, to Ravel's *Bolero*, long before Bo Derek in the film *10*. I was sufficiently fond to go down on her even while she was menstruating. Teresa said she didn't mind about my bisexuality – 'My previous affair was with a moody musician,' she added irrelevantly.

Great student houses are passed on by word of mouth and 52 Palmerston Street was no exception. It was a warren with more than ten rooms, a cobblestone courtyard and that greatest prize, an L-shaped second-storey loft. To be a loft-dweller was the ultimate in bohemian hipness, for garrets were also exceptionally rare.

Teresa and I never made it to the loft but those couples who did tended to marry eventually: Irving Reid and Yvonne Mitchell, Peter Hall and my ex, Judy Gardner. In our room at the front my relationship with Teresa began falling apart. The extreme scunginess and domestic apathy of this group house didn't help. As a consequence, plates lay in the sink with chops still on them for weeks on end.

Doone had approved of Judy Gardner but she didn't like Teresa, calling her 'bog Irish' – and a Catholic to boot. She was also offended that Teresa and I were openly living together. One night after we had been co-habiting for months, my father arrived unannounced and delivered one of his irregular

'Father and Son' lectures.

He had parked his Holden station wagon outside and nervously knocked on the door of our boudoir. I took him downstairs and he addressed me in the courtyard. He declared that our living together was 'causing a problem'. Why was that? I asked defiantly. He said he liked Teresa personally but that the 'connubial relationship' between a man and a woman was the strongest known in society and must not be taken lightly.

'In wartime it is the young unmarried males who are called up first, because they have no attachments. Then it is older unmarried males – up to the age of forty-five. Always the last men to be called up are those who are married, because they are the hardest to separate, the ones whose deaths leave so many dependants,' he told me.

I was captivated by this analogy but I didn't see how it related to a non-warrior like me. Father manfully maintained his case. He said if I was going to live with a woman I really should get married, since that was 'the way things are done' and I was taking a short cut. He said he had to wait four years before he could sleep with Doone – he had to get married first. That was always the 'decent way things are done', otherwise women 'lost their value'. And if I wasn't going to marry Teresa I should cease the affair forthwith as I was using her. Men could do this, he said, but it was grossly unfair on women.

His homily was a classic parent/child clash of the sixties but it was a fight which the older generation was doomed to lose simply through the effluxion of time. Astonished by Alan's sudden interest, I promised to think about it. As I waved him off, I noticed Doone was sitting in the car. She had badgered him to come to Carlton to confront me, to make sure I didn't marry Teresa. Years later, when they knew I was gay, they were desperate that I should marry any female who would have me.

*

The person who terminated my affair with Teresa was Beatrice Faust, the distinguished feminist and author. It happened slowly. I wanted Teresa to partake in a threesome with my schoolboy lover Ian Dodswell, but she declined. I thought that was both unsporting of her and excessively Catholic. Ian and I had been in frequent contact since we left school, but he was now keen to avoid me as he wanted to get married. No matter how many other males I suggested grace Teresa's bed, even those whom she liked personally, she categorically refused to share her bed with two men at once. It was an impasse. Further, her fertility was starting to scare me. Teresa was pregnant by this time but I absolutely did not want the child. Apart from a lifelong pedophobia, I was probably enacting my mother's proscription of Teresa.

In a sisterly way, Beatrice took Teresa in her vintage brown Dodge Tourer to High Street, Prahran, to an abortion clinic. Teresa was told the foetus was extremely large – possibly twins. It cost sixty pounds to do it. The thought of twins was an even greater nightmare to me, the father who was a long, long way from settling down. The Prahran abortion terminated both our child and our affair. Later Teresa became bitter about Beatrice, calling her 'a wheezing, walking coathanger' and referring to Faust's eclectic, often gay collection of friends as 'Bea's zoo'.

I was intellectually attracted to Beatrice. As co-editor of *MUM* I published a piece of hers in which she revealed her background as a 'renegade Irish

Catholic' resented by her father because his wife had died giving birth to her. A fairly heavy burden for any child to carry. She was doing English/History Honours with a Psychology sub-major. In matriculation she had topped the state, sharing her exhibition in English Literature with the late Dinny O'Hearn. Her further studies were interrupted by the 1966 Kay enquiry into abortion. She played a big part in reforming Victoria's Victorian abortion laws and starting up the Women's Electoral Lobby in 1972.

Our romance was very courtly: for weeks, months we saw each other but nothing carnal happened. With her small frame, prominent shoulders and bronchial wheeze, she may have been no campus beauty, yet she was gutsy, clever, experimental – and female! She even looked boyish and was a fag hag before anyone had heard the term. I was hoping she would tolerate my bisexuality, and the fact that I had a dose of the clap.

She was still hopelessly in love with Bill Walker, a gay man who later married for a while, and who was the lighting operator for the early Barry Humphries shows. When Bill left Bea for an Englishman,

Beatrice and I started up. We spent afternoons in her Elgin Street flat screwing and discussing Lorca's theory of *duende*. Ours was a literary not a musical affair. I marvelled at her truly Karma Sutran flexibility in areas that then had hardly been named, like the epicoccygeous muscles and the G-spot.

Midway through our affair, Bea became pregnant and our child was terminated for another sixty pounds. Brian Davies lent me the money. This was Bea's third abortion. (She later had a son, Stephen, by the second of her two husbands.)

At the time I was firewatching for the Forests Commission at Briagolong in Gippsland to earn money to go overseas. Sitting in the Pinnacles firestation hoping for fires to break out was hard to reconcile with a gregarious type like me. I read voluminously. Bea made a welcome visit in her trusty Dodge and I handed over the abortion money. We went to have a drink at the Briagolong pub. As I was ordering the publican said, 'You must be a university student.'

'How did you know that?' I asked, miffed that my ocker cover had been blown.

'You've still got all yer teeth,' was his reply.

Bea returned to Melbourne and I went back up the cloudy mountain for my last few weeks as a firewatcher.

While Bea and I were on, my love for Ian Dodswell remained undiminished and mostly unrequited. Since Ian was still a virgin with women, I flashed with a bright idea: Bea could 'educate' him while at the same time I could resume our affair, even though all parties would now be sharing. This could be a most satisfactory arrangement, with Ian finding out about women, while Beatrice could taste another of the '1001 Delights' which she had once written about for *MUM*. These trysts with a twist occurred at her new house in Park Drive, Parkville, overlooking treeless Royal Park, and on weekends down at Ian's parents' holiday home in Mount Eliza. Sometimes they got quite operatic. I wrote bad poems about meeting Ian's orchis in Bea's yoni and took to reading Sappho, Catullus and other pagans.

It was an exhilarating time mentally and sexually. There was one great French film that year, *Jules et Jim*, part of the New Wave that predicted the polymorphous perversity of the seventies as well as the great sexual divas of the eighties. Set in the carefree days before World War I, this subversive masterpiece showed us that a threesome with two males and a female could work. *Jules et Jim* deliciously inverted the standard hetero French *ménage à trois* which assumed two women and a man. Catherine (Jeanne Moreau) played teasing games with her two attractive young men, bedding them separately and together. She wasn't a beauty but she was wacky, wilful and very much the boss. Raving about her performance, *Time* magazine said she had a mouth like a 'badly opened can of sardines'. Her frayed looks were part of her wicked impulsiveness as she drove the two young men wild with jealousy, their mutual desire binding the 'three crazies' into one psychosexual whole. It was French in its insouciance but we persuaded ourselves it was Australian because it examined the homoerotism between two mates.

We drove everywhere in Bea's veteran 1927 Dodge. Soon after seeing the film, Bea bought a camelhair skirt and grey rollneck jumper *à la* Catherine and delighted in teasing us by undressing in front of us. First Ian would fuck her then I would, always excited by the sight of a man's *gluteus maximus* muscles hard at work. Other times, we both fucked her together,

I lying underneath, Bea in the middle and Ian on top, both our *lingams* in her *yoni* at the same time. Gymnastically hard to achieve, these meetings were sensationally intimate. Ian and I got to feel each other while Bea gained double the pleasure. We called these rare events 'Two-in-Ones'.

In a memorable scene from the movie, Jules and Jim analyse Catherine's erratic actions. Jules explains: 'Don't worry, when she feels slighted she always overtrumps!' This is how our troilistic adventure ended. Our *ménage* became unstable and fissile as they inevitably do. Bea was miffed because I loved Ian more than her. Our open sex games only confirmed it. She said she wanted to be honest and tell my mother about everything, especially my longstanding love for Ian. I was horrified. I warned Bea that if she told Doone it would be the end of everything. But Bea insisted. I said her 'honesty' was really sadism. She denied this. She rang up Doone and arranged a dinner at Balwyn between Doone, Bea and myself. It turned into a confessional crisis. She got to the house first and told Doone that my relationship with Ian even went back to my schooldays. When I finally arrived on my motor scooter I was astonished to find them sitting ensconced together on the floor, openly discussing my shameful secret.

Doone was upset and weeping intermittently. She was smoking, something she hadn't done for years. On the one hand, she seemed appalled. Homosexuality was an awful thing – 'quite vile', she said. I said she was protesting a little too much, given the intensity of her own sporting friendships. Her Presbyterian mores came to the fore when she said to me contemptuously, 'So you've been throwing your cap at Ian, just like a woman!' On the other hand, she also seemed grateful to know and thanked Bea, saying, 'It explains so much now' – the failure of my relationship with Judy Gardner, for example. She said I should be careful because homosexuality was in the family. I replied it was in every family and it was no big deal. She disagreed and implored me not to tell my father as it would kill him, but I felt her paranoia was absurd.

Although Bea and I are now friendly, I never really forgave her for telling Doone on that day in 1963 and our lovely, Truffaut-inspired threesome ended that afternoon. She was mystified as to why I was so angry. She was only telling the truth, wasn't she? I told her she was jealous and seeking revenge. In love, I said, the truth can be a terrible weapon. I was in tears, Doone was in tears, and Bea was quietly satisfied. All I wanted was to earn some quick money and get away from horrible, awful Melbourne, the old sow that eats her farrow.

World's End and Back Again

I learned from him that sex is not a game,
it is a disease of the feelings, an itch, a rage, a mania
HAL PORTER, *THE WATCHER ON THE CAST IRON BALCONY*

Ah London! Once mighty and glorious, now raddled and spavined like a broken-backed old harridan.

You, the empress of the augustan world, now a painted whore of the colour supplements, a very Gross Britannia indeed.

Those clean-limbed young men, those innocent maidens, from every corner of your far-flung Empire, you lured them all – many to their ruin!

From the ovid hillocks of Otago, the wheatfields of Western Australia, the prairies of Canada, the kraals of Africa, the nursing colleges of Melbourne, the gargoyled dental schools of Sydney . . .

Yes, I too came to Carthage, to that delicious cauldron of unholy loves singing all around. . .

As a young acolyte of Empire, I saw Churchill in his home in Hyde Park Gate being carried by two nurses, his V-sign wilting; I went later to his funeral and wept the death of 'England's greatest son'; I, too, hymned the glories of the two-party system, saw Harold Wilson's mistress in the corridors of Westminster and went water-skiing in Essex with a closeted Tory MP . . .

I, too, visited Wren's London, heard the bell of St Mary's of Woolnoth clanging on the ninth stroke, got drunk in the Prospect of Whitby singing 'We All Live in a Yellow Submarine' and went home with a young pup to the Isle of Dogs . . .

I, who sodomised rent boys from Hull, had sex with actors from Slough, was undone by the Tree of Knowledge on Hampstead Heath, watched police raiding on horses, was buggered by a bikie from Wapping . . . It was I who rode sidecar around Scotland with a blond Borstal Boy huge of dick but minute of brain, and I, on a Channel ferry, who misled a sweet young girl from Dorset whom I took back to my Chepstow Road lair in Paddington, to promise we'd live in England forever . . .

I, too, devoured the Sunday papers as the 28 bus trundled down to Earl's Court and giggled over Gerald Scarfe's lampoon of Macmillan and at P. J. Proby when his crutch split open on stage for the twenty-third time . . .

Watch over us Saint Christine of the two-way mirrors, remember us Saint Mandy who always had the last word, sanctify us Saint Stephen, osteopathic in your ossiary, and pray for us Saint John in the poor houses of your guilty memory. Intercede on our behalf, oh Lord Harold, architect of many abominations, high priest of Tory hypocrisy, purveyor of perversions, Creator of Carnaby, in your crofter's cottage in the sky!

IN WHICH I EXPLORE THE UNDERWORLD

In 1964 boatloads of Australian physiotherapists, seemingly all called Gail, berthed and soon were fornicating, two couples to a room in Hampstead bed-sits, before doing Europe in Kombivans. There were young farmers from Quilpie, jewellers from Sydney, and thousands of Aussie doctors and dentists intent on rogering randy debs in the Royal Borough. They all came to London in the mid-sixties for the music, the career, the freedom, the fashions, and that once-in-a-century spectacle of an Empire imploding in opalescent decay.

The above is one way of putting it: generalised, sociological, well-armoured and flip, provocative yet aching with bravado and defensive in the extreme, my thirty-year-old hindsight has little to do with what actually happened when I arrived in London in March 1964.

I was afraid of going alone but I didn't care, so keen was I to leave the horrors of Melbourne, forever I hoped. It was not one of those epic voyages on the Chandris Line. P&O's liner *Canberra* was an air-conditioned nightmare, under way for Southampton. On the boat I made no friends.

In February 1964 the *Canberra* was a jinxed ship. For some reason it carried a number of suicidal passengers. We became aware of this after Colombo when a man had tried to kill himself by jumping off A-deck. He landed on Ddeck instead, hospitalising him for the rest of the voyage. A more sensational attempt came in the Red Sea – traditional theatre for weird happenings – with the call, 'Man Overboard!' We lounging passengers were able to see a man wildly beating the water in a shark-infested sea. Rapidly the crew let down a small motorised boat which went towards him as he flailed. A steward beckoned from the boat and insisted the man come aboard. He refused. He wanted to stay in the water and die. Foolishly, another crewman got in the water to try to hoist the passenger into the boat – and was taken by a shark! We saw his threshing, his screams for help, the blood in the water and his comrades who could do nothing. The attack was so frightful the intending suicide panicked and climbed back into the lifeboat. It was a silent journey as the lifeboat returned to the ship.

Next morning there was an eerie, moving burial at sea. The man who had caused the crewman's death became the most unpopular person on board, occasionally glimpsed scurrying away from people as he returned to his cabin, where he spent most of the voyage.

Within a month of arriving in London, I rented a bedsitter in Hampstead for six pounds, six shillings a week, which I shared with Ted, an English trainee zoo-keeper who had done his apprenticeship at the Whipsnade Zoo. The bed-sit looked over the Heath – eight hundred acres of copses, ponds and parkland. English habits appalled me, like most Australians:

the queuing, the greasy cafs, the grisly ads on the tube like 'Underwear that's Fun to wear', watercress sandwiches, jellied eels, dogshit everywhere, even the dogs fighting in restaurants without their owners batting an eyelid. Such a grey, fey little island filled with people who love pets more than people.

I was shocked by the verbal frankness of the English. Ted took me to innumerable pubs and parties where I met many 'birds' who were zestily outspoken on sexual matters and often made the first move. 'Come on,' he'd say, 'let's go and get some crumpet.' We quite often 'scored' and brought the birds home. Birds didn't become chicks until later in the sixties. A heterosexual cockney, Ted was astonished at how a colonial like me attracted such interest, which only increased when I demurred shyly, overcome by these tough-talking English women. Ted used me as bait in his bird-snaring, but soon I wanted out of this hetero aviary around the Heath. I craved something less 'vanilla' but I didn't know where to look. Ironically, the answer lay on the Heath itself, though it was not until much later that I discovered the largest open-air gay beat in Britain. Meanwhile, doing all the pubs with Ted from the Flask to Jack Straw's Castle simply had me depressed.

A month later I ran into a friend in Piccadilly whom I had known in Melbourne. It was Brian Shattock, an *homme fatale* who knew the city's underbelly – and I left the birds of Hampstead forever. Shattock had been educated at Melbourne Grammar then Trinity College. Musically accomplished, he was a startlingly beautiful teacher of the 'liberal arts' with cold blue eyes, black hair and a taste for rough trade. Since he had arrived in London before me, he was able to guide me around a demi-monde which made Melbourne seem like Mudgee.

For six months Brian and I shared a flat together at 52 Chepstow Road, Paddington, while, like Charon, he showed me the Underworld. He took me to gay pubs in the East End, and to the Elephant & Castle south of the river. He took me to the Calabash, a piss-elegant club, and the amazing gay wonderland of Earl's Court, where I spent too much time.

Brian loved teasing men with his Italianate good looks. But like E. M. Forster, he fell for working-class navvies and adventurers. He showed me the cruising pubs around Piccadilly Circus, especially the White Bear, where rent boys could be had for a few quid, just as in the time of the great Oscar.

The most fascinating, squalid dive we visited – unique in London – was called the Place, off the Kings Road in World's End. It was definitely the end of something, this subterranean fuck 'n' suck bar; probably civilisation as we knew it. It was all sighs in the darkness and fumbling hands and oozing walls, perspiration pouring down them like the house in *The Amityville Horror*.

Except for the occasional sounds of muttering, sucking and (un)zipping, the cellar was silent. There was the dirty sock aroma of amyl nitrite, a stimulant for angina sufferers which was adopted by queens as a sexual top-up. In the rectal-mucus dankness, you could just make out a seething mass of men, some topless, some bottomless, some in denim, some even in the Kings Road floral shirts, kissing, frotting and fondling. They were approaching or repelling each other like amoeba in a stately, wordless ballet of male desire as old as humanity. Indeed, lust like this, be it Ortonesque rough trade or the later cult of the leatherman, is much more elemental and 'male' than that of any husband sitting meekly at home with his family. I became addicted more to the sense of danger than the sex.

In the Place, some young men were serviced by several hobbit-like old men who moved on all fours like sea-floor crabs, searching at fly level for a proffered member whose owner did not reject them. When accepted, they blissfully settled down and performed their work, sucking greedily like waterbabies on a nipple until orgasm, whereupon they were roughly pushed out of the way, while the dick-owner zipped up and exited the cellar of sighs, home to Pimlico, Shepherds Bush or Earl's Court on a London Transport bus.

I found this nightspot incredible. Dantesque. It was so anonymous and anomic, so fascinating and, at the same time, so defeated and repulsive. The dissociation of a person's emotions from his sexuality made him a piece of meat, a mass of ganglia. This schizoid split became more widespread as the sixties wore on into the seventies and eighties – as the gay revolution 'took root', as it were. Wasn't this what Gay Liberation had hoped to reform?

Because gay sex was illegal in Britain at the time, and the owners probably paid off the bobbies, the atmosphere of contempt and degradation was intensified. And yet the Place could also give you an ultimate high. The first time Brian took me there, I was worshipped as New Flesh. We moved zombie-like through the cellar, tarried a while here, cockteased there, hurried to avoid a Groper – a horrifying old desperate inhabiting the darkest corners. While we had no compunction feeling others up, Brian and I made sure that we did not touch each other. We might have been flatmates, even 'sisters', but we certainly weren't on together. Gradually, gratefully, we climbed up the cellar stairs to the streetlights on the Kings Road, to air and comparative freedom from obsession.

'God,' I said. 'It's amazing!'

'Some people live there, they come here every night,' Brian laughed.

'But it's not for me,' I replied, 'not really. I prefer lights, a drink, a chat, a bit of a laugh. . .'

'Yes,' he said. 'The one thing that's taboo down there is laughter.'

When I went to Europe for a weekend, Brian moved John, a labourer, into our flat and his room. Although they claimed only to be sharing a bed, I often heard them doing more. John was an attractive-enough Irish layabout, who had the impertinence to despise me because I was an honest 'shteamer', as he called me, even though he himself had had sex with Shattock for months. Brian was crazy about John, but when they tried to avoid paying the rent I threw them out.

I frequented either Bolton's in Earl's Court, or the Colehearne opposite – a large cavernous, late Victorian pub specialising in leather, rough trade and foreigners. I became obsessed with this part of Earl's Court – monomaniacal, as addicted as a junkie. Walking down Earl's Court Road became a *via paradisa* for me. For two years these pubs, along with a nearby drag bar called the Chepstow, were my Nirvana. I would come home from work, eat a quick dinner of omelette or fish fingers and frozen vegies, get dressed in something vaguely leathery, and walk down Chepstow Road. At Westbourne Road I jumped on a 28 or 31 bus and alighted at Earl's Court once, twice, sometimes four times a week.

This erotomania is a common enough experience for every gay man when he first comes out. I would stand around drinking tepid pints and eyeing off other young men eyeing me off under the Watney's ads and framed pictures of Edwardian chorus girls. There were plenty of cigarette machines and this gave the opportunity for enquiries about change, or the weather, or the time, or any other of these endless obvious gambits in pick-up land.

Usually I approached my prey with some lost-boy, marsupial routine: 'You wouldn't have a half-crown for one of these bloody machines?' was one of my cornier openers (the diphthongs very much in evidence). I was often rejected but just as often I scored, preferring good-looking effeminates. Since I was then a passable twenty-four, it wasn't too hard to notch up a score approaching one hundred. But I quite often fell in love too, and was regularly impaled on Cupid's arrows.

To the Colehearne I took many visitors including, one night, painter Keith Looby and economist Paddy McGuinness, who was then working at the Moscow Narodny Bank. Paddy watched the English queens cruising the baby-faced Keith and myself, but ignoring him. He said bitterly, 'Nobody ever tries to pick me up.' Hardly surprising since even then he was red-faced, plump and sacerdotal, not a good look in a gay pub.

Paddy, then an anarchist, lived with one of his several French girlfriends and his Australian foil, Ian Parker. Parker and Paddy had studied economics together at Sydney University and become one of the Push's oddest couples. It was not sexual, but there was a weird S&M about them. In those days and for many years after, Paddy couldn't live without Parker. They nagged, tortured and supported each other like any old couple of many years' standing. Paddy was large while Parker was small. Paddy was gruff, Parker imploring. Paddy could handle his grog while Parker couldn't. Paddy was successful, Parker a failure, having stuffed up his PhD at ANU. Random phosphorescent shards of his former brilliance would show when he went into raves against the Tories, the 'Reverse Bank' of Australia (as he called the Reserve Bank where he had worked) and the general bastardry of landlords and people on the make. Sadly, Parker was slowly sliding into alcoholic paranoia. His dingy ground-floor bedroom in Paddy's apartment, which was opposite my flat, had at least twenty quart-sized Bulmer's cider bottles. Some were full of cider, others full of Parker's piss. Jobless in London, Parker found cider and perry (pear juice) a cheaper inebriant than beer. Dressed in anarchist black, bespectacled and looking like Oblomov, Parker shuffled off every afternoon to the local off-licence for more Bulmer's at half a crown a bottle.

Like Parker, McGuinness was also right at home in the anarcho-Marxist traditions of London. Paddy sided with his co-tenants and denounced the upwardly mobile as 'coppers' narks'. His finest act in Chepstow Road infuriated his landlord, who was trying to sell the house. Paddy put up a large sign in the window which said: 'Don't Buy Us. The Roof Leaks. The Walls Are Cracked And The Drains Don't Work.' The landlord tried to evict them but couldn't because of rent control.

After the departure of Brian and John, I invited another Push character to move in. Chester Graham was a talented Sydney University writer and theatre person who was in the throes of deserting his large blonde wife, Sue, an American heiress. Chester and I had a desultory affair after he left her. He was keen on me, for this was his first gay relationship, but I preferred his mind to his body.

He was tall and nerdish with a wit like a whip, a scintillating ectomorph. Starting with Berlitz schools, he later became an acclaimed English language teacher in Rome and Lisbon, finishing up in Brazil. He used to boast how often he'd arrive at European frontiers carrying bags filled with nothing but dirty washing, or relate how Roman slaves used to get off with each other in the catacombs and used the special intimate greeting 'Ciao', indicating another slave. (Was he having me on? In any case, I was a slave to his raves.) He was full of Sydney University Dramatic Society gossip about Clive James, who was revered even then, and whom I saw at several expats' parties, down from Cambridge. Germaine Greer, whom I did not come in contact with for another twenty years, was also one of Chester's favourite topics. Chester and Germaine had been close at Sydney University, but unlike other men who talked about her, Chester never made stupid sexist cracks. It was hardly surprising he did not see her in sexual terms, because he was gay.

Not that Ms Greer would know. In a 1972 interview with Bob Ellis in *Nation Review*, Germaine claimed to have fallen in love with Chester back then in the sixties. She was lolling in the bathtub when Chester had dropped by, eager to read some lines from a play he hoped to produce: 'Chester paid absolutely no attention to my nakedness,' Germaine said. 'Altogether it was one of the most extraordinary unspontaneous situations I've ever been in.'

After Chester headed off to teach on the continent, Christopher Pearl turned up to take his place. Though my passion for Chris remained unrequited ever since our friendship at George Patterson's agency, this time things would change dramatically.

Christopher was only in London to earn money to go back to Greece, his Hellenic fixation cultivated after nine months living in Athens where he had picked up almost fluent, demotic street Greek. Initially he stayed in Earl's Court with his friend Liz McLean until I was invited to a dinner party there in celebration of his arrival.

Because London Transport in those days effectively terminated at 11.30 pm, Chris suggested I stay the night. We ended up alone in the same room (was this by design?) and early in the morning my wandering hand found Christopher's and, within seconds, other equally eager parts of his anatomy. At last my love had been reciprocated and when he later moved into Chepstow Road my first experience of living together as a gay couple began.

IN WHICH I BECOME A SUPPLY TEACHER

I landed on my feet in London, getting a job within a month through a Miss Rickus, Personnel Officer of the Borough of Brent. The job was supply teaching: filling in for permanent teachers who were absent or having a nervous breakdown. In those days it was quite a rort. Part of Middlesex, Brent contained a number of Secondary Modern schools in spirit-draining North London bearing such doleful names as Willesden, Harlesden, Brondesbury and Queens Park. The schools in this vast wasteland of lower-middle-class brick terraces were connected by the Bakerloo Line and by the quaint above-ground carriages of British Rail. Even today I can smell chalk, dust and fear and see a room full of laughing black faces when I hear again names such as Dollis Hill or Salisbury Road.

I taught largely West Indian adolescents in classes of thirty, for the huge sum of twenty-five pounds a week. It was tax-free for a period of two years in the UK; if you stayed longer, all the accumulated tax had to be repaid. Supply teaching was the perfect way to see Europe on a working holiday. One could hitch-hike to Sicily for a month (as I did later at three days' notice) and then immediately resume work.

The West Indian schools tended to be better than the schools where English pupils predominated. The West Indian girls were more effervescent, more responsive, more willing to learn and more filled with hope: in other words, they were more educable. Even so, one was not required to teach so much as to entertain in this cynical perversion of the welfare state so well portrayed in L. P. Braithwaite's novel and later in the Sidney Poitier film *To Sir, With Love*. Everyone living in Supply-land was filling in time; the teachers until the day ended, and the students until they reached fifteen.

My charges' parents tended to be train drivers, cleaners or Portobello Road fruit sellers. Academic rigour was minimal. Many of the girls wanted to be hairdressers in salons in the nearest high street. Most were counting the days before they escaped to a 'reality' they would regret within a year. That's why some classes contained girls who had returned, with a few who were nearly twenty.

One such student on the rebound was Cleopatra Dobson, a mature, exuberant young West Indian woman who regarded the meticulous combing of her best friend Dolores' crinkly hair as infinitely more important than the fate of the Tolpuddle Martyrs, whose story I was telling at the time. My students were even less responsive to Oliver Cromwell and the Long Parliament, although the story of Pocahontas always struck a chord. It was difficult not to adore these kids. Spontaneous and demonstrative, they would swarm about the teachers they liked, bantering and seeking autographs.

The trick was to be friendly while maintaining a suggestion of dignity. Like most Australians, I was too easy-going and informal. I soon realised this spelled disaster, as one became a patsy, a sucker, a huge mug. If it were reported back to Miss Rickus that a teacher had 'discipline problems', one's future work could be curtailed severely. The authorities didn't care about education, any more than the teachers did. They just wanted no trouble.

It was not uncommon to hear the words 'Get fucked, Sir' from children, both white and black, in answer to the simplest request. One had to stay patient, realising such statements were not insubordination so much as the *patois* of north London. But when Cleopatra said to me, 'Gee, Mr Blazey, I'd like to take your bag to de tube station, and then we could go to dinner and I could fuck you,' I should have coldly rebuffed her. Instead, my inappropriate response – 'Not tonight, Cleopatra' – inspired shrieks of laughter. Seeking to retrieve the situation, I said, in Joyce Grenfell tones, 'We don't speak to our teachers like that do we, Cleopatra?' Quick as a flash, she retorted, 'Yes we do, Sir, when dey come from Australia.'

Christopher Pearl was another Australian teacher having some droll adventures of his own. With my help, he too had a position in the Borough of Brent and while working at Queens Park Primary School came the extraordinary tale of the turd in the shoe. The turd had been discovered, quite large and fresh, in a sandshoe in a change room at the school. Arriving to work, Christopher discovered the staffroom in an uproar as the large, vinegary, grey-haired headmistress Miss Lumley sought to accuse one of the teachers present.

Bearing the sandshoe like a trophy into the staffroom, Miss Lumley said, 'We all know enough about biology to know that this didn't come from one of the children. We all know it came from an adult.' The teachers present were indignant to be accused of this enormity and denied it vociferously. One said that in thirty years of teaching he had never been so insulted. 'For God's sake, take the thing outside!' he demanded. But Miss Lumley said, 'I'm sorry, I cannot accept your denials. We're going to get to the bottom of it.' Weirdly, she persisted: 'I know it's not the caretaker, I know his toilet habits, and besides this is quite fresh. Maybe it was one of the supply teachers.' She asked Christopher, one of the two supply teachers at the school, where he'd been earlier in the morning.

Christopher declined to answer. Instead he said, 'I'm sorry, Miss Lumley, but the list of possible culprits should be extended to six. You yourself are not above suspicion. You certainly have the frame for it!' After that the suppressed laughter took over and Miss Lumley was forced to beat a retreat with her *objet trouvé*.

*

It was apparent that certain schools were quite beyond the pale. From other teachers one heard bloodcurdling rumours about schools which were dangerous, of teachers departing them in County of Middlesex ambulances. It was like hearing rumours about atrocities during a far-off war. The first news of Mai Lai or Srebreniza must have been passed on in the same halting, hushed tones as I heard about hammers, bottles, knives in the schools of Brent. My friend Julia McKay left one school after a knife was pulled on her. A New Zealander was brained with a wooden compass, a Canadian hit with a broken bottle. One heard of fourteen-year-old girls spending all day in headmasters' studies in states of déshabille.

Time and again the names of several schools recurred, but at the top of everybody's list was Pound Lane. This was the Great Mother of all Slum Schools, the Babylon of Evil, the black hole of English liberal education where most students were illiterate. It was the last resort when all other schools had turned down a student. Great bad schools are not born, however, they are made – and incompetent headmasters have a lot to do with it. So I was more than curious when Miss Rickus told me that the turnover at Pound Lane was 'higher than usual' and that I could do a week there. As a courtesy we were allowed one free period for travel to get to the school for the first time. When I finally arrived at Pound Lane, I was impressed. The school stood on a hill, there were plane trees all around the extensive playgrounds and marvellous views of the rolling terrain of north London, including a much more famous school, Harrow-on-the-Hill. I asked my way to the staffroom from a sullen youth dressed in a leather jacket who regarded me with contempt: 'Not anuvver bleeding teacher. Where you from, huh?'

Ignoring him, I went to the staffroom during lunchtime and was astonished. It was more like a lobotomy ward. The teachers seemed to be in a state of shock: some were giggling, others had strange compulsive tics. I announced myself as a new teacher and heard bitter laughter. Several of these craven people said they'd lost count of new teachers and one said, 'Best of luck, cobber.' I walked over to the tea urn, which was rusted and disused. An elfin teacher called Sally approached and tittered, 'Oh, we haven't used that for ages. You should try this.' She felt into her handbag and pulled out a hipflask of gin. 'Go on, take it – it's the only "tea" you'll get in Pound Lane.' I took a nip and noticed others doing likewise. It was necessary in order to perform one's duties, Sally informed me.

The teachers started talking about two feared boys named Wilcox and Pascoe, about fires being lit in classrooms and about one headmaster who left his own office via the window, screaming, 'I can't take this any more.' There had been a fight that morning in which a teacher had been hit on the head by a cosh and taken to a medical clinic. I was his replacement. They explained: 'It doesn't matter what you teach, you must *never* turn your back on them.'

'What about writing on the board?' I asked, starting to get nervous. Traditionally, an army of Anzac teachers disfigured the blackboards of London with pictographs of kangaroos, wattle, kiwis and moas.

They chorused with derision. 'Nobody writes on the board in this school. Far too dangerous.'

How then was one expected to teach? I asked. Sally took a large toke from her hipflask and said one had to keep them entertained, so as to get out 'in one piece'. And what about the syllabus? Several people stared at me as if I'd said 'Hail to Hammurabi' or 'How do you get to Jeparit?' The syllabus? They scratched their heads. The syllabus *had* been followed a few years ago, but not any more. 'These days, it's a matter of playing it by ear,' said someone in a Welsh accent.

In this crowded, demoralised staffroom, with an oculist's eye chart in the corner, one of the few things functioning was a large clock, which was being watched warily as it edged towards H-Hour: 2.15 pm. A siren sounded. Lunch was over and the staffroom went silent. Some teachers took a last puff on their cigarettes, then tumbled out of the room. Sally kindly showed me my classroom and left.

It was a boys' class. They were about fifteen years old, half of them black, half white, dressed as toughs in jackets of synthetic fur, leather and vinyl. They looked surprisingly smug. I told them I was a replacement teacher. To rising noise, I called the roll. At the end of it, one boy of considerable bulk said, in a bored voice, 'We know you're the replacement, Sir. Pascoe decked Mr Robb, who was a silly old cunt, and he'll do the same to you – if you stay long enough.'

Instead of being scared, I was incensed by the boy's insolence, his cynical acceptance that nothing would change. As Pascoe was being questioned by the police, I asked the name of the boy who had first spoken to me. Fallon, he replied. I told him to get out of the classroom. He refused. I gave him one more chance, saying, 'Fallon, if you don't leave now, I'll personally throw you out!' I was amazed at how icy I sounded. Fallon hesitated. He looked around for class support, but it was wavering. Maybe they were fed up with disruption for one day. I moved threateningly towards him. When he stood up I realised I was much bigger. That was one thing Australians had over the poms, a healthier diet. We stared defiantly at each other. I knew if I got Fallon in a headlock, I could drag him out the door, but I didn't have to for he seemed to sense my dominance. Suddenly he bent down, picked up his bag and walked out the door, calling me a 'flash Australian cunt'.

It was a minor miracle. There was a sigh of relief and after that everything was OK. The students told me what had happened. How they had had a succession of lousy teachers who only stayed a day or two. When I asked the headmaster, a seedy, defeated man called Moyle, if I could remain at his school, he practically blessed me. I'm not claiming anything heroic, but I taught at Pound Lane for two months, which was a long stay for me. Later I heard that several hopeless cases had unexpectedly passed their exams.

IN WHICH I SELL ENCYCLOPEDIAS IN GERMANY

Unfortunately the Furies were descending in the form of a taxman who required the last two years' tax on my teaching salary to be repaid in order for me to remain in the UK. Like cicadas Christopher and I had sung through two summers, never thinking of the winter. There were few prospects for me. Christopher's father Cyril, on our one meeting, coldly told me to write to the chief of staff of the *Guardian*. Cyril didn't like me, suspecting (years since Adland) that I was now having an affair with his son. He was right, but our relationship was entering its final stage of bickering and malice due to extremes of jealousy and poverty.

At least Christopher had hit on a brilliant plan to reverse our fortunes. We would go to Munich and sign on as part of the Grolier International sales team who were selling encyclopaedias to illiterate

US servicemen on Germany's many army bases. First, however, we would sub-let the Chepstow Road flat, the scene of so many joys and parties in earlier days. I slipped a card in the window of a Notting Hill newsagency which promised an airy flat with 'two bedrooms, white carpet, smart, elegant, modern, on major bus lines. Three months' rent in advance.' Soon two delightful Danish girls wrote saying they were interested. We met them and everyone was charmed, especially after they handed over the advance rent. We said we were returning from Germany within three months anyway. Some time after we departed, they discovered the rent was already three months in arrears, so they had to pay another six months' rent just to stay in the place. They were not pleased. They wrote a furious letter to *poste restante* at the Munich Post Office, saying how awful it was that two seemingly 'nice boys' were really 'total swindlers' who had completely ruined their trip to London. Christopher and I did feel a little caddish when we read this letter. It was a bit rough, but how else were we to get out of England?

We joined up with the Grolier International team in Munich, which was actually a couple of 'wide boys', ie spivs. The head of the team was cockney Tim who, with his brassy girlfriend Cheryl, drove a sales team of about ten people all over the US army bases of south-west Germany. These salespeople were dropped off and spent afternoons and evenings trying to sell encyclopaedias to ill-educated, non-commissioned officers, SP4s and the like, who were often black. The absurdly detailed knowledge in the twenty-six volumes could hardly profit them in their current circumstances, and the repayments of 'merely $30 a month' for years wouldn't either, even though the profusion of coloured pictures was attractive, especially to their children. If allowed into the quarters – which occurred about once in ten attempts – we put the main book on the floor, plus a few updates. Our standard pitch was to say the encyclopaedia itself was free but the annual updates cost only four hundred dollars a year.

One had to be ruthless and think only of the $200 commission to get a sale out of these poor people. Several times Christopher and I were near to closing deals but stopped, warning the vulnerable SP4s that the whole thing was a huge rip off.

Much of the money went on accommodation

and petrol for Volkswagens which Tim and Cheryl drove from Stuttgart to Mannheim, to Frankfurt and back to Munich. Some members of the team were quite brilliant, notching up scores of three or five sales per week. But Christopher only sold one and I didn't sell any. The truth is neither of us had our hearts in this fraudulent operation and it showed in our pitches. It finished, as it had to, six weeks later by Christopher and I being dropped off in Munich with our belongings and a few hundred marks between us.

We were now seriously broke and decided to try to get to Garmisch-Partenkirchen, a ski resort at the Austro-German border. But first we had to get out of Munich. We had booked into a pension near the station with insufficient money. We told the owner we were expecting large sums from England soon. Then began a tortured scramble for survival. We sold blood several times until we were expelled from the hospital with a touch of anaemia. I wrote letters to friends in the UK, pleading for money. Among the few replies was someone who offered to leave a five pound note at the Calais Post Office so I could catch the Channel ferry. We chatted up people coming in on the Orient Express, mostly Turkish guest workers who were happy to pay for our breakfast if we entertained them with German stories in our polyglot of broken languages. Daily trips to the Deutsche Vereinsbank still yielded nothing and I cursed my so-called 'friends'.

We became desperately hungry, as the pension had ceased serving us meals. It was now October and getting colder every week. We were reduced to begging, which grew more difficult as our appearance deteriorated. Each day we visited the HofBrauhaus with four pfennigs which allowed entry and the purchase of a roll. After this it was easy to steal food from tables as we moved from one to the next singing dreadful German drinking songs. I became an expert shoplifter. After various run-ins with shopkeepers and police we discovered that Germany is lenient about food theft – it's called *mundraub* (mouth rob) and it's hardly a misdemeanour. That was nice to know.

The bill at the pension had mounted to the huge sum of three thousand marks which made it necessary to spin increasingly improbable stories to the manager who sat at a desk on the first-floor staircase. We decided to go to the Australian Consulate, where they tagged our passports and lent us fifty dollars, enough to get out of Munich. Meanwhile, the manager was becoming more and more hostile, so an escape was arranged for after 7.00 pm, when the night manager came on.

We had three suitcases in our fifth-floor apartment and these had to be removed by means other than the main stairs. We threw the suitcases out the window. Although two of the cases didn't open, one hit a Kombivan and showered underwear all over Damenstiftestrasse. Christopher gathered it up as we both ran to the BahnHof. We heard the sound of police sirens and of cars roaring as we escaped. Paranoid that they were still after us, we broke the journey halfway at the charming Bavarian town of Mittenwald. Finally, we got to Garmisch.

Chris secured a job in the Hotel Eibsee. I found a job in a Heimsauna factory, making saunas for personal use at home, and worked only with Germans for several months, getting my Deutsche sprechen up to scratch. Signs on the walls implored us to 'Say pleasant things all the time' and 'Be nice to one another'. Was this an example of post-Hitler social engineering?

Or was it part of the all-pervading Bavarian kitsch: niceness and sentimentality gently snowing down and settling over unthinking racism? Bavaria, like the American South, was very ethnocentric.

All through 1966, my adoring mother had been working hard on my future. Earlier, in London she had sent the middle brother Antony to visit, ostensibly on Hortico business, but really to check up on me. Antony stayed several weeks at Chepstow Road. He and Christopher got on well, Chris managing to persuade Antony to strip down to jockettes while he drew his athletic body in pencil. It was an inspired drawing and Antony was quite flattered. My brother berated me for being gay, however, saying he had once hero-worshipped me, but could now do so no more. Although he was rooting three birds a week, he attacked me for my immoral lifestyle.

Naturally, when he returned to Melbourne he told of the infamy which had befallen the firstborn of the Blazey family. My resourceful mother hatched a plan. In saccharine letters, complete with application forms, she reminded me that I only had a year to go before I was no longer eligible to be a Junior at Peninsular Golf Club, Frankston, a great boon that saved thousands of dollars and conferred benefits for the rest of one's life. She wrote: 'Please, darling Pete, fill out this form and send it back. You'll never regret it! Love, Mother.' Since I disliked golf and loathed the private school jocks who were club members, I wasn't tempted. She was disappointed at my lack of 'sporting spirit' so evident in all the other family members.

Her next and final plan had to do with Clive. He had met a wonderful girl, Penny Hiscock, and it was likely they would be getting married at the end of the year. The Hiscocks were such a nice family. I really should come back for the wedding. Its date, 25 February 1967, approached. After three European winters, suddenly an Australian summer starts to appeal. Freezing and with few prospects, I decided to swallow my pride and accept my mother's offer of a Lufthansa air ticket from Frankfurt to Melbourne.

Christopher and I had a heart-wrenching farewell. On our last night together at the Hotel Eibsee, we softly sang 'our' song which summed up our marvellous, doomed six-month relationship: 'Though it's forbidden and I'll love you never, / I'll keep my love hidden forever and ever . . .' We really did have one of the great affairs, we decided, but it was not fated to last. Christopher went on to Greece, and I flew resolutely to Melbourne.

Clive and Penny's wedding, held at St John's sandstone church, Sorrento, was sumptuous. Everyone loved it. Lots of people told me how thin I looked. 'My dear, what have you been *doing* over there in England?' Antony had already preceded me with gossip. But Doone was happy that night. She had her three sons, all in dinner suits, dancing with girls on the one floor.

The Strange Death of Harold Holt

I loved him, but he never loved me.
Zara Bate

In my determination to become a 'useful member of society' I landed a job at the *Australian* within a month of returning and started a postgraduate degree at Melbourne University. I maintained my honour, I thought, by not joining any golf clubs. Graduates were not appreciated in journalism then, being considered slow and pompous, but I gained a position on the recommendation of Michael Keating, who had become a Treasury official.

Taking the job with Murdoch meant declining my father's offer of a position at Hortico. As a believer in primogeniture, he was thrilled at the thought of all three sons working in his firm; but a trial of five days at the Port Melbourne works convinced me otherwise. Here were grey-coated chemists, sweaty labourers and executives eating peanut butter sandwiches amid the pungent smell of blood and bone. People were horrendously polite to each other.

As one of the most inexperienced D-graders on the *Australian*, I alternated with another, Jonathan King, on night shift at the Melbourne bureau situated on one floor of the old *Truth* building in La Trobe Street. This involved the impossible task of competing with the locally based *Age* and *Sun*. It was a valiant attempt to 'cover' the city and condense all the crimes, strikes and parliamentary news which had occurred after our extremely early deadline of 4.00 pm into a single late news box or 'fudge' printed in red ink for the second edition. The Sydney-based *Australian*, with a Victorian circulation of about 17,000, was regarded by the Melbourne press corps as an exotic joke.

So it turned out to be incredibly lucky for me that Harold Holt decided to go for his last swim at Cheviot Beach on Sunday 17 December 1967 while I was staying nearby. Not only was the death by drowning of a Liberal Prime Minister the start of a series of events leading to Labor's victory in 1972, but it greatly assisted my own career.

Clive and I, holidaying at Whimsy, had gone down to Portsea's surf beach for a swim at about

11.30 that morning and were astonished by the water. There was a raging westerly, and the beach was closed with crossed flags, a very rare event and something that would not normally have dissuaded us. But the boiling fury of the waves, more than ten feet high, stopped us in our tracksuits. 'I dare you,' I said, but Clive, more practical than I, baulked before the wildest surf he'd ever seen. We went back to the house for breakfast.

When we heard the first radio messages at about 3.00 pm that Holt was missing in the water at Cheviot, a mere four beaches away from the Portsea back beach, we were dumbfounded. For one thing, we must have been better surfers than Holt (who was really a dog-paddling Bay snorkeler) and we hadn't dared put a toe in the water.

I went to the gates of the Quarantine station, which also housed Portsea Officers' Cadet Training School, and watched the frantic movement in and out of police vehicles. After talking to some army men, I rang Max Hollingsworth, the Sunday duty editor of the *Australian*, telling him to send several journalists to Portsea to cover what seemed to be a 'major, major' story. Of course it was. For the next three weeks journalists lived in Whimsy racking up a huge phone bill and providing a sensational scoop.

Several elements made the story bizarre. First it happened at Portsea, which not only is snobby Melbourne's most exclusive resort but is also the base for the glamorously sleazy 'Portsea set' – a group of raffish, swinging, hard-drinking, skindiving spouse-swappers. Living at Portsea or in Toorak and the wealthier suburbs, their style was anti-suburban: it comprised a throwaway elegance in which ostentatious display was despised as 'nouveau' even though many of them were just that.

The 'old money' owned a 'high water title' on the 'golden mile' which meant they had private beaches. They belonged to the Sorrento Golf Club, not Portsea (which was public) and their MGB-driving sons drank at the Nepean, not the Portsea, and skied at Falls Creek in the winter. These public school groovers were named Andrew, Jonathon or Antony and they invariably married girls named Caroline, Sophie or Jane from schools such as Merton Hall or Lauriston. Owning a house as far away from the front beach as Whimsy could only place the Blazey family in the category of new money (or no money).

However, our family's prowess at golf and other sports (with my exception) was a definite social asset. Thus we participated in the summer 'season' which started at the Christmas service at St John's, Sorrento (where Clive had married Penny a mere nine months earlier), and ended a month later, after a welter of balls, barbecues and tennis parties, at an all-night dance on the Australia Day weekend at the Sorrento Golf Club.

Zara and Harry Holt were the undisputed monarchs of the Portsea set, having vacationed among those tea-tree-shaded houses for many years. They owned a small block of land, bought with Zara's money, at the Weeroona estate on the high water bayside cliffs; their neighbours on the estate were the Gillespie family.

Harold Edward Holt was a solicitor who came from a family of theatrical entrepreneurs. He was born in 1908, the same year as Henry Bolte and one year earlier than my father: Holt was therefore another male from the blighted Depression generation. Marrying a richer woman didn't upset my father one bit, but then Holt was a playboy with a more fragile male ego. He won the Liberal seat of Fawkner in 1935 and his rapid rise was helped by Menzies' deliberate elimination of formidable rivals like Richard Casey and Percy Spender. Holt became Menzies' deputy in 1955. Finally in 1966 when Menzies retired, the faithful and dogged Harold was elected Liberal leader unopposed. Not long after becoming Prime Minister, Holt lost two by-elections and induced a swing to the ALP of six per cent. There was serious party disaffection that he knew about before his death. This gave rise to rumours, for which there is little evidence, that his death was a suicide caused by depression.

Zara was affectionate, zany and spontaneous. Her quotability and popularity were such that Holt later called her 'my secret weapon'. Zara was a very sixties person, a career woman before her time. Daughter of the wealthy Melbourne merchant S. E. Dickens, she met Harold in late adolescence when he was a penniless law student. Despite her family's wealth, Zara had always earned her own money. She sold her first dress shop, Magg, in Little Collins Street for a profit of 1500 pounds, a vast sum in those days, and said to Harold, 'Let's get married.' Harold rejected her, saying 'in no circumstances' would he marry on a woman's money. He was also playing the field with others. Incensed, she bought a first-class round-the-world trip, married British officer James Fell on the rebound in Poona, India, and had three sons. After divorcing Fell she married Harold at a private ceremony in October 1946. While Harold was Treasurer, Zara recreated Magg in Toorak Village and by 1960 she was queen of the Melbourne fashion scene.

It was around this time that I knew the family vaguely. I frequently saw Zara's son Sam lounging near the University Law Library, with his strange strawlike hair and pockmarked face. He had a stocky figure encased in a Harris tweed jacket and was always surrounded by beehived girls and ambitious young Liberals like Andrew Peacock. Rather than looking like a go-getter, he had an air of dreamy passivity and later lost a fortune during the eighties. My mother knew Zara, and I once dropped into her St Georges Road house to pick up some outdoor flares for my twenty-first birthday party.

Harold's three stepsons married bouffant-hairstyled, buxom wives. A photo of him spearfishing in a wetsuit with his bikini-clad stepdaughters-in-law became the photo of the Prime Minister's two-year reign. But, like much about Holt, it was slightly fake: his stepsons came from Zara's first marriage, he himself could hardly swim, and his marriage was a sham. Harold had had an affair with his Weeroona neighbour, and this was the occasion of our scoop.

At the first press conference on Monday 18 December, Holt's press secretary, Tony Eggleton, a saurian Englishman and former navy PR officer, said that Holt was alone when he drowned at Cheviot Beach. I had heard from Portsea locals, however, that there were four other people on the beach including Marjorie Gillespie, wife of Holt's friend Winton, a professional carnation-grower.

Journalist Don Hewett and myself pressed Eggleton on the phone on this point in several intense calls. At first he denied it. Then he pleaded with us. We threatened to publish regardless. Finally, after consulting Zara, who was now at Portsea, he relented. I'm positive that Zara in her grief wanted the truth to be told. So, after 10 pm on Monday, Eggleton formally admitted to us that there were others on the beach, including Marjorie. This was exclusively reported in the second edition of the

Australian and won me a rare compliment from the paper's proprietor, Rupert Murdoch. The unsmiling Eggleton's TV demeanour made him a national hero and greatly prospered his career.

Despite crews of hundreds of army and navy frogmen who continued searching for weeks, it was obvious by Tuesday that Holt's body would never be found. It had probably been carried out to sea on a mountainous flood tide and was being devoured by fish and sea lice.

The joint police report, released in January 1968, sheds some light on his last minutes. He had invited the Gilles – pies along, having run into Marjorie in a fish shop in Sorrento the day before. In two cars, Harold leading in a maroon Pontiac, they had all entered the Quarantine station to watch the lone English yachtsman Alec Rose go through the Heads on his epic world journey. Then Harold had impulsively suggested going to Cheviot for a swim. Two of the young men went in but quickly got out, later complaining of a 'tremendous undertow'. Holt observed their retreat, saying, 'I know this beach like the back of my hand.' He then walked purposefully towards the smooth-looking rockpool, took off his sandshoes without laces and plunged into the water. Marjorie watched him swimming and being swept slowly towards the pool's opening and the ocean. She noticed the water begin churning up around him, then suddenly swamp him. And that was that. On TV she said colourfully, 'He was sucked out like a leaf. There was nothing we could do.'

Was his competitive sense activated by the sight of young men retiring from the water so quickly? Was he showing off in front of Marjorie? Either way, he was soon out of his depth. He had entered the water just after the turning of the high tide when rips become vicious.

The drowning was reported worldwide and the reactions were incredulous. It was unbelievable that a Prime Minister could just vanish. Why didn't he have a security guard? Why wasn't he rescued by friends on the beach? How like Australia's 'she'll do' mentality that Holt simply disappeared and a body was never found. As Louis Nowra put it: 'How typical. No real crisis; just an Australian Crawl into nothingness.'

Despite his Vietnam record, Holt was liked as a jovial, decent leader who had successfully promoted the 1967 referendum to bestow full citizenship on

Aborigines. He was a portent of what was to come, a first melting of the Menzian glacier. He changed the focus from cricket to surf, from Savile Row to wetsuit, from regality to razzamatazz. He was the first PR PM, not seen again until Bob Hawke. Zara was good copy too: she disclosed that her pet name for Harold was 'Puss'. I wrote illustrated pieces on the Martin Collins back page of the *Australian* sending him up as Puss in the bath, Puss in boots, Puss-ywhipt. It would have been unthinkable under Menzies.

There was a memorial service for Holt at St Paul's Cathedral on Thursday 21 December. The British Prime Minister, Harold Wilson, HRH Prince Charles, US President Lyndon Johnson as well as leaders of seven Asian nations attended. The funeral became a camouflage for crisis talks about Vietnam. At the same time, there was incessant manoeuvring, producing a dam burst of inspired newspaper leaks as the Liberal Party sought to elect a new leader.

LBJ's presence in Melbourne caused mixed emotions. His huge black bulletproof limousine with its motorcycle escort made him look like a Mafia boss. An exquisite moment occurred the night before the Memorial Service. At a state reception at Victoria's

Government House, the lanky Texan approached Prince Charles with open arms. Johnson treated all the VIPs as guests who had come to honour 'his friend' Harold Holt. My bureau chief, John Dunn, reported the following exchange which was widely related as a perfect squelch for the brash American:

'Oh your Highness,' said LBJ, his hand outstretched, 'I thank you for coming so far to honour the death of my friend Harold Holt.'

'On the contrary,' replied Prince Charles with immense *sang froid*. 'It is *I* who should thank *you*. And indeed I do so on behalf of my mother who is Queen of Australia.'

*

I was always intrigued about Zara's fate. She later married a knockabout rustic Liberal member, Jeff Bate, in a barnyard media wedding with poddy calves tripping over TV cables. He drank himself to death in 1984 and she was a widow again. She had now became a modern folk heroine, always marrying the wrong man. Soon after, she retired to the Gold Coast for a while. She was often visited by her three sons (all of whose marriages broke down after Holt's death) and her new grandchildren.

In 1985 Marjorie Gillespie went public in a TV interview which was reported in the *Sydney Morning Herald* as 'I was Holt's lover'. 'Rubbish,' riposted Zara in New Idea. Marjorie was one in a long queue. 'Harold had lovers all over the world, in Melbourne, Canberra, Sydney, even Hong Kong,' she said. 'There were dozens of women in the woodwork.' As for herself, she said: 'I was pleasantly faithful. It sounds dull but that's the way I am.' To another interviewer she said she knew about his womanising all through their marriage. 'I had to learn to live with it,' she admitted, adding resignedly, 'I loved him. I don't think he loved me. But I suited him. I ran my business well. I looked tidy and neat. I was a good public speaker.'

Zara Holt was one of the most remarkable First Ladies Australia has ever had: honest, loving, without pomp and utterly modern. She died peacefully of a heart attack at the age of eighty on 14 June 1989. One hundred and fifty people attended her funeral service at Toorak. She was buried at the Sorrento Cemetery which faces the turbulent green waters of Bass Strait rather than placid Port Phillip Bay. Her large white marble headstone is a miracle of simplicity. It is inscribed: ZARA KATE BATE – 1909 to 1989. A PROUD AUSTRALIAN.

The whole Harold Holt experience was exhilarating professionally, helping me to become Victorian state roundsman on the *Australian*, quite a promotion for one who had been in journalism less than a year. I may have been ALP, but Liberals kept assisting my career.

IN WHICH I DISCOVER I HAVE A POLITICAL FATHER FIGURE!

At Victoria's Parliament House where Sir Henry Bolte held daily press conferences, I spent eighteen months observing this impossible, reactionary, wily old premier. Although the *Age* and the *Sun* didn't attend, I did because I found him fascinating copy. If he was tense he clicked on a biro and the conference terminated quickly. Most of the rather supine press gallery discussed racing with him and faithfully printed what he wanted. They rarely asked tough questions. This clubby, cosy situation was an outrage against journalistic ethics and encouraged me to write a truthful biography of him.

Bolte was exceptionally intelligent, yet he despised academics and played up the dumb farmer. He was an old-time Aussie with a vulgar knockabout sense of humour. After he had escorted the Emperor Haile Selassie to Tullamarine, he jumped out of his desk and started hobbling before the ten or so journalists in front of him: 'Did you see the way he walked? He looked as if he had pooped his pants!' Meetings with Aborigines were no problem, he said, because he offered them 'a few combs and mirrors'. Another time he declared, 'I am as opposed to the legalisation of poker machines as I am to the legalisation of homosexuality.' He clownishly mimed pulling the arm of a pokie till he was bent double, then pretended he had been 'goosed'. He didn't care who he offended.

Of course by this stage he had been in power for fifteen years, mainly by virtue of DLP preferences, and had become extremely arrogant. When I first met him during the Ryan hanging I hated him, but two or three years later my feelings had changed. Having had two hangings in his reign, he would say, 'If you want to win an election have a hanging. I've already proved that it works.' He was so un-middle class. Unlike most politicians he never reneged on anything he had said, even when drunk. So that one of the most frequently asked questions after the Ryan hanging was, 'What were you doing at the time, Sir Henry?' He simply said, 'I was having one of the three Ss.' When I wrote that he said he was having a shit at the time, he was angry at the inaccuracy, saying, 'Don't you young whelps know what the three Ss are?' (Shit, Shower, Shave.) He was furious about my book, commissioning another more flattering biography. It flopped. When I saw him nine years later at a Liberal fundraising function in Prahran he was sozzled. He leaped at me with delight. He was trying to disengage himself from the grey Liberal ladies intent on steering him towards grey Liberal money.

'Jesus, you snake in the grass! What are you doing here?' I told him I was representing the *Nation Review*, but he misheard and said, 'The *National Times*?' I repeated that it was the *Nation Review*. His contempt was immense. 'Gar, it doesn't matter. They're all the same: pinko rags, for pinko ratbags.' Then he told me he hadn't read my 'stupid' book on him because it was all fiction and he'd instructed all his friends not to read it. A few minutes later, he told me the book had really disappointed him.

'But Sir Henry, I always said I was an ALP supporter.'

'It was nothing to do with that,' he replied. 'What you did was make me look like . . . a clown. I had such high hopes for you when you got that job with Andrew Peacock and now look where you are.' He was then determinedly steered away by a large Liberal lady who had decided he had dallied enough. Drunk as a skunk and knowing he was in captivity, he gaily waved at me as he was wheeled off to talk to Liberal donors. It was the last time I saw him.

On the Road with the Show Pony

Liberal policies are the headlights of Australia's future.
ANDREW PEACOCK IN A POLITICAL ADDRESS, 1971

Peacock and I had been in the Scotch College debating team together and later he appeared as a mere Roman soldier beholden to my Julius Caesar in the Dramatic Society's 1957 production of that play. Though we were at Melbourne University, we hardly saw each other since he was studying law, girls and sports cars when I was mixing with the scruffy, puritan members of the ALP Club. While he was rising in the Liberal Party, I was plumbing the depths of Melbourne's snooty class system. But as the Vietnam War gathered pace, Carlton's social lepers became morally superior to South Yarra's silvertails who had manifestly backed the wrong horse.

Soon after Gorton's narrow election victory in 1969, Peacock became Minister for the Army and he rang me at Parliament House to ask if I wanted to be his press secretary. I was horrified. During the

Vietnam War, such an invitation could only come from the devil incarnate. Instead of dismissing it outright, however, I used it to try to gain a promotion from my editor, Adrian Deamer. In those days, four years after its founding, the *Australian* was a left-wing paper and Deamer legendary. He was appalled: he said Peacock was a lightweight and a charlatan, that Liberal policies were atrocious, that I should reject them and be more patient: 'Some of us have had to wait for more than three years before we got to the top, you know.' He wouldn't give me a rise, nor would he promise that I would be the next Melbourne staffer to go to Canberra or Sydney – or anywhere for that matter. Deamer's final plea to me was astute. He said I was a good writer and far too young at twenty-nine to be going into public relations. 'You'll spend all your time in the Strangers' Bar looking for people to drink with.' He was certainly right about that. Over the next five years, I was to spend thousands of hours in that marvellous methylated hellhole, the gossipy guts and soul of the old Parliament House.

Because I got nothing from the paper, I had decided to accept Peacock's offer when he visited me at my parents' place in Balwyn. He was my local member. Having inherited the electorate of Kooyong on Menzies' retirement in 1967, he now lived just three streets away in Victoria Road, Canterbury. He had already been married for seven years to his first wife Susan; their friends called them Droopy and Soupy. They had three young daughters.

'Do you want the job?' he asked eagerly in my parents' lounge room on this Saturday morning.

'You must be joking, Andrew,' I replied. 'You know I'm a member of the Labor Party.'

'That doesn't matter. It means you'll get on better with the press gallery.' His urbanity was starting to appeal, but he undercut it by saying, 'I thought that since we'd been to school together I could trust you.' Being a true rebel, I had long ago rejected the claims of 'school spirit', yet I found his belief in it endearing. I offered him a beer in a cut crystal glass and noted how darkly good-looking he was with his expensive casual clothes, his Levantine nose, his brown, poached-egg eyes and his unnatural tan. Even then his wavy black hair was greying, which pleased him greatly. In those days, he wanted to sound youthful while actually appearing to be older than he was. Most people would kill to be a federal minister at thirty, but to my amazement he saw it as a liability. Being the youngest minister meant he could trust nobody since all the older Liberals were out to knife him.

I told him that he was the only Liberal I'd work for and he replied that he was the only Liberal who was 'mad enough' to employ me. I liked that answer and said if I joined his staff I'd have to 'open up a new can of friends'. He said that friendship had never affected him in 'really important decisions'. I later discovered that while Andrew was as matey as hell, he had few lasting male friendships. He said he was offering me a challenging job with lots of travel. The salary was about ten thousand dollars, a huge sum in those days and a good deal more than the C-plus wages I was getting at the *Australian*.

Since Melbourne with its moratoria was the hotbed of Vietnam resistance, I had nightmares for months. I was castigated as a sellout, a weakling, a fascist shit and a ridiculous fraud. I was spat on in Jimmy Watson's Wine Bar and expelled from the North Carlton branch of the ALP. The job made me defensive for a while and it showed up in strange ways. A university friend approved, saying I would be his 'Trojan horse' in the government. I blurted out, 'Trojan whore, you mean!'

Soon after taking up the position, I was regaling a group of journalists in the Imperial Hotel in Melbourne. 'Don't worry about Peacock,' I declaimed, 'I'll have him supporting the NLF [North Vietnamese Liberation Front] within six months.' This was reported back to Peacock within hours who then rang me and asked had I actually said that? Yes, I replied, I had. 'Well,' said Peacock, 'my informant told me to let you know you were heard saying it, which I have just done.' I was starting to appreciate his cool, unrecriminating style.

The new world of cars and planes and inside information soon became addictive. I sent Commonwealth cars to the Manuka shops for cigarettes, wrote out my own air tickets and found a phone call from 'the minister's office' often performed wonders in the department. But I worked hard also in this most paranoid of ministries.

In my office, I was bound to report every movement I made, even a trip to the lavatory. If I left the room I had to tell security. The goons then entered the room and checked every drawer and file. At night the door had to be left open to facilitate inspection. I found it farcical. If a file were missing or out of place, this was a 'breach of security' and a pink sticker was placed on one's desk. It was called an 'occurrence' and could only be cleared by an explanation to Bruce White, the head of the Department of the Army. I got a number of occurrences – another omen.

Upstairs on the first floor there was an Orwellian phantasmagoria of precedence and suspicion. The army was run by a troika comprising the military board headed by the chief of the general staff (CGS), the minister representing the parliament, and Bruce White. The hawkish Defence Department in the next building, led by its brooding minister, Malcolm Fraser, applauded the war's aims and wanted greater involvement. But the army, which actually did the fighting, was not quite so gung-ho. They realised there were no more troops and the war was unwinnable. Their motto was, if we can't win, we should get out.

In the first few weeks, I met Prime Minister Gorton's chic principal private secretary, Ainslie Gotto, and received a long briefing from his press secretary, Tony Eggleton (who had survived the job after Holt's death), nicknamed the Maltese Falcon. By now, the gallery detested Gorton and was impatiently awaiting the Whitlam government in which many expected to find employment. Eggleton told me the five most 'unreliable' elements were the two youthful Walshes, Max and Eric, Mungo MacCallum, Peter Samuel and Laurie Oakes. These 'irresponsible' journalists often wrote things which were 'hurtful' to the Prime Minister. The difficulty was that the 'irresponsible' journalists tended to be smarter, tougher and more industrious. Eggleton advised me to build up confidence between the department and the press, for the quality of the man made the job – some press secretaries were cyphers, while others were respected colleagues. This was excellent counsel. Within days I had irresponsibly reported most of it to the *Nation Review*'s Mungo MacCallum, who was delighted to be accused of being hurtful.

TRENDY MATTERS MILITAIRE

My first year under Gorton was an exciting time. Weekends were spent in Melbourne, where I occasionally went to functions with Andrew. I would also take weeks away with Peacock, either in

Canberra, or visiting army bases in Australia and the Pacific.

Though I sometimes mixed socially with Peacock, he didn't encourage it and we moved in different circles. When he introduced me as 'my press secretary', it sounded like 'my publicity agent'. But there were moments of piquant role reversal. One night we were visiting the house of the local state member, Julian Doyle, who was cultivating Andrew since he wanted a federal seat. Being at Mount Macedon, we were some distance from Melbourne. A station wagon bearing an ABC camera crew suddenly arrived and Andrew flew into a petulant frenzy. 'What the hell is all this? I didn't give them permission!' he ranted. But the 'Four Corners' crew had come not to see him, but to interview me about the impending retirement of Sir Henry Bolte. Since I was known to be writing an MA thesis on Sir Henry, I was by now one of the world's leading Boltologists. I pointed to Andrew and told the producer to 'see my press secretary' and Andrew laughed. Momentarily he had reverted to being that Roman foot soldier to my Caesar again.

As Andrew was political head of the army and because Vietnam was humungously unpopular, we soon worked out that my task was to write speeches about anything but the army. Of course at army events he spoke about military matters. But at political and general functions he poured out speeches about pollution, the environment, mass media, youth rebellion and the need for open decision making. It is remarkable now that such bland truisms could have even been widely quoted in the media. One of my early successes was a speech delivered to the Young Labor Association of Kooyong – an invitation Peacock accepted to emphasise his small 'l' liberal grooviness. Smart, warm, trendy and modern, he was marking himself out as a future Liberal leader.

Andrew's new reputation for thoughtful social commentary somewhat astonished those who knew him previously, and it began to infuriate both his Liberal rivals and his army colleagues. One colonel asked me, 'Why is it that whenever the minister opens his mouth he never mentions the army?' A general said, 'He never seems to defend the army in public.' Understandably, I denied this, since I couldn't tell the truth, which was that the minister thought the war was lost and couldn't wait to get a decent portfolio.

In his speeches and answers in the House, Peacock's decorum and his rapport with the army was superb. He was a natural as a service minister. His predecessor and rival, Phillip Lynch, had been awkward and tense, returning speech drafts with notations like 'more big words, please' and even vomiting before he made it to the dais. Andrew, a horse-owning man, was magnificent at ceremony and beloved by the troops; we both enjoyed visiting army bases, getting briefings and going to dining-in nights (where I could perve on the soldiers and he could show off his exotic clobber and his zany wife Susan). All his training in the Scotch Quarterguard and in the Citizen Military Forces was being put to good use. The CGS, Sir Thomas Daly, responded to his ability and flair. Indeed the friendship between them and their wives was jealously observed from afar by Andrew's volatile Jacobean boss, Malcolm Fraser.

In one fabulous three-week sweep we took the RAAF's small executive jet *Mystere* and visited bases in every state except the Northern Territory, to get to know the army. We flew from Melbourne to Rockhampton in two hours fifteen minutes, refuelled and went on to Townsville within three hours twenty minutes, a trip which would take the best part of a day on a commercial aircraft. Here we inspected the Tropical Training Establishment at Innisfail. Since we were visiting the Townsville army base, it was a ceremonial occasion which required Susan's presence. One of my functions was to hold Susan's hand as the jet took off and landed, since she hated flying; another was to act as court jester. I recall one trip just after the *Mystere* returned from Townsville air force base and everyone suddenly became expansive. The crew brought out champagne and we got down to the delights of the VIP fleet. Present were Bruce White and the CGS, his wife and several generals.

'Well now, Peter,' grinned Andrew, a glass in hand, 'how do you with all your socialist principles justify sitting on this plane drinking champagne? Haven't you compromised just a little?'

'Not at all, minister,' I said coolly, 'we're in the people's plane and we're drinking the people's champagne!' This riposte got a large laugh and ensured more trips in RAAF silver birds both big and small.

We dropped into Enoggera and Canungra Jungle

Training Establishment behind Brisbane, where I flew in my first Sioux helicopter, an almost cosmic experience since its perspex bubble leaves you suspended thousands of feet above the earth. We jetted down to Tasmania Command, to inspect the Royal Tasmania Regiment, then across to Central Command in Adelaide and on to Western Command where Peacock put on his politician's hat and delivered a speech at Hervey, WA, for the Western Division of the Liberal Party.

I had laboured over an especially futuristic speech which contained images that a metaphysical poet might have recognised. It seemed to hit a nerve with the stalwart Liberal ladies who shortly after mobbed Andrew and sang his hosannas. Of course they had always appreciated his good looks and seductive banter. (As Phillip Adams once commented to me about this time, 'That's the trouble with Andrew, he's so damn poisonously likeable.') Overnight we stayed in Perth at the house of Liberal strongman Sir Charles Court, who was 'courting' Andrew as a power in the federal party.

At the Swanbourne barracks, home of the Special Air Services, I had an unexpectedly thrilling adventure. Being in the ministerial party was a bit like Princess Di doing a meet-the-people walkathon. It was easy for me to approach the most attractive soldiers and engage them in intimate enquiry. At the Swanbourne officers' mess I was ensorcellated by a young soldier called David. Telling him I was a keen surfer, he revealed that over the sand dunes there was a good nude surfing beach. I said I'd like to go there and he promised to meet me. Feeling jaded after having been cooped up in the *Mystere* for a week, I told Andrew I wanted the day off.

Swanbourne's sand dunes are the sexiest in Australia. Discovering other men naked in such an environment brings on a sort of delirium with me. This pervert's paradise of sun, salt, sand and subliminal sex are what makes Australian summers unique, for no other country has such wild and lonely beaches. Better still, most Australian nude beaches, which are invariably gay-friendly, are in areas near Defence bases: Lady Jane and Obelisk in Sydney, Somers in Victoria, Casuarina in Darwin (which offers concrete pillboxes for privacy) and Swanbourne in Perth.

Close to the city, Swanbourne was then a busy gay beat. And being an olive-skinned sun bunny I stripped and went for a dip in the cold Indian Ocean. I loved the ozone, the freedom, my own nakedness, and rushed back up to the sandhills where I'd left my shorts and towel. There was nobody else in sight.

At eleven o'clock exactly, I saw a figure sauntering along the beach wearing a pair of blue Speedos – almost as infra dig on a nude beach as carrying a Polaroid camera. I waved from the dunes and David approached. He was tall, tanned and well built. He smiled and sat down. He said how impressed he'd been meeting the minister, how engaging and youthful Andrew was and how lucky I was to be working with him. I quite often got this line, usually from people I didn't respect, but I liked David, especially his sensitive, slightly femme quality.

He said he was a cook at Swanbourne and a conscript. He quite liked cooking for the SAS, who were friendly but as 'tough as nails'. They often teased him, he said.

'They tease you?' I asked innocently.

'What about?' 'They call me a "choco" because I'm a conscript and a cook. They say that I could never kill a man – as if I'd want to.' He looked indignantly at me with eyes as blue as his Speedos.

'Well, that's what the SAS do. They're trained killers, aren't they?'

'I know,' he replied. 'They go on these all-night marches with black on their faces and luminous watches and leather thongs so they can strangle someone from behind. They're like Boy Scouts who've gone bananas.'

He hoped he wouldn't have to go to Vietnam and I told him Australian forces were being pulled back under the government's 'Vietnamisation' policies. I asked him if he had a girlfriend; he replied no, that he didn't have time. He laughed and settled into the warm sand. There was a frisson between us but I was still unsure if he was just being hospitable or whether he batted for my team.

As the sun got hotter, I grew bolder. I said being on a nude beach while wearing a pair of Speedos was 'incorrect dress code' and maybe he ought to take them off. He hesitated. Then he slipped out of them elegantly and lay down close beside me, his stomach on the warm sand. I cautiously brushed my leg against his own and soon we were both aroused. He started laughing when I went down on him: 'If only the minister could see us now!'

*

At breakfast next day in Perth's posh Parmelia Hotel, Andrew asked me if I'd had a good day off. Yes, I said. He grinned knowingly, thinking I'd been with a girlfriend. He liked the idea of working and playing hard.

We were approaching the high point in our platonic affair but Susan was proving a little spiky. Her mood wasn't improved by being trapped with three young children in her dismal Canterbury house, while we were gallivanting all over the South Pacific; she was also an ambitious socialite and model who craved the limelight. One day Andrew discovered her in his Melbourne office using his ministerial letterhead to tell media chiefs of staff she was available for interview. He reprimanded her in my presence, which was calculated to offend. It was evident there were serious strains in their marriage.

One weekend we were in the Sands Motor Inn in Surfers Paradise, having delivered a speech to the Twin Towns RSL in Coolangatta. A weekend in Queensland was always desirable during a southern winter and it wasn't too hard to drum up some organisation that wanted to hear a speech. We were lounging around the apartment, drinking beer and watching the sun set over Mount Warning, when the phone rang and I picked it up. Thinking I was Andrew, Susan said bitterly, 'How come you're in Surfers with Peter instead of being at home with me. You *knew* it was our eighth wedding anniversary!' Andrew took the phone and made a series of disclaimers, not wholly believable, and lamented having forgotten it yet again.

IN WHICH SUSAN SPINS OUT IN THE HIGHLANDS

Susan accompanied us to New Guinea in July 1970 to inspect the Pacific Islands Regiment which was then a command of the Australian army. In order to prepare Papua New Guinea for its independence, the army suddenly realised it would have to become more 'localised'. This meant more Papua New Guineans in all ranks, especially officers. There was resistance to this from many old-style officers and NCOs who regarded the 'natives' with amused contempt. In a regiment of about five thousand, there were still only nine indigenous officers, none above the rank of captain. Although both races worked well together, it was obvious that many adept and intelligent Pacific Islanders were being held down.

Susan and Andrew made a terrific impression at many dining-in nights on this trip, mixing and drinking with the officers. They were the epitome of a groovy young seventies couple – a species rarely seen in these stuffy environs. They created a minor sensation when they both jumped on a table at Murray Barracks near Port Moresby and drunkenly danced the twist to Chubby Checker.

The tour was quite a triumph. After visiting the Highlands, we flew up the north coast to Lae, Popondetta, Wewak and Vanimo, a tropical paradise on the Irian Jayan border. Bruce White, who had fought in New Guinea during the war, proved an amiable companion. He was droll about his previous ministers, saying that Phillip Lynch had 'photographic constipation – he couldn't pass a camera' and 'I don't mind carrying ministers, but I do wish they wouldn't drag their feet'.

The high point of the trip for me came in an

officers' mess in Lae at yet another dining-in night. It was casual so I wore a white silk shirt with a necklace of love beads I had picked up in the Koki markets. I was approached by an army colonel who was somewhat under the weather. He hated localisation and made a reference to 'rock apes' getting promotions too easily. When I reproached him about his language, he sneered at me: 'The press secretary for the Minister for the Army does not wear the things that natives wear!' 'Who says?' I replied, becoming so angry that I nearly took a swipe at him. Peacock's private secretary Maurie Barry separated us and led the colonel away. His parting shot was to call me 'a queer' (of all things!).

The tropics affected us all. Susan went mad buying up hundreds of Sepik River masks, headdresses and figurines at cheap local prices, then weighing down a VIP aircraft transporting them to Melbourne, which caused a minor media scandal. Otherwise the 1972 trip had been a notable success. It put the mainly white Pacific Islands Regiment on notice and Andrew's decolonialising experience made him the most acclaimed (and the last) External Territories Minister.

When we got back to reality Susan became even more unsettled. She had finally got herself a gig with the Sheridan sheet company modelling their new range of floral bedsheets as 'the wife of Australia's youngest federal minister'. With her dark eyes and madcap vivacity, she was quite a dish in those days, even though the tabloid press later rubbished her as 'Australia's most famous serial bride'.

As soon as the Sheridan ad came out in the *Women's Weekly*, Andrew's many enemies passed copies of it around the House and in the party room. Party shellbacks were appalled. Within days it had blown up into such a media kerfuffle that Andrew offered his resignation from the ministry because his wife had 'abused Westminster conventions'. This was a highly arguable and pompous interpretation, but he couldn't be talked out of it. It seemed to me, he was motivated by the desire to humiliate Susan in public.

The English columnist Clement Freud, visiting Australia at the time, declaimed in the *Age*: 'Of all the rotten, unchivalrous and egotistical actions, resigning because his wife appeared in an ad for bedlinen, this is the most puerile thing I have ever heard of . . .

In any right-thinking community, Pea-hen [Susan] could get a divorce on the grounds of mental cruelty.' Freud, who called himself a 'professional grandson', had a point. I remember thinking this as Susan wept uncontrollably on the phone while I forced her to authorise press statements in which she deplored her own 'immature' behaviour and promised to give the model's fee to charity. She was distraught and Andrew was coldly furious. The only person who behaved well during this silly episode was a rather worldly Prime Minister Gorton, who refused to accept his minister's resignation, telling him to withdraw it and take a few days off. This Andrew did.

The affair was really a matter for a marriage guidance counsellor rather than the federal government. Their marriage dissolved seven years later when Susan ran off with the first millionaire who made eyes at her, leaving Andrew to bring up three daughters. By becoming Mrs Susan Sangster (and later Lady Renouf), she got her revenge for the Sheridan sheets incident and a lot more.

The major victim of the Sheridan sheets fiasco was Andrew himself. It confirmed a perception that he was fickle and narcissistic, a show pony obsessed with appearances. Worse, it aroused the issue of his marital instability, which ultimately cost him the Prime Ministership. Although he was married during the 1984 election, he was really in love with Shirley MacLaine, whom he had met in 1977 after Susan dumped him for Robert Sangster. Susan liked older men while Andrew liked older women! When he made his second attempt at the Lodge in 1990, Andrew was divorced, which may have cost him enough votes to lose a very close election.

Instead of resigning, Peacock spent the next four years keeping John Howard, a man whose suburbanism he loathed, out of the Liberal leadership. He performed this remarkable, Calwellian feat of political sour grapes by backing first Dr John Hewson, who lost the 1993 elections, and then the Pooh Bear-ish Alexander Downer, a former staffman. Peacock's resignation from Parliament in October 1994 to join a business introduction consultancy with MacLaine lifted the ban and soon after, John Howard became Leader. Later Peacock was appointed Ambassador to Washington, which was a dream come true.

WHY I GOT THE BOOT FROM THE PEACOCK CAMP

During 1970 I had become friendly with John Hogan, a maverick sugar farmer from Tumbulgum in northern NSW. John was one of three brothers, then in his forties and unmarried as well as an amateur lobbyist for the Labor Party. Nicknamed 'Planter Hogan', John was absurdly generous. He would send crates of Moreton Bay bugs and mangoes to his friends in Canberra. John had been drawn to the ALP by his lobbyist friend, Eric Walsh having gone to school with him.

As Hogan's friend I was a frequent visitor to his homestead, Laurel Lodge, near Murwillumbah. He was a political groupie and his house on stilts became the base for junketing politicians such as Bob Hawke on their (too) frequent trips to Queensland and the Gold Coast. In these tropical purlieus I met the late DLP Senator Vince Gair, who knew Hogan as a baby, as well as many of the 'Irish mafia' who later dominated the Whitlam government. Then federal ALP secretary Mick Young and Eric Walsh were a hilarious team to drink with. Eric had such a brilliantly quick and inventive line of repartee he could have had a stage or media career. Instead, he chose a courtier's obscurity, becoming a rich but influential lobbyist selling access to Asian governments; among his biggest clients was his old friend Rupert Murdoch.

One ill-fated weekend in October, I went up to visit John. First we went to Coolangatta for a seafood dinner, then to a function at the Kyogle Show which was washed out by rain. A really big tent, which belonged to the Kyogle Girl Guides, had collapsed in the downpour, leaving the guides wet, chattering and bedraggled. We were forced into the only tent still standing, the banana fritter tent. It was crowded and steamy and everyone was eating. John slyly introduced me to someone called Withie, who happened to be the best mate of then National Party Leader Doug Anthony, although I didn't know and John didn't tell me.

Withie asked how I thought the government was going. Being a National, he was easily able to rubbish the Prime Minister, McMahon, who had just become Father of the Year, which was felt to be a ridiculous honour for a sixty-five-year-old man. 'What are we going to have now? Baby-burping sessions in

Cabinet? What do you think?' he asked casually.

Devouring a fritter, I replied that it was without doubt the most awful, frightful government since the war; it had neither style, authority nor purpose; ministers were warring with each other constantly; there was no respect for the PM who was a national joke and the most ridiculous incumbent since Billy Hughes. I said the government was like the Titanic. The question was: would it actually get to the iceberg, or would it sink from leaks beforehand?

Within hours, my words had been quoted to Doug Anthony, who reportedly broke three brandy balloons in disbelief at my slandering of the party. Of course, he was no friend of Peacock. Next morning Andrew was summoned to the PM's office in Canberra and told that he would have to ask for my resignation. I had been seen going into Whitlam's office too often and I was 'vedy, vedy disloyal and hurtful,' the PM said.

Within an hour Andrew sacked me, saying, 'Sorry, I have no alternative.' Within a week, my honour intact, I was back in Melbourne, a long, long way away from that creepy administration. Whitlam saw me before I left. 'All the good men are going,' he laughed. He told me there would be a job for me in his government, as indeed there was.

Back in Melbourne I drank at the boozy and decadent Albion Hotel in Faraday Street, Carlton, then one of the great bloodhouses of Australia. On Friday nights I caroused in a 'school' including John Halpin, Terry Counihan, Michael Rubbo, Pete Steedman, Dinny O'Hearn and David Wilson. I had met Wilson ten years earlier, when he wrote a blackly humorous column for *Farrago* and worked in the university bookshop. He had an anarchic, goonish sense of humour which we all loved.

But my greatest achievement that year was to finish my biography of Sir Henry Bolte, published by Jacaranda Press and launched, with Sagittarian luck, in November 1972 on my thirty-third birthday. It was two weeks before Gough became Prime Minister. Sometimes when you Go Too Far, you find you can go a hell of a lot further.

Wedding Fiasco

When a man marries, he divorces his mother.
JEWISH SAYING

During my first year with Peacock I was looking to complete the ultimate fantasy in the trifecta of job, higher education and romance. I felt sure that this third leg would be consolidated through heterosexual marriage. Perhaps it was my father's prompting which had me crossing sexual boundaries once again. He considered that thirty was a dangerous age to be still a bachelor, for one had not yet reached the 'first base in life'.

It was Jonathan King who had introduced me to Joanna O'Rorke back at Melbourne University in the summer of 1968. Jonathan and his girlfriend Kay Cardwell and Joanna and I became that cliché, the campus quartet. Our affair was all the more powerful for being between two black sheep from Melbourne's *haute bourgeoisie*. Joanna was the daughter of a socially conscious doctor from Ireland, who'd married a

Melbourne heiress. Of their four children, Joanna was the most striking. She ate too much and smoked too much, yet everyone loved her Italianate generosity of spirit. She was a giver not a taker.

Joanna had been educated in one of Melbourne's top Catholic convent schools. Paradoxically, Australian nuns have been the loving and competent teachers of a whole generation of determined and lapsed Australian feminists from Germaine Greer downwards. But Joanna had never really lapsed, she just wavered. She was subjected to those fabled idiocies of Anglo-Irish Catholic convent prudery like having to sit in a bath with talcum powder sprinkled on the surface of the water to veil the body beneath, or scuffing the shine off her shoes so boys couldn't see the reflection of her underwear. Such institutional dirty-mindedness always leaves guilty traces and Joanna was said to be brilliantly 'neurotic'. If we overlook the Freudianism, we can say that in the late sixties we were a colourful, contemporary couple: Joanna steadying herself after leaping the convent wall and me trying to go straight after deep immersion in the gay leatherworld of Earl's Court and Europe. Was I misleading her? Not really. I told her about my past but she thought she could convert me.

Melbourne was still as staid as ever but Joanna was living in Carlton, where the Presbyterian rigours of Bleak City had been leavened by bohemia; a parent-free zone to which Melbourne's frazzled, beat-worshipping adolescents repaired. Joanna's edenic, tree-spangled apartment overlooked Grattan Street, the teachers' college and the university. A glowing but neglected eyrie, this flat had two bedrooms, a bar and a huge lounge with a cork floor. She had laid the floor herself but had forgotten to seal it so it soon became filthy. Joanna, like myself, was fashionably untidy.

Still, at the time it seemed to me like the centre of the universe. It became the cockpit of our relationship. In my romantic memory I shall always see her pottering around with her long titian hair, intense blue eyes, sculpted lips and those magnificent breasts which the nuns' sense of shame had taught her to minimise by hunching her shoulders. More powerful than her quattrocento beauty were her monologues, which she delivered with the rapidity of a race caller on speed. Should the Pope be sacked? Was a certain law lecturer a criminal? How could young students be helped? The vice-chancellor was an idiot, someone else criminally corrupt. I always wondered if these rapid-fire rodomontades were a consequence of her mental agility or her convent-induced neurosis. Joanna was an artful fabricator; the further she strayed from the truth, the faster became her diction, almost as if she didn't want God to overhear her. She was endlessly argumentative, provocative and challenging and could have been a great lawyer had she persisted in that male-dominated profession.

She was not only studying law, but was an heiress (with three siblings) to a department store fortune. Her apartment contained a whiff of inheritance as strong as a mink farm and certainly as strong as the marijuana which we smoked there. It also bore all the mementoes of the period: NLF and Castro buttons, the *de rigueur* poster of the Christ-like figure of Che Guevara, Aubrey Beardsley and Mucha posters and, in the bathroom, another one of a laughing naked man and woman captioned, 'Save Water, Shower with a Friend!' in reference to the Melbourne water shortage.

This was a Make Love, Not War household similar to millions of others all over the world. There was that late sixties mix of political engagement and hedonism. Bob Dylan records, Penguin books by Danny Cohn Bendit and later the hardback edition of *The Female Eunuch.* Visits to Grattan Street were frequent and effulgent with Alice B's hash cookies often turning up for dessert. A long string of lefties became habitués.

One of the trendy places in the music-mad sixties was Smacka Fitzgibbon's in Chetwynd Street, North Melbourne. Smacka, a jolly, moon-faced man, was a jazz musician, head of a popular Dixieland band and one of the first to exploit the clever seventies format of jazz/theatre restaurants. Joanna and I went there often, occasionally running into the city's Beautiful People, the sons of Harold Holt, the Andrew Peacocks and such remnants of the Seekers as Athol Guy. Twenty-five years later, Smacka's cavernous North Melbourne site is now owned by painter Jan Senbergs and his wife Helen (nee Beresford) – two good friends.

Joanna and I were not officially engaged but we were 'promised' to each other. We certainly relished the social acceptability of our phantom engagement. This was necessary for both of us since she was having trouble graduating, partly because she was running a cafe in Carlton. Christopher Pearl did the sign in the window and met my father at the opening. Alan rounded on him, asking in a hostile manner what he did and what was his profession? Since reading my diaries when I was seventeen, he knew about my obsession with Christopher and was acting like a Victorian father, asking Christopher his intentions. Christopher provoked him by saying he was a signwriter, which left Dad unimpressed.

Although Joanna and I believed our sexual connection was good, I insisted on continuing erotic encounters with men and bringing home diseases, which didn't thrill her. In the midst of our affair and quite unbeknown to me, Joanna started to fall in love with the drummer in Smacka's band, a tall and lugubrious person named Jim. In those days he seemed tragically old at the age of thirty-nine. I can remember sneering about his decrepitude and what an unattractive 'creep' he was, so I must have been jealous. Naturally Joanna did not disclose too much, though I knew they were going out.

I proposed to her in June 1970 and she accepted. We were fond of each other even though our engagement was socially driven. Because we were both uncertain and I was still travelling with Peacock as his press secretary, the wedding was slotted to happen in six months' time. Andrew congratulated me effusively on hearing about my intentions. He said, 'It's great, Knuckle, you're just at the right age, but my advice to you is, long engagements are disastrous – get married as soon as you can.'

To mark our new social position, Joanna's father, Dr O'Rorke, threw a lavish engagement party at his Toorak house with hundreds of guests. They came from journalism, Melbourne University, architecture, law and politics. But on that most glamorous of nights, our mutual indifference was apparent to the discerning observer. Friends later pointed out that we hardly spoke two words to each other, although we greeted guests with robotic charm. Actually, we were shocked by the enormity of what we had done. This engagement party was so public, its irrevocability ominous.

That night we had icy presentiments about the impending marriage. Joanna later confessed she was having a fling with the drummer. I didn't have my heart in it any more than she did. But we were locked in. Going through the motions, not the emotions. Grimly determined to Get Married.

After the engagement, we were on a connubial juggernaut, entrapped in our very own *folie à deux*. There were morning teas, afternoon teas, shower teas, baby's booties' teas, it just went on and on. Suddenly I met scores of uncles, aunties, older children, younger children, infants everywhere and a cousinage that was breathtaking. There were grand aunts from Scotland, third cousins from Poland, beloved octogenarian priests and favourite nuns. Had I loved her more I wouldn't have cared, but I did.

My dislike of Australian Catholicism was intensified. Hardly surprising, considering the attacks on the 'wily papists' delivered at Scotch College. This prejudice wasn't helped when I agreed to take instruction from a Catholic priest. By 1970 the rules had been relaxed slightly after Vatican II and 'mixed marriages' were now permitted so long as the non-Catholic party agreed to learn about the 'one true faith' and sign over some of the progeny to a Catholic education. Once a week I would go to see the priest in North Balwyn to be taught about the Mysteries and Sacraments of the Catholic Church – then, as now, it was mumbo jumbo to me. I tried to absorb it, I really did, but I felt I was falling head-first into a vat and there was nobody to hear me as I drowned.

My friends, sensing a disaster, suddenly made themselves very scarce and this became painfully evident when we tried to find a best man. Various friends were asked and politely declined: George Negus, at whose first marriage I had been a witness; Michael Keating, who agreed to it in principle since I had been best man at his wedding to Rosemary, but was unable to do it since he was in Paris; likewise Jonathan King, who was at the London School of Economics; John Paterson, the economist who later became a cost-cutting Social Welfare honcho in Jeff Kennett's government, manfully agreed to this onerous duty but was rejected by my bride-to-be because, as a dwarf, it was felt he would not look good in the bridal photos; and Christopher Pearl, returned from Europe over Christmas, declined because he felt it would be too cynical. Finally I was left with the social disgrace of having my brother Clive to be my best man. Did this mean I had no friends at all?

The madness grew apace. There were choices of wedding rings, wedding presents, bridesmaids and groomsmen – all the absurd paraphernalia of a Melbourne wedding. After the wedding was postponed twice, the nuptial vows were finally to be taken in February 1971.

One day Joanna was due to arrive from Carlton in her Mini Minor, having delivered a series of gifts to friends. Her parents, two brothers, one large married sister and I were present, but not the bride-to-be. At three we started panicking. At four we rang police, hospitals and all friends. At five, her builder brother Johnno and I got into cars and visited her empty flat. We searched every street from Carlton to Toorak. We rang the police again. Finally, Joanna arrived at seven, looking quite demented.

Where had she been? Didn't she realise what was happening? She said she had fallen asleep in the sun in Fitzroy's Edinburgh Gardens and had only just woken. Since we were overjoyed to see her, we didn't press her further, but she and I cried when left alone by the family. I understood her disappearance was because she feared the upcoming marriage, felt utterly trapped and was taking evasive action. Much later, she confessed she had spent the afternoon talking to Christopher who was adamantly against this – or indeed any – marriage. Christopher's mediation even extended to sleeping platonically with Joanna in her double bed. Any feelings of affection she might have held for me were fast vanishing as he outlined to her the manifold reasons why marriage to me would be a calamity.

Over Christmas, when the Melbourne bourgeoisie commutes to the Mornington Peninsula, the situation got grimmer. On Boxing Day Joanna was due down to visit Whimsy, but she didn't make it for two days, with similar excuses – falling asleep at the wheel, et cetera et cetera. The awful thing is I was unable to comfort her: I had relapsed into a dreadful, stiff, patriarchal mode, talking about 'my fiancée' and other horrible possessives of marriage. When she finally got to Portsea there was a family crisis meeting. By this stage we were both out of our minds with anxiety but incapable of doing anything. We both spelt out what was wrong and tearfully asked whether we should go ahead. My father said sagely, 'I've seen a lot of engaged couples in my life, but I've never seen one as unhappy as you two.' He recommended cancellation on these grounds alone. But my mother said, 'Don't be silly, Alan. They can't cancel. The wedding invitations have gone out.' And so they had – this time for 21 February, a date which everybody was by now dreading. The service was to be at St Peter's, Toorak, followed by a reception at the Dorchester on the Yarra.

Ten days before the big event, Joanna and I met at Grattan Street, for the last time as it turned out, to make final arrangements. She had invited a friend, Yvonne Allen, and the three of us got thoroughly drunk. Yvonne became more and more contemptuous of marriage. She said she and her husband fought constantly and she regretted having got married and could not see why any modern intelligent woman should, since it was men who got most out of it.

It soon became a slanging match. Yvonne turned on me and accused me of neglecting Joanna, of dithering, telling lies and being 'negative'. We started screaming at each other. Yvonne said I had failed at organising the wedding and had repeatedly said to Joanna, 'Trust me, baby.' Having sowed dissension, Yvonne left at about one o'clock in the morning. Joanna became very agitated, calling me a bastard and a shit. She started throwing crockery and vases at me, but none of them hit. Then she attacked me physically, trying to pummel my face, but her blows mostly missed. I grabbed her, put her over my knee and spanked her. It was a ludicrous situation and had there been any spark we might have had sex, but matters were too far gone for that. As a final flourish, she tore off her engagement ring and flung it at me, shouting, 'You can take back your ring. I never liked it and your mother chose it anyway.' It hit the hardback edition of *The Female Eunuch* which had been lavishly quoted during the night and fell to the cork floor where it lay between us. We stared at it, dumbstruck.

At that moment Joanna's Afghan hound Alf lazily stood up and approached the ring. First he sniffed it; then, evidently approving of my mother's taste in diamonds, he wolfed it down, returning to his resting place one thousand dollars richer from the experience. At last the nightmare was over. We fell about with relief, laughing – for the first time in months – at this canine caper.

The next day I went around to her father's house to apologise. Dr O'Rorke had already placed an ad in the *Age*, declaring the wedding between his daughter and me cancelled. I had always liked him. When I sat in his lounge room with Joanna staring at me disdainfully, I broke down and cried. I blamed myself and said in a strangled voice, 'It's my fault. I am terribly sorry this has happened. It got out of control for both of us.' I told him we had been fighting too much and were incompatible. I did not mention I was gay. Joanna also began to sob. I realised it was finished when he, and not she, offered me a cup of tea. I followed him out to the kitchen and said, 'John, I want to deeply and sincerely apologise for any embarrassment –'

'Too late. No. The wedding is off.'

Gulping down my tea, speechless, I melted out the front door. News of the fiasco spread, causing stunned amazement and hilarity. More than forty wedding presents had already arrived at the bride's house; the dining room table in the front room was piled high. There were plate warmers, casserole dishes, toasters, Jensen's silver services, cutlery canteens, crisp linen sheets, gleaming stainless steel saucepans and so on, many of them bought from lists left at Myers, Buckleys and Georges. Protocol demanded they all be returned by the bride's mother.

Because the wedding was cancelled during the

mid-February holiday season only nine days before it was to be held, many people had not seen the notice and arrived at the Dorchester in evening dress on the night. Paddy McGuinness was more than a little testy, having flown down from Sydney. He was heard saying, 'Blazey's gone too far this time.' Michael Keating learned of the cancellation in Bahrain and turned around and flew back to Paris.

That night, while Joanna's two dinner-suited brothers were explaining the catastrophe to arriving guests on the porch of the Dorchester, I was far, far away – in Alice Springs on a trip exploring the outback. Coincidentally Joanna, who wittily called herself 'the bride-to-be that never was', was also losing herself in the deserts of the Northern Territory.

The final grace note was provided by Alf, the dog. Joanna asked me if the ring he devoured was insured. It was not. We agreed the only way to recover it was to have someone follow the dog around the streets of Carlton with a cake fork. This mournful duty was carried out the next day, but the ring was never found.

BOLTE
A POLITICAL BIOGRAPHY
BOLTE

The Eggwit and I

Some of you have written that I was immortal...
I am not just for this time, I am for the ages.

Gough Whitlam,
tongue in cheek on his eightieth birthday

The Opposition Leader's office, overlooking the Lombardy poplars in the courtyard of the old Parliament House, was a magical place in those buoyant, prosperous years of the early seventies. It seemed to be always morning with the sun streaming in, the aroma of coffee percolating around packed filing cabinets, ALP posters, the potted palms. Hippies would call it a 'power site', for it radiated energy and hope. These poky, white-painted rooms were the locus for the future transformation of Australia. In a policy sense, Whitlam was really in power for seven years, from 1968–1975, since he changed the conservative political agenda as well as Labor's.

Out of his offices came speeches, position papers and policy statements and into them poured pollies, academics, unionists and journalists seeking either Whitlam or his gifted staffmen, Graham

Freudenberg, Race Mathews, Dick Hall and later Jim Spigelman. Having gained sixteen seats in 1969, it seemed inevitable that Gough would be Labor's next Prime Minister in 1972.

In the meantime I was still hedging my bets politically and sexually. While working with Peacock, I started having an intermittent affair with someone in Whitlam's office.

Jenny Tudor was one of 'the girls', as Gough called the family of minders, typists, bag-carriers and diary-keepers who maintained his great Oppositional enterprise. They all adored him, calling him 'Eggwit' from his initials E. G. Whitlam. They shared his droll sense of humour and, unlike Liberal staffers, were open about sexual matters; he might buy them a chastity belt on his return from a European trip. Gough used to tease the girls about their boyfriends and I was welcome in the office, being an enemy trophy. Jenny was wonderful, theatrical, competent yet self-effacing – perfect for Whitlam's office. She had gone to a 'good' school but seemed to have boyfriend problems. She couldn't stand 'ockers' as she called them and so fell for rather more dreamy types. Somehow or other, Ian Marsh, who was Malcolm Fraser's private secretary, and myself started a troilistic affair with her. Surely here was an event of interest to ASIO!

We would spend Sunday afternoons performing low-impact aerobics on Jenny's gigantic double bed. We went to restaurants in Sydney as a three-way, but in Canberra used more conventional binary configurations. I even gave Peacock Jenny's phone number for weekend contact. As one of Gough's secretaries, she got a great charge from saying 'Halloo' in a fluting voice and finding a Liberal minister on her bedside phone, then passing the phone over a tangle of hairy legs to his press secretary. Though he never knew who she was, Peacock was delighted I had a girlfriend in Sydney. But coupledom is soon exhausted by the brio of a trio and the affair ended in tears. While it lasted, I spent a lot of time visiting Gough's office and my comings and goings were reported to the Liberal's petty new Prime Minister. When I was sacked, my familiarity with Whitlam's staff was cited as a reason.

Initially, John Gorton had posed immense problems for Whitlam who, it was widely agreed, had got the measure of Harold Holt before he disappeared in the surf. After being elected Prime

Minister in January 1968, Gorton enjoyed a wild media honeymoon which stressed his Australian populism; but when Eggleton briefed me two years later, Gorton had exhausted his credit. He was paranoid and friendless, with only one more wilful year to go. One day, after Gorton had been sacked in March 1971 and before I had been dismissed by McMahon, I walked into the offices and Gough was there, arm resting on a filing cabinet, holding forth.

He was so gargantuan he nearly filled the room, but it's what he said that stayed in my mind. 'Gorton had so much and he threw it all away,' said Gough. Gorton had not been born into a true blue, silver-spoon upper middle class Liberal family (like Gough) and because of his bastard birth, had a chip on his shoulder, a huge resentment of his party and the establishment. All that was obvious enough, but I was intrigued when Whitlam, then fifty-four, observed that Gorton was a 'shallow, trivial man' because he had hired an attractive young woman like Ainslie Gotto and had wanted it to be thought they were having an affair when they weren't. 'For a man who was nearly sixty, it was a very vulgar thing to do,' he said.

One of Gough's staffers mentioned Gorton's

amazing PR surge and Gough admitted that for the first nine months he had been a very worried man. 'I knew that Gorton could talk to farmers, drink in Leagues clubs and be photographed in surfboats at Maroubra or wherever it was. I knew he could do these things and I couldn't. I'm a bookish, staid, bourgeois sort of person and I knew if I got into a surfboat I would look ridiculous,' said Gough. 'Of course I rationalised these things by saying it was beneath Prime Ministerial dignity. But really I knew I couldn't do it.' Gough finished with words which would come back to haunt him: 'In a mere three years Gorton destroyed his Prime Ministership because of character flaws. I can assure you, that won't happen to me.' This was a significant conversation for me.

I admired Gough's candour, his serene intellect. Compared to the tepid, querulous hypocrisies of the Liberals, he embodied both original analysis and courage, the two qualities by which I wanted to live. Of course, it was easy for him to admit these things after Gorton had been overthrown. Still, I liked him categorising himself as staid, bookish and bourgeois. That day I became the most devoted Whitlamite in the McMahon government.

IN WHICH I BECOME EVEN MORE OF A GOUGH DEVOTEE

I first met Whitlam at an ALP Club conference in Warburton, outside Melbourne, in 1963, two years after he had become deputy leader. Although we young socialists considered Gough an up-and-coming man who would one day overthrow his geriatric leader, Arthur Calwell, we thought him a little too middle class for our sixties tastes.

In 1968 I met him again. I was introduced to him this time at the Bendigo by-election and must admit I found him even more pedantic and bourgeois. He was pedagogically intoning about half senate elections and how the House of Representatives represented the 'will of the Australian people' – that life-obsession by which he was made and unmade. Max Hollingsworth, a gifted journalist and a friend, said: 'Mr Whitlam, here's someone I'd like you to meet.' Whitlam stood there with an amused stare. He looked very Brylcreemed in those days, before his fluffy seventies hairdos. He said he was 'honoured' to meet a friend of Max's. He had the ability to make you feel special, especially if you were from the media, which he was courting in his bid for power. He asked me what I thought of his speech and I replied, 'It was hardly electrifying.' He seemed miffed, saying one had to go through these motions at by-elections, but it was good to get an opinion from 'a trained observer like yourself, Peter', laying it on with a trowel.

We next met in 1970 when I was with Peacock, at a function in the Great Hall of the National Gallery of Victoria. I had written Andrew's speech about youth, leadership and compassionate vision – a load of seventies feel-good codswallop. Whitlam invited Andrew and me back to Canberra on his small VIP jet. In those days they got on favourably, since Andrew was a small 'l' Liberal, a young trendy rebelling against the party's aged Tories. On the plane, Andrew told Gough that I had been a member of the ALP when he hired me and Gough was intrigued by this. On that night in Gough's plane in the first year of the seventies, I wore long hair, sideburns and a mustard-coloured herringbone suit from Henry Buck's. I was trying so hard to be respectable and straight.

Eight years later, when he was well and truly

out of power, Gough recalled this meeting with an accuracy that took my breath away. He said: 'I certainly do remember, Peter. You were wearing a brown suit but black shoes.' How amazing to recall such an incongruous detail. Was he reproving a sartorial gaffe? He continued with the campest flourish: 'And I thought you and Andrew made a very handsome couple!' By then he knew I was gay, so it was Gough at his most feline. But he himself had by now become a very camp person indeed. All great stars from Greta Garbo to Mick Jagger have this mysterious androgyny. It was Gough's double-edged, gay-friendly theatricality that captivated me and secured my devotion. I always thought that Gough had more than a touch of Oscar about him. On his eightieth birthday in 1996 he proved this to be true by quoting Oscar and bringing forth his own well-thumbed copy of Richard Ellman's biography of Wilde. It is certainly a book few other Australian Prime Ministers would know about.

In 1973 the platonic love affair between Gough and me blossomed since I was now working in his government, albeit for one of his most unpopular ministers. Moss Cass was forty-seven when he became Whitlam's Minister for the Environment. He only just squeaked in, twenty-sixth in a ministry of twenty-seven. Moss was a home-loving, intellectual doctor who had won the seat of Maribyrnong in the pro-ALP surge of 1969. A medical researcher, he had come to prominence in the Footscray trade union clinic and was a staunch supporter of the left-wing Victorian ALP. Bearded and short, he was a quietly spoken, left-wing liberal Jew. Though he despised the crude histrionics of politics, he was passionate about many radical causes – feminism, multiple member electorates, the decriminalisation of marijuana. He was friendly with painters like Cliff Pugh, film people such as Tim Burstall and Phillip Adams; his political allies were Bill Hayden, Lionel Murphy and the Gietzelt brothers.

Cass's strengths were remarkable: they included an uncompromising determination on policy and a laterality that was visionary. Among his creative reforms were the restructuring of the Australian Conservation Foundation, the introduction of environmental impact statements and the Gorton/Cass motion in favour of homosexuality in the ACT and the Northern Territory. This historic free vote of the House of Representatives, on which we had all worked for months, passed easily and disclosed some surprising bedfellows, as it were. Bill Snedden, Bill McMahon and Paul Keating voted against it, while Whitlam, Peacock and Doug Anthony voted for it. I saw Anthony in the corridors soon after and asked him why. He said, 'You Labor blokes think you're all so trendy. What you don't realise is that a lot of us went to Public Schools.'

Despite Cass's good works, he developed a personal monomania about Whitlam which damaged the government, especially at the end. Moss's dislike of the towering, patrician Prime Minister started early. When Gough first looked at the twenty-five new ministers elected by caucus, he said to his cabinet, 'Lance [Barnard, Deputy Prime Minister] and I were doing a great job as a duumvirate. We don't need you bastards at all.' Of course it was a joke, but Moss used it time and again as evidence of Gough's arrogance.

As Whitlam got into deeper trouble, instead of being supportive, Cass became more rebellious. One day after caucus, Whitlam denounced Cass in the corridors. It was exactly the sort of thing a Liberal would never have done and certainly not the leader of the government. He shouted that Cass was a 'captious little cunt!' Rushing to a dictionary we discovered that captious meant hypercritical, carping. We were disappointed. It sounded worse.

*

The year 1973 was an *annus mirabilis* for both Whitlam and me. A vast amount of reform legislation had been passed or foreshadowed, even though much was already being obstructed by the Senate. My Bolte book had been a hit in Canberra. For some weeks *Bolte: a Political Biography* shared billing on the *Sunday Telegraph*'s bestseller list with such books as Malcolm Muggeridge's *Chronicles of Wasted Time, Volume One*, Solznenitsyn's *August 1914* and Frederick Forsyth's *The Odessa File*. For one week it was number one.

That year I lived in a large group house in the suburb of Curtin which I shared with Henry Rosenbloom, Neil Swancott (a clever Scrabble player who later worked for Dr Cairns when Treasurer) and Paddy McGuinness, then adviser to Bill Hayden, the Minister for Social Security. Like the rest of us, Paddy was a radical, fired up with the mission of reforming Australia. He was obsessed with the greed of the doctors whom Hayden was fighting to get Medibank going. Paddy's friend Parker occasionally stayed in the laundry of the house when he wasn't living in the psychiatric hospital in Goulburn.

I now had houses in two cities, a prestigious job in a historic, reformist government and I had just written a bestseller. I commuted weekly between Melbourne and Canberra, being at home in neither but lionised in both. From being a bum with Christopher, stealing food in the HofBrauhaus five years previously, I had indeed landed on my feet. It wouldn't last, of course. It never did with me.

ON THE MAT WITH MOTHER

Having bought a cottage in Carlton in 1972, I encouraged a sixteen-year-old German-Australian boy named Udo to move in. He ran away from his parents and set up in my house for a three-month gay idyll. In those days, this harmless enough arrangement had caused scenes of outrage from my blokey pals in Melbourne. Udo, a tall, exquisitely handsome schoolboy, had a mane of tumbling brown hair and was immediately nicknamed 'the sheep' by my friends. But since I wasn't really out, dealing with Udo socially was difficult. Fearing the sissy in me, I neglected him by spending too much time beerily bonding at the Albion Hotel.

With a mother's ESP, Doone suspected something was up although she had never heard of Udo. She took to visiting me unannounced at my house, dubbed the 'Purple Palace', in her Alfa Romeo. She arrived frequently and very early in the day, as I frantically slid the barely clad Udo out into the backyard, putting 'the sheep' to grass, as it were. On one epic occasion he stayed there shivering for twenty minutes as I made my mother a cup of Nescafé au lait.

'You seem very tense today,' Doone said to me with laserlike accuracy. I muttered that I was worried about some work. She suddenly became agitated, starting to walk from room to room with the aplomb of Lady Bracknell. 'I get the feeling there's someone else living in this house,' she said, examining the bathroom cabinet and seeing two toothbrushes.

'Oh, that belongs to Christopher Pearl. He sometimes stays here,' I said airily.

Her scorn was immense. 'You're not still seeing him, are you?' remembering the scandal of our alleged affair fifteen years ago.

'Yes I am, as a matter of fact,' I said, finding my elaborate nonchalance was curdling into irritation.

She got angry herself: I'd ruined my life, I'd run away from everything that had been offered me and I had totally wasted the last three years in Europe. 'What's more,' she wailed, 'you once had the chance to become a Junior at the Peninsular Golf Club and you totally threw it away – as if it were dirt! You're nothing but a flibbertigibbet!'

The use of this word was so bizarre that I laughed outright and she did her block. She rushed towards the back door and grabbed the handle, saying: 'Don't lie to me, Peter! There's someone in the backyard. I know!' She threw her body at the door. Terrified, I rushed to cut her off, grabbing the door knob and saying that recent rains had swollen the jamb so it wouldn't open.

Horrible to recall, we wrestled violently in front of the door, knocking over a pile of Carly Simon LPs onto the carpet. I prevailed because I was stronger, and put my mother in a headlock. I told her to get out and leave me alone. I was now thirty-three, I shouted, and she couldn't visit unless she rang up first.

'I know what you're up to,' she sneered as she stormed out of the house and got into her Alfa with her labrador and the golf clubs in the back. I hated her at that moment, particularly because she knew I was a closet queen and she would use it against me forever, if I permitted it.

Naturally such cowardly displays didn't impress Udo who, shaking with cold, had shuffled back into the house. He asked me why I had denied him? Had I no *mut* (courage)? When I asked him if *mut* was short for *mutti*, he laughed bitterly and said that I had too much *mutti* but not enough *mut* and that I would never be able to have a boyfriend while I had such a terrible mother. Soon after, he left Australia sending me a contemptuous letter from Stuttgart. It was the terror of the closet, an exponential fear which eats into every aspect of your life like acid until you have the courage to face it.

I brought Udo to Canberra for a week in October. He was lonely living in my Carlton house, so I took him to the national capital to meet my friends. I introduced him to Moss Cass, almost as a trophy of the Gorton/Cass motion. Moss was charming to Udo, he had no problems about homosexuality. Only recently, Moss had encouraged me and Henry Rosenbloom and other staffers to smoke a marijuana joint openly in the Members' Dining Room. This was another historic first for Moss, who didn't inhale himself (since he didn't smoke). He was simply making a point about the stupidity of the anti-dope laws and later helped bring about reforms in the ACT with Attorney-General Murphy.

All through that year I would run into Gough in the corridors and at functions; he made cracks about how, being bearded, I looked like an Old Testament prophet. After Moss and his staff made a well-publicised trip to try to save Lake Pedder from being flooded by the hydromanic Tasmanian government, Gough delighted in a new sobriquet for me – I was now a 'Pedder-ast'.

IN WHICH WE MEET GOUGH'S NEMESIS

Many other remarkable things were happening. As early as September there were straws in the wind foretelling disaster. Minister for Energy, Rex Connor, lost his temper with 'the apes of the press'. This old man in a hurry, nicknamed 'The Strangler', was becoming paranoid and, by some weird alchemy, he intimidated Gough and the caucus. Connor was finally sacked on 15 October 1975 when the Melbourne *Herald* revealed that Connor was *still* encouraging Tirath Khemlani (a complete fantasist posing as a financial guru) to raise petrodollar loans, despite his authority having been revoked four months earlier. This act was the trigger for the blocking of supply, which occurred on the same day Connor was sacked. In November 1995, at a convention held twenty years after the dismissal, Fraser admitted supply would never have been blocked but for Connor. If only Gough had sacked this cranky old monomaniac along with Cairns in mid-1975 or earlier, he might have lasted as a Labor Prime Minister, instead of becoming a Labor martyr. Whitlam was not scared of Cass, or Cairns, or even Clyde Cameron and certainly not of the late Lionel Murphy (whom he called a 'cowardly cunt' to his face), but he *was* scared of Connor and that fear brought down his government.

*

In September 1973 at a public diplomatic lunch, Gough called himself the 'greatest Foreign Minister in Australian history' – not bad for a man who had only been in the job for nine months. It was obvious we were dealing with a most unusual politician. Was he mad or was he just brilliant? In those days we believed the latter. Gough's hyperbolic statement was not Bonapartist as many feared, just another Gough *gasconade*, tongue-in-cheek exaggeration. But this sort of talk was starting to scare people, as was the radical rhetoric of his ministers, not to mention the sheer unstoppable flow of reforms. That was the problem with the birdbrained critics: they were so literal minded. But then politics is a fairly low- to middle-brow activity.

In October things started going really sour: there were strikes, industrial trouble, rising inflation and interest rates, and the National Party announced it would use the Senate to get rid of the Labor government as soon as it could. Liberal Leader Billy Snedden was uncommitted on this, since many Liberals thought Labor had a right to three years. But not Doug Anthony. Bob Hawke was attacking Whitlam like static, accusing him of political idiocy.

He was jealous that Gough was the star and he wasn't. He was also manic-aggressive, which I believe was due to the bad sugar-energy of alcohol. A mere nine months after being elected, it was becoming quite likely that Whitlam would be in for just one term. How did he take all that? His stock response to his staffmen was almost carefree. 'Well, it was fun, wasn't it?' Another time he told Mick Young, 'If we've got to go, I think it's better that we go out gloriously and not like Harold Wilson.' Gough's 'crash through or crash' style was evident right from the start.

The Christmas party in Gough's office that year was a gala event. But there was little to celebrate really. Gough's 8 December prices and incomes referendum had been resoundingly defeated throughout the country. Although many backbenchers realised they were likely to be 'oncers', spirits were high and the booze was flowing in the Prime Minister's recently enlarged suite at the corner of the old Parliament House. The place was packed with ministers, members, journos and flunkies. The ebullient Mick Young was running around calling Gough 'Darling', which delighted him – almost. Gough was standing in the corner of the outer office, a warm beer in his hand, towering over this event like a Roman emperor.

'I see Bolte's being nasty about your book,' he said to me. 'My own biographer wasn't all that objective,' referring to Laurie Oakes's book *Whitlam PM*, 'but they always have to find something critical so they can prove they are objective.' He laughed at this human absurdity. Gough said the thing that most distressed him about the referendum result was the misuse of the Latin plural: 'In the end I was talking about referend-ums because people were talking about referend-as!' He laughed again at the ignorance of his subjects.

*

The last time I saw Gough was at a birthday held for Anne Summers at the Moore Park Bowling Club in 1995. Since I hadn't seen him for years, he was much older and seemed less serene. In the smoky, blokey atmosphere of the bar, he was surrounded by wellwishers, former staffers and the curious. Gough now looked puffed and florid; yes, rubicund, his grey hair definitely thinning. He was still immense but he also looked wary, almost at bay, like an old tiger.

He moved up and down on the balls of his feet, his head bobbing more than it used to as he searched for the *mot juste*. Then he would deliver it, his chin thrust forward, his mouth snapping shut like a huge barramundi.

He was pleased to see me, murmuring about Boltes and biographies, saying that it was time for another biography on him. I told him that Tim and I had gone to the recent Mardi Gras parade dressed as Bob and Blanche, me wearing a five-dollar blonde wig and Tim sporting a cardboard face mask of Bob Hawke drawn by a *Daily Telegraph* cartoonist. We both wore white bathrobes and loafers as Bob and Blanche had done when they announced their engagement for '60 Minutes' and *Woman's Day*. 'We were mobbed,' I told him excitedly. 'Everyone recognised us! People shouting "G'day, Bob! Good on yer, Blanche!" It went on and on. For two hours we had constant adulation. Now I know what it's like being a pollie or a star. It's *wonderful*. It's like a drug,' I said. 'Oh, I don't know,' said Gough drily, 'you get used to it.'

When I showed him some photos, he wanted to meet Tim, who he said looked much more interesting than the 'original of the effigy' who was a 'man of straw'. I then asked Gough if he had seen us walking in the Mardi Gras parade up Oxford Street. He was, after all, in the VIP viewing room in Taylor Square. Was it, I asked, his first Mardi Gras?

He stared at me with a feline smile. Then he deadpanned: 'Yes, it was my first Mardi Gras. I may be nearly eighty. But I've decided to come out. Margaret's come out too. We're a very out couple these days, Peter!'

Who is Sylvia?

There's more to be learned about wearing a dress for a day, than there is to be learned about wearing a suit for life.
Mario Mieli

I may have been a mere journalist, dunked in a urinal of greed, venality and power-worship, as all journalists are, but I also loathed being a courtier and flunky, even to someone whom I worshipped as much as Gough. Part of Whitlam's great alchemy was in encouraging people to throw aside caution and to follow their star. These are not political virtues, they are the attributes of a visionary. For me, 1973 was the year I succumbed to Gough's rather reckless counsel – in this case falling in love with David Wood.

We were introduced by Suzy Dark, a hippie who worked in the Minerals and Energy minister's office. Suzy was keen on me and was intent on converting me to the values of hippiedom. She smoked an excess of hashish and had a huge network of potheads throughout Parliament House and the press gallery. Undoubtedly David Wood was her dealer, amongst many others. Later, when David and I were living together, Commonwealth cars were used to deliver parcels marked 'urgent' to senior ministers' offices.

With David it really was love at first sight. He wasn't working nor was he a student, though he hung around the fringes of the Australian National University and the Union bar making a passable income selling cannabis and sometimes hallucinogens.

Tall, lanky-limbed with a thatch of brown hair, he had an open face distinguished by one eye being hazel, and the other brown. He had strong psychic powers and had the capacity to make people fall under his sway or else despise him. He was a flamboyant and lively figure, a natural cricketer who had been born the son of an Anglican preacher in Mittagong, the heart of Bradman country. But now he had thrown in his lot with the hippie movement, the Vietnam protesters and those who believed drugs conferred superior truths. David was impressed by my job with the Minister for the Environment. Like all hippies, he was entranced by 'ecology'.

Our night of bonding occurred when Suzy introduced us at an improvised concert in the Albert

Hall. Normally a distinctly sedate venue where First Assistant Secretaries in black tie listened to Ravel piano trios or a Mozart flute concerto, this performance by contrast featured Sylvia and the Synthetics, a collection of drugged-out drag queens from Sydney. Sylvia's shows were notorious for their finale which often transformed into an orgy.

It started with drag queen Miss Jacqueline Hyde (I later discovered), appearing on stage as a housewife, wearing pedal pushers with rollers in her hair. While the tapedeck played Johann Strauss's *Blue Danube*, she vacuumed her carpet, smoking a cigarette and affecting great boredom. The suction tube of her Hoover was called 'Mel' and she began talking to it in the most intimate fashion. Then she started licking, sucking, even fucking it in a pantomime of eerie power. Finally she snapped and said, 'Mel, I'm tired of shoving shit up your chute!'

Then there was six-foot-tall Miss Danny Aboud, lip-synching to 'Big Girls Don't Cry' in front of the burghers of Canberra, who had no idea this was going to happen. Suddenly she slipped out of her canvas 'Miss Lebanon 1947' frock, and stood naked on a debris-scattered stage, her large schlong swinging idly from side to side. There were few cries of horror or surprise – just a stunned silence from the public servants although there was an enclave of hippies in the audience starting to buzz with anticipation. It was not too long before one of Sydney's best-known drag queens, Doris Fish, dressed as a mermaid, leapt off the stage of the Albert Hall and began to simulate fucking with a semi-naked hippie at the front. Soon the hippie's underbody bucked forward and he started shouting. Miss Fish, whose faculties were dulled by substance abuse, mistook this activity for the throes of orgasm. It was only when Danny shouted from the stage: 'Watch out, Doris, he's having an epileptic fit!' that she recoiled, slipped her penis back inside her gold lamé tail and returned to the safety of the stage.

Although I hardly dared to laugh that night, for fear of giving myself away, I was enthralled at this gender confusion and mayhem in the national capital. A thirty-four-year-old closet queen with a good job and a government car, I felt my hypocritical life starting to crack down the middle.

When 'Sylvia' played in Sydney, it was greeted with howls of laughter, but here in Canberra the mullets were aghast except for a few titters from hippies, some of the friends of James Mollison – the hip director of the National Art Gallery – and some members of Whitlam's staff. The maddest thing of all was there was no Sylvia. At the start of each show a solemn announcement was made: 'We're sorry Sylvia can't be here tonight. She was decapitated by the fins of a '57 Chevy on her way to the show.'

Suzy required a few joints to get right into Sylvia's stage routines. She had spent that whole day with her friends dyeing loaves of homecooked bread green, purple, pink and red. They played Stevie Wonder and Pink Floyd while they worked, dressed in long white muslin gowns. There was rice (coloured with natural dyes), brussels sprouts, cabbages, fish, marsala dhosas, chapattis, oatmeal cakes, cupcakes and a myriad of other foods on long trestle tables at the side of the hall. Lovingly cooked and presented, they had all brought 'plates': it was half CWA, half Hindu prasad, an offering of love presented with incense and madness. They called it the All Senses Ball.

It's almost too easy to deride the naivety of hippie idealism back then. All those bruised love-children in their caftans, their robes and their Gujarati jerkins, smelling of patchouli oil as they raved on about love and the need for liberation.

But Sylvia had wackier ways of resisting oppression. When the performers started throwing brussels sprouts and offal at the audience, the show was getting under way. Some of the crowd returned the fire, others hid behind chairs, for there were ox bones among the offal. Now nobody could pretend they were observers. We were all participating. The air was alive with screams, abuse and insane laughter. There were flying objects everywhere. There was the smoke from beedies, kreteks, marijuana and hash; there was acid, mushrooms, mescaline, mandrax, Jim Beam, Southern Comfort and flying cans of Foster's.

Then there was Danny Aboud, naked, crouched on the stage singing John and Yoko's 'Woman is the Nigger of the World', but it was too late. One of Sylvia's roadies, a beautiful long-haired boy called Tim, laid a trail of gunpowder right around the wooden parquet floor and lit it. It went up with a huge, fiery WHOOSH. The Albert Hall filled with smoke and consternation and the show was over. The ACT police and the fire brigade had been called. It was apparent that Sylvia would never get a gig there

– or anywhere else in the national capital – again.

Later David, Suzy and I walked to Suzy's home in Narrabundah. We smoked some hash. David and Suzy started making out on the cushions. I was watching, aroused. Finally Suzy said, 'Why don't you boys both come up to my bedroom?' Suzy loved 'mixing it', as she said. So we all trooped upstairs. Very soon Suzy was naked on the bed while David was going down on her. 'Oh David,' she moaned, 'you give better head than anyone I know.' He looked at me and winked, saying, 'You look very overdressed there, Mr Environment.' My Henry Buck's suit was on the floor in seconds. We had a marvellous scene. We were doing it for Sylvia.

I told my journo friends about Sylvia and the All Senses Ball at the non-members' bar the next day. They were amazed. What, men fucking on stage, surely not in Canberra? One or two closets blushed, looked at the floor and said nothing.

I later discovered that Sylvia and her ten regular performers grew out of gay liberation and performance art. They were powerfully influenced by the burgeoning feminism of the times. Their show was actually performed only about forty times (the

Vice Squad was always chasing them), but they altered the mind-set of everyone who saw them.

The Synthetics came out of the freedom offered by the Whitlam government which said, if you want to liberate or change yourself, go ahead and do it. We'll encourage you. We might even fund you. That's why, I believe, in the Whitlam years there were more de facto marriages and divorces, more relationships started and stopped than any other three-year period in Australian history. Many rejected the Whitlam challenge. But many others – Kooris, artists, women, ethnics, gays and lesbians – didn't.

I wanted to be my own man, to write something profound. Soon after, I asked Moss Cass for three months' leave to complete an MA thesis on the politics of the environment for Melbourne University. Moss was annoyed. He wanted my services and had a low opinion of political sociology, while my project seemed unoriginal to him. He said, 'Make sure you write it, otherwise I won't re-employ you.'

I retired to my Carlton house during a memorably infernal Melbourne summer, and started on the convolutions of this thesis. I was supposed to be writing a thousand words a day; instead, I was doodling, drinking at the Albion Hotel, and thinking about David Hugh and the All Senses Ball.

'The Politics of the Environment' might have been a cute idea, but was there a thesis in it? Why did some people get steamed up over 'symbolic' environmental issues like the damming of Lake Pedder, while others saw the environment as clean waterways and no dogshit on footpaths? I devised a trendyism scale which went like this:

Trendy	Nontrendy
muesli	*cornflakes*
drop out	*drop scone*
co-habitation	*marriage*
Pink Floyd	*Burt Bacharach*
counter culture	*counter lunch*
lemon scented gum	*plane tree*
blow job	*blow wave, etc*

The more I thought about it, the more I realised that I was less interested in getting an MA (Env.), than enacting the trendy scale which I had tabulated.

By late January I had grown sick of the farce of my ill-conceived MA and I wrote a postcard to

David in Canberra. 'It's hot, hot, hot here. I need you to cool me down. Come down soon, love, Mr Environment.'

David arrived only days later. We commenced an affair, one of the biggest in my life, but one constrained by the proviso that he was basically straight. Within weeks we had gone back to Canberra and set up a commune at 30 Canning Street, Ainslie, a famous anti-Vietnam resistance site much raided by police and much visited by draft evaders and anti-war campaigners such as Dr Spock, who stayed there after speaking to a Canberra rally, as well as Jack Waterford, now the editor of the *Canberra Times*. It was a historic site but it eventually became a terrible slum.

As head tenants we were meant to be responsible for up to ten students, artists and others staying in the house. Bourgeois sensibilities found no favour here. Clothes and newspapers were converted to confetti within days by a voracious empire of vermin, while in the kitchen a permanent cloud of flies flew in a congested holding pattern, waiting for landing rights on the Klondike of spilled, rotting and lidless food spread across the benches, stove-top, sink and floor. Some time later it was revealed that the vile stink coming from the laundry was none other than Sweeney, the house cat (named after the chief drug enforcement officer for the ACT police), who had died beneath the washing machine.

It was the sort of group house in which the culture demanded that no one would be uncool enough to refuse access to any visitors. This caused major problems well after I had moved on. According to my good friend Julia Perry, a former resident and now a senior bureaucrat with Social Security, when the psychiatric hospital in Goulburn began discharging its inmates many drifted down to Canberra and found their way first to the Union bar and then inexorably to Canning Street. She recalls coming upstairs one morning to find a psychotic redhead known as Barbarella wearing some of her clothes and having apparently moved in during the night. The household froze her out in silence, hoping she would go away. Barbarella was finally expelled after she set fire to someone's wardrobe.

Of course I was oblivious to the sordid domestics going on, being completely fixated on David. But he had other things on his mind, notably drugs and sex, preferably with women. Although we slept in the same double bed for a year, we always moved into threesome country on the weekends. David had a tremendous capacity to please and women seemed to adore him. 'To be a great Casanova, you have to be a pussy slurper,' he told me. I agreed with this rather jejune summary of male–female relations, based on the fact that as a budding homosexual I was not mad about cunnilingus. When we started living together in the commune he would say, 'I just can't help myself, mate' (he always called me 'mate' as if to deflect the homoerotic implications of what we were doing), 'I just love going down on ladies.' Still, we were inseparable. I liked to think of him as my boyfriend but he was sure that I was his best mate.

You've got to remember this was the polymorphous seventies. It was the decade in which most straight men and women wondered if they might be bisexual and whether they couldn't play with sex like plasticine. People who called themselves 'bisexual' were either on their way to becoming hardened heterosexuals, as Hugh later did, or a sort of a staging post during which gay men and lesbians discovered their final, true sexual orientation, as I did. I believe there are a few true bisexuals, but many more claim they're bisexual because they fear they might be gay. Fortunately, queer theory, which arose in the late eighties, is helping to break down some of these calcified positions.

We all bear the marks of the seventies. Those years changed Australia forever. Unfortunately the era started glamorously and ended daggy. Satin jackets, platform shoes, lurex jumpsuits and flares went with decent drugs and serious drag (especially in Sydney). But mid-decade came the oil shocks and the thrifty Fraser years. The postwar boom burst and stagflation set in. Along with that started the 'systemic unemployment' that has never ended.

In Australia, glam androgyny seemed to last longer than in other countries. Skyhooks, Sherbet and Hush were the top three bands in 1975, with also-rans like Ray Burgess and Taste. Let's face it, when the now nearly-forgotten Supernaut sang 'I Like It Both Ways', something gave way. Many marriages quivered with instability. The seventies was the 'Countdown' decade, with word-mangler Ian 'Molly' Meldrum burbling, bumbling and clanking through language like Ned Kelly on beta blockers. It was also the decade when I was seized by a form of sexual dementia.

Realising I would never get my thesis done in time, I resigned from Cass – who seemed relieved – and picked up my back pay. I relinquished the Apollonian (and heterosexual) heights of Parliament House for a more uncertain, more Dionysian life with David. It lasted two years until we again discovered to our great pain that two into three didn't go.

I suppose my mission had been to resolve my sexuality. The trouble was, in those days, there was no such thing as 'a gay man'. Although the Stonewall riots had happened, gay liberation had hardly reached Canberra. The great gift of the movement was for a person to be able to declare himself gay, and live on his own or with another man, without going through all the bullshit of dishonest marriages, fake bisexuality, male odd couples, or any of the other devices by which many homosexual men delude themselves.

Though there was no going back to a career in the government, there was at least something practical accomplished from my aborted MA experience. I transmuted the remnants of my thesis into a book about the 1974 double dissolution, *The Political Dicemen* (Outback Press), co-authored with Andrew Campbell. It was launched with great panache in the

Ainslie Hotel by Deputy Prime Minister Jim Cairns and as a Christmas quickie it sold well but was not a critical success, being a little too Gonzo in style. Whitlam's adviser, the late Dr Peter Wilenski, called it a 'curate's egg', which was accurate enough.

David and I had some high times together, but were they enough to compensate for me having 'thrown away' my career? The irony is, that those who stayed faithful to the Good Ship Whitlam only lasted another eighteen months, while I, though I hardly knew it at the time, was fitting myself for a sojourn in a much bigger, much angrier commune.

FREE

London Bollocks

Pussy cat, pussy cat, where have you been?
I've been to London to look at the Queen.
NURSERY RHYME

After Gough's 1000-year Reich terminated in less than three, it was time to get out of Australia. In the crazy, historic year of 1975, I had gone back to Parliament House and got a job on the ABC (radio news) and I was also a tutor in political science at ANU. Since both these jobs were part-time, they ended the day after Malcolm Fraser blocked supply on 15 October. David Wood and I were still in the commune but we had separate bedrooms as he'd decided he wanted to be straight and no longer 'Blazey's Daisy', as a friend put it.

During the year, another male had come onto the scene. Answering an ad for Canning Street which said 'exotic house requires ambidextrous tenant', he moved into a room of his own and soon after into my bedroom. His name was Philip Juster, a student at Canberra College of the Arts. We started a relationship that lasted, with several breaks, for fifteen years.

At twenty-two, Philip was bright, bearded, good-looking. He had read deeply on feminism and was a promising artist with a touch of the naive. He had grown up in Queensland, the son of a Bjelke-Petersen-voting baker, but soon left after fighting at school and at home over issues ranging from Vietnam to long hair. He visited Indonesia on his own at eighteen and stayed in mining camps in Western Australia.

As I began drifting away from David's hypnotic power, I found myself falling for a person who identified as a gay man. This was a unique situation for me. I thought I was bisexual but Philip told me I was deluding myself. I was misusing women, identifying with straight men and denying my own true nature, which was gay. We spent endless nights arguing about it under the massive, brooding Mount Ainslie, which he called *Gunung* Ainslie from his time in Java. We bought air tickets to Indonesia at the end of December and left, supposedly for two months, but actually for two years. Philip needed to settle down in a relationship – so I, for better or for worse, became his first boyfriend. But for me, he lacked that magical sexual 'oomph' which had been a central feature of all my lovers from Ian Dodswell to Chris Pearl and, most recently, David Wood. So Philip and I became a companionate gay couple, a version of what the Germans call an *ehepaar*.

Before leaving Australia, I reported on Gough's horrendous 1975 election campaign for the *Melbourne Observer*, then owned by Maxwell Newton. Following Gough's bus was depressing: endless speeches to faithful audiences of how unfair the dismissal was, how there had been no notice, how so much of Labor's program had been left undone, how if re-elected Kerr would be dismissed . . . (As a gay friend said years later, 'Australia's history was changed because two old queens had a tiff.') I heard one of Gough's final fiery speeches at Woolooware Football Ground and sadly followed him around other places in his old stamping ground of the Sutherland Shire. But to the trained observer it was obvious that the general electorate had turned massively against him. The media were uniform in their anti-Labor denunciations. Most poignant was Labor's 'inspirational' rally in the Domain. By then we knew the louder the cheers for

Gough, the greater would be the Liberal landslide.

At campaign's end, I asked a pointed question of the Kerr-appointed Liberal Prime Minister at Canberra's national press club. Was it true as rumoured, I queried, that you, Mr Fraser, have been seeing Melbourne psychiatrist Dr Ainslie Meares for depression and did you think the mental health of candidates was a matter of public interest?

Fraser half rose then sat down, staring at me with withering contempt. There was a chorus of hissing and boos from the small businessmen who were associate members of the club, but scattered applause at the spectacle of me Going Too Far again. Max Hawkins, the press club president, asked Fraser if he wanted to answer the question. Fraser declined, declaring stonily, 'To answer a question, I've got to have some opinion of the person who asked it.'

Later in the same forum, I asked the identical question of Whitlam. He responded with elegant humour: 'Neither myself, nor my wife nor my dog, are now seeing a psychiatrist, nor have we ever seen one in the past. I think it's a measure of this wretched campaign that such questions are not being answered. The mental health of the Prime Minister is a matter of public interest, Peter.' (Of course by this stage, many Australians doubted Gough's sanity!) It was the last time I saw Gough for years and it was a poignant farewell.

*

Philip and I went to Bali, to Jogjakarta and Jakarta. (I had sold my Purple Palace in Carlton for a little more than I'd paid for it in the mid-seventies.) It was cheap travelling in Asia in those days anyway. We stayed in Thailand for six months where I wrote freelance articles for the Thai tourist board about the glories of Pagan and the wonders of teak elephants. We travelled well since Philip had his own ethnographic interests and I had never been to Asia before. I still had occasional erotic dreams about David but the yearnings petered out when we flew to Greece and rented a house on the isle of Lesbos for six months. Here Philip hoped to finish some art and I thought about writing a novel. Later, we heard that gay activist Dennis Altman had arrived on the island. Having travelled with his vivacious sister Vivian by rail through Java, we invited him to stay. Dennis never said no to a free bed, but the Turkish primitiveness of Lesbos failed to impress him. When one morning he popped uninvited into our double bed, Philip was horrified. He said, 'It's like waking up next to Woody Allen.' Totally unabashed, for he is no stranger to rejection, Dennis proved to be enchanting company – humorous and lively – for the rest of the week.

We posted a card to Gough who was Opposition leader at the time. We said we needed him in Lesbos because we'd just discovered a new scroll of Sappho's poetry and only he could translate it. Philip did some intricate collages; I wrote an epigrammatic diary but I didn't finish (or even start) a novel. We started drinking ouzo, a terrible, powerful rotgut while I fantasised about the Greek soldiers who were stationed all over the island. We had jealous fights and vicious fisticuffs because Philip alleged that I was giving some Socrates, Nektarios or Adonis 'the eye'. In fact neither of us was unfaithful to the other for the whole six months.

Christopher Pearl, who was in Athens, came to stay. He has always cropped up at crucial times of my life, like a Joanna. Usually his advice is unwelcome but accurate. He formed the opinion that my relationship with Philip was not a healthy one. By then, he was only pointing out the obvious. After one particularly ugly drunken fight in which we were both bruised by blows from hunks of wood, Philip said bitterly, 'Why did my first homosexual affair have to be with a monster?' There didn't seem much point in staying together, so we separated. I flew to London, my old stamping ground. Philip followed later.

IN WHICH I JOIN A TROT SQUAT

I arrived in July 1977, at the height of Queen Elizabeth's Jubilee and the birth of punk rock, as it turned out. The Silver Jubilee was supposed to celebrate the twenty-fifth anniversary of the reign of Queen Elizabeth II. Historically, it should have been held in wintry February but by postponing it for four months and holding it in June, Britain picked up the summer bonanza of six million tourists.

The boost to a flagging balance of payments was important, but it also meant London in the summer of '77 momentarily regained its status as the cultural capital of the world. Planes queued in the sky like schoolboys, awaiting their turn to land at Heathrow at the rate of one every five minutes. Tourists from Europe, the Middle East and America poured in by the hundreds of thousands each week. Prices soared. Everyone was banking on the Jubilee. It was hoped it would be a superb tele-spectacular of Imperial Nostalgia – the best production yet in that series of Noble-England-on-the-Skids, a Royal pageant which has been running non-stop since 1940.

Despite the official optimism, political and cultural truths kept breaking through. For 1977 was the apotheosis of punk, a reaction against that staggering period of high prices, falling income and inflation at sixteen per cent. It was also a time when the trade union movement under the leadership of recalcitrants had started to go feral, laying the foundation for the merciless nightmare of Thatcherism from which the UK has still not recovered. In that late-seventies recession about the only things that were prospering were circuses and scapegoats.

By now gay-identified, I went to the Old Bailey during the blasphemy trial of *Gay News*, a paper which had printed a homosexual poem about Christ. Morals campaigner Mary Whitehouse had set this one up. Many literary figures like Margaret Drabble spoke on behalf of *Gay News*, but the British judicial system (unlike the US system) is so biased and corrupted with ancient prejudice about sexuality that there was no chance of obtaining justice.

At a demonstration outside the Old Bailey, a tall Cambridge-educated queen named Paul noticed the bowler hat I was wearing satirically and said, 'You're not a Bruce, are you?' I admitted I was. All Australians were Bruces that year due to some Monty Python sketches. He asked me if I wanted to go home with him. I did. We went to the East London Gay Centre which was the squat where he lived. We had desultory sex and he asked me if I wanted to move in. I said yes and that was that.

For six months I lived in this Trot squat which was plastered with graffiti such as 'Bollocks to Royalty', 'Boring Old Farts Rule OK?' and other attacks on the Queen. The squat was a once-deserted three-storey building in Redmans Road, Whitechapel, near where Jack the Ripper had stalked through Victorian fogs. Every Saturday morning about ten of us gay Trots ventured forth to nearby Brick Lane to sell the *Socialist Worker* and provoke squads of National

Front bovver boys who were taunting Pakistanis (Paki-bashing).

Invariably these encounters erupted into running street fights with milk bottles, half-bricks and insults flying wildly between 'Fascist shits' and 'Queer cunts'. Every year or so these skirmishes turned into set piece battles with thousands participating and many injured, such as the Lewisham and New Cross riots which I attended. Of course, militant Trot theory believed in provoking the bourgeois state so that capitalism would show its worst face, thereby precipitating a revolution of the maddened proletariat. That was the hypothesis and on that day we helped enact history in our own minor way, but not in the way we intended. The riots got totally out of hand with bricks, bars, pipes and even stoves being thrown at us as we marched down the main street of Lewisham shouting, 'Down with Racism!' Many were injured at this unpleasant and bloody event. My special friend Paul, a flaunting, flaming queen, a gay La Passionara who would have starred in the Stonewall riots eight years earlier, acquitted himself heroically on this day.

During Lewisham, I got separated from my

comrades and was chased by a gang of National Front skinheads through nearby parks. When I fell to the ground they started kicking me. A larger band of Socialist Workers Party (SWP) comrades only just rescued me from a severe beating and we escaped through back lanes. The entire fracas had been terrifying and accomplished little except increased hatred on all sides. It certainly made me appreciate the peace and comparative generosity of life in Australia.

Although I stayed at the squat another few months, I decided after Lewisham I just didn't want to live the rest of my life in this provocative way. For one thing, at thirty-seven I was rather too old. The riots received international coverage and represented a turning point in the British people's intolerance of political activism. Far from creating a better world, the major beneficiary of all that perfervid activism was Margaret Thatcher.

I stayed on in the squat because it was cheap – about ten pounds a week for the shared kitty. The political education may have been a tad puritanical, but there was lots of sex and adventure. Because its schema for social change was a dramatic one, it was attractive to someone as unresolved as I and perhaps my guilt glands at coming from comfortable Balwyn needed massaging. I zealously followed most of the squat's dictates during those tempestuous six months and it certainly extended my political radicalism.

IN WHICH I STUDY TROTSKYISM

Based on principles of 'Democratic Centralism', the squat was run by a revolutionary Trotskyite from Jo'burg called John Lindsay, a tireless worker, speaker and organiser for the SWP. Lindsay spent his days recruiting young men to his liberationist cause but, since he was bald, rotund and squat with a Vladimir Ilyich beard, he found it harder to attract them to his bed. This was the cause of great tensions within the commune. To what extent did the political obligation to 'make the world a better place' override the anarchic impulses of gay attraction? If you were drawn to someone, to what extent should this be denied because they are politically unsuitable?

We were ahead of our times. For in this grimy slum in Whitechapel we were partaking in an early, rather scandalous school for political correctness, then called ideological soundness. With Lindsay leading us, a band of fifteen or so gay young Trots, we went on endless rallies, meetings and demos. We gave talks in pubs, we sold our publications on street corners, we recruited young gay men and lesbians to the SWP cause. We hated the corrupt Tories and the Labour Party but most of all we hated those sects which claimed to be more revolutionary and chiliastic than ours: the Maoists, the Stalinists, the Workers' Revolutionary Party with their mascot, actress Vanessa Redgrave. We spent up to four nights a week on these agitprop activities, but we also went to East End pubs to hear punk bands and occasionally visited such discos in London as Bangs and (my favourite) Napoleons, where, dancing to a combination of amyl nitrite and the sultry, sexual beat of Donna Summer's 'I Feel Love', one could be guaranteed a bed partner for the night.

Five of us slept in a large communal bed adorned with silver paper, where sex was supposedly free, constant, available for all comrades and lacking that 'possessiveness' deemed to be bourgeois. There was an orgy several times a month with sometimes up to six young men from places like Basingstoke screwing each other through the night.

Paul was a gifted linguist and spoke French and German. Although we were in love for several months, we had indifferent sex. I found him too cerebral and unraunchy and being a rather precise queen, he probably found me too grubby and sluttish. He always called me Bruce. Sensing my affinities, still present after the Lesbos 'marriage', he would say, 'Bruce, dear, you don't belong to me. You are free to go with whomever you want.'

Having overcome the class conditioning that oppressed our homosexual desires, we were supposed to have liberated ourselves and become sexual revolutionaries. But, as we all know, it's never that easy. At 19 Redmans Road, sexual jealousies were often expressed in the context of ideological denunciation. There were endless rows on such subjects as consciousness raising, idealism, direct action, fundraising and seriousness of commitment to the punk-led 'Rock Against Racism' front.

We saw one of the first screeching performances by Johnny Rotten and the Sex Pistols at a rowdy, dirty, smoky pub in Mile End. We responded to the song 'Liar' and its message of contempt, directed not only at politicians but also at the money-obsessed 'establishment' of the music industry. It was one of many punk gigs we went to and I liked their homoerotic energy. With his ripped singlets, torn jeans and green teeth Johnny R. looked hypnotically seedy as he gyrated around, and he became unforgettable as he caterwauled the lyrics of 'God Save the Queen'. This song certainly hit the mood of the times and soon the Sex Pistols were signing the highest-priced contracts since the Beatles.

I rarely saw Philip. On the one occasion we went out together, to Bangs, we had a fight on the dance floor and were thrown down the stairs by several bouncers. We never went there again. He was living in a squat in Villa Road, Brixton, working in a North London bookshop and seeing a Reichian shrink. We spoke about every three weeks on the phone.

The most beguiling thing in my revolutionary house was the endless sorrows emanating from the Socialist Men's Group, a weekly meeting of straight men in the basement. Many of these trendy young men were guilty because they still showed signs of heterosexism and bourgeois individualism. They held 'consciousness raising' meetings in which they broke down and confessed to impotence with their wives. The most attractive of them were recruited upstairs to experiment with their bisexual leanings. Failing to perform in the orgy room where we all slept, some wept because their unreconstructable heterosexuality condemned them to be masculinist oppressors of women and gay men for the rest of their lives. Others were troubled that women were no longer interested in them because they had become such total wimps.

IN WHICH I SEDUCE ONE OF MALCOLM'S BODYGUARDS

Having been in darkest Whitechapel for several months, I was feeling nostalgic for both Australian accents and my Canberra past when I read in the papers that Prime Minister Fraser was arriving for a Commonwealth PMs' conference. Although I had ceased working for Peacock (now Fraser's Foreign Minister) six years previously, we were still friendly. From the gloomy basement of the squat, just next to what we called the Men's Crying Room, I rang him direct at the Savoy Plaza. The ever affable Peacock told me journalists Laurie Oakes and Michelle

Grattan were in his room as I called. Would I like to attend a function he was hosting at Australia House that evening?

The potted palms and marble pillars of the oval-shaped Reception Room at Australia House were a marvellous contrast to the squalor of the East End. I put on the best clothes I had, my Saturday morning NF-provoking brown leather jacket, denim pants and brown boots – a tad underdressed I realised, as I surveyed the sea of dinner suits and tuxedos.

I noticed Malcolm Fraser, tall and gawky, talking to 'Piggy' Muldoon, the New Zealand Prime Minister, who came up to Fraser's fly. They were alone in the middle of the hall watched by hundreds of officials. The gargantuan Laurie Oakes described Canberra after the sacking of Whitlam as a morgue full of dull, grey staffers trying to do the right and proper thing. He said the press gallery was full of juvenile sycophants. Looking at me with narrowed eyes, Laurie remarked, 'All the decent people have gone. But some of us stayed on to fight the good fight.'

Peacock joined us, looking resplendent in a dinner suit, tanned, confident and radiating that Oxbridge aura of glittering prizes that accompanied him in those days. He greeted me effusively and was intrigued when I told him what I was doing. He had always regarded me as nutty if not completely unhinged. He looked every inch the 'Foreign Minister from Central Casting'. He was a man to whom many more things have been given than taken away.

But the biggest thing that had been taken away, or rather had withered away from neglect, was in a hotel nearby: his estranged first wife, Susan. The fact that she was staying there with her new husband, millionaire Robert Sangster, was the cause of much ribald speculation. Although Andrew had neglected her in their fifteen years of marriage, her departure was immensely humiliating for him. Susan had run off with Sangster in Hong Kong recently and the whole delicious story had been plastered all over Australian papers with endless puns on foreign affairs. This public cuckolding had taken its toll on Andrew. His hair had gone completely grey since I had seen him last. I mentioned this and he said, 'I guess I have a few more worries than you.' That was debatable.

Fraser now looked very happy. The last time I had seen him was before the 11th of November 1975, when he was walking round the place like a zombie, wondering if his scheme to depose Whitlam would succeed. The muscles on his slab-like, pitted face would occasionally break into a pained grimace to prove how relaxed he was.

'Yes, he's a changed man now,' said Peacock. 'He's much more confident than when you saw him last. His gamble paid off – although I never thought it would. He acts as if he owns the joint now.'

Later that night I went dining with some journalists, members of Fraser's staff, Peacock's private secretary and Sir Alan Carmody, Secretary of the Department of Prime Minister and Cabinet. We walked through Soho to get to the Mykonos Restaurant. The streets were very festive, packed with tourists wearing bowler hats, Union Jacks and other Jubileeana. One of the journalists recalled for my benefit that Sir Henry Bolte had been to Buckingham Palace that day. Later he had been discovered sitting in the Cafe Royal. The journalist approached him saying, 'Ah Sir Henry, did you know that Oscar Wilde used to drink here?' And Bolte replied, 'No I didn't. What team did he play for?'

Walking with us was Jeremy, a willowy security

officer, seconded to Fraser's party. A blond nineteen-year-old with a very light gait, I was drawn to this most unconventional guard. He said he'd secured this unusual gig at the last minute, ordered by Australia House to guard the PM's party and that his usual job was as a window dresser. I told him where I was squatting and he grinned, saying, 'It's such a gay city, don't you think? I spend nearly every night at the Sombrero' (a disco at South Kensington).

We sat next to each other at the table. Opposite was Sir Alan, who had once helped found the Federal Narcotics Bureau and therefore took a great interest in 'low life'; next to Sir Alan was Caroline, a member of Fraser's staff. We started an animated discussion. They all made jokes about 'gillies', retainers in Scottish castles. In fact the humour of the Fraser party relied on protocol, correct form, title and class. Sir Alan was very jolly. I had met him before when working for Moss Cass, who had arranged a meeting with Attorney-General Lionel Murphy to discuss the decriminalisation of cannabis. In Murphy's office the attorney-general, Cass and the Minister for Health, Dr Everingham, decided possession of cannabis was legal in the ACT. I recalled Sir Alan as smiling and obsequious, the master bureaucrat who promised and delivered, qualities which helped his rise to the top of the Commonwealth Public Service. When I met him in 1973 I disliked him, thinking he was sly, treacherous and a staunch defender of the DLP. Now at the Mykonos a staffer made a derogatory reference to Murphy, at that time a judge of the High Court. Sir Alan replied, 'Don't say that about Lionel, he's a friend of mine.' But he said it with a pervy grin, indicating he didn't really mean it. As we got drunker, I found the knockabout Sir Alan much more likeable.

Our talk livened up when Jeremy and I raised the subject of homosexuality. I said it was monstrous that it was still illegal in most Australian states. Caroline agreed and so did Jeremy, rubbing his knee against mine under the table. This frisson inspired me to further eloquence which reverberated around the restaurant's stucco walls. Now well in his cups, Sir Alan said that as a small 'l' liberal he was in favour of decriminalising homosexuality, but there was the problem of the protection of minors. I pointed out that most cases of child molestation actually occurred between heterosexual men and little girls. Sir Alan then wheeled out the old argument about the future of the race, which everyone at the table pooh-poohed. He finally resorted to the scoundrel's defence: that it was unnatural. Encouraged by Jeremy's knee, I protested that Judeo-Christianity had been poisoned by both Jewish homophobia from Leviticus and the toxic misogynistic ravings of St Paul, who was undoubtedly a closet queen.

I challenged Sir Alan to recall anything that Christ had uttered about the topic, saying that if He were here in London for the Jubilee, He would probably be meeting some of His disciples up the road at the Salisbury (a local bar for theatre queens). Sir Alan laughed and said that Christ didn't drink beer, while Jeremy pointed out that Heneky's Wine Bar in South Kensington was full of gay tourists from the Middle East, most of whom preferred beer! After further drunken nonsense, Sir Alan left with Caroline for the Savoy Hotel to prepare some papers for the next day's meetings. Caroline said to me, 'Take care of Jeremy. He's a very spunky young man.' As the table laughed, Jeremy called out, 'Hey, wait on. You can't all have me!'

Jeremy and I also decided to go to the Savoy where

there was a party in one of the Fraser suites with a great number of Treasury boffins. On the way to the hotel I told Jeremy that my last train to Whitechapel went at 11.30. He told me not to worry as an extra mattress could be arranged and that I could sleep with him in the hotel's Prime Minister and Cabinet suite which he was 'guarding'.

Jeremy and I settled down in the suite to enjoy the largesse of the Australian government. It was an L-shaped late Victorian room with a grand table at the centre which might have seated a war cabinet. There was an enormous marble bathroom with two chains hanging from the ceiling, one labelled 'Valet' and the other 'Maid'. Jeremy gave the 'Maid' chain a big tug saying, 'This is definitely my chain, Bruce.' Even he called me Bruce!

I lay on my mattress, thinking about what I would tell my Trotskyite friends back at the squat the next day. Jeremy absented himself, saying he had to visit someone on the third floor. He returned an hour later, waking me to say, 'I've had a marvellous experience. I've just been fucked three times.' I forbore to ask by whom, since I knew he wouldn't tell me. After much kissing and fondling, we made it a sloppy fourth.

Jeremy had to depart in an hour to make arrangements for the PM's plane to go to Brussels. He told me that when I woke I should leave the premises as quickly as possible. Maybe we could meet some night at the Sombrero? Yes, I said. We both fell asleep.

Some time later I was woken by a key turning in the door. Looking over to Jeremy's mattress and seeing he had gone, I gazed out the window at the London dawn starting to break, as dismal and grey as Portland stone. Panicking, I thought I would find it difficult to explain why I was lying naked on a mattress under Malcolm Fraser's Cabinet table. As the door closed, I heard the sound of a person approaching me. I decided to feign sleep. The figure walked down the side of the table and affectionately kicked me saying, 'Jeremy, is that you?' It kicked again. 'Jeremy?' I turned around, looked up and beheld Sir Alan clad in a huge white bath towel looking like Colonel Blimp. He moved back in shock. 'Oh it's you, Peter,' he said. 'I thought it was Jeremy!' Now very flustered, Sir Alan said that he was hoping it was Jeremy as he had some papers for him to put in the safe.

I said, 'Sir Alan, do you mean to say you haven't

got the keys to the safe?' Defensively he replied, 'Of course I have, but not on me. Anyway, it doesn't matter. I'll get them later and I must be off now. It was nice meeting you.' He waddled rapidly towards the door. Just as flustered, I got dressed, picked up a wad of Savoy notepaper and left in a hurry without being seen. I went straight to the Westminster tube station to await the first train home.

Oddly, my London adventures in Liberal strongholds lessened the animosity I had been feeling for the now conservative Australia. In the two years I had been away, I felt such hatreds could not be maintained. A man whose government could organise such outstanding security guards couldn't be all bad. I took these thoughts back to Whitechapel where I stayed another month or so while deciding to return to Australia. When I told John Lindsay that I was returning home he didn't berate me for being a trifler, as I had expected. Instead he said, 'You're lucky. You've got a home to go to. We Jaapies can never go home.'

EARLWOOD NEEDS GAY RIGHTS:

VOTE 1 PETER BLAZEY
GAY LIBERATION GROUP CANDIDATE

There are 100,000 homosexuals in Sydney. Fashion companies and bar owners want our money, policemen want to arrest us if we walk the streets as homosexuals. After the Mardi Gras at Kings Cross on June 24-25, 60 gay men and women were arrested. Many were bashed. At the Central Police Station pol illegally closed the court to the public because they dislike homosexuals. Police think they can do poofters a lesbians over, well they can't.

The Gay Liberation Group wants:

1. The Repeal of all Anti Homosexual Legislation.

2. A real Anti-Discrimination Act which allows people to be openly homosexual without losing their jobs.

3. The dropping of the charges against the 60 gays who were arrested and an inquiry into police behaviour.

We want honest and open discussion of the gay rights issue.

We want both major parties to make specific commitments about gay rights, before the State elections in October.

We want to show politicians, if they don't take notice of us, they may lose their seats!

VOTE  BLAZEY,

Ring Ian Purton, 78 6862 or Peter Blazey, 827 3254.

Authorised by Colin Semmler, Charlie's Place, Homer Street, Earlwood.

Gay Riots

Pickin' out people, knocking them down
Resisting arrest as they're kicked on the ground
Searching their houses
Calling them queer
I don't believe that sort of stuff happens here.
Sing if you're glad to be gay.
TOM ROBINSON, 'GLAD TO BE GAY'

Stranded in London, a socialist without a razoo, for the second time in a decade I relied on my mother to rescue me. Doone secured me an air ticket with Qantas and I was invalided back to Australia. It was beginning to look as though I had a taste for it.

Miserable in Melbourne, Sydney was beckoning me with its cynical, bright money-loving aura. Other Australian cities were born in various forms of rationalism or enlightenment, but Sydney is the Hobbesian exception. It is the only Australian city which has that fatality, that materiality, that sneering cruelty so well summed up by the admonition, 'Beware the mockers of Botany Bay.' Once a subtropical gulag, punishment and death are still subconsciously engraved on the city's mind, which accounts for its hedonism, its ripe and slatternly ways. Cemeteries perch crazily on headlands above the beaches. Always a harlot, Sydney is still the scarlet woman of Port Jackson, but refined and housebroken: a reader of *Vogue Living*, she dresses up for the Mardi Gras.

IN WHICH I CONTRIBUTE TO THE DIVERSE CHRONICLES OF THE TIMES

I made the decision to move there in the summer of 1978 and gravitated to Balmain, that great bohemian cliché of the seventies. I rented a house with Annie York, who had once been a casual 'threesome' participant from my days in Canberra. Some friends assumed we had shacked up together and called her 'bent Annie', for she was well acquainted with my peculiarities. Our Balmain house quickly became a hub of drugs, androgyny and political activism.

The house was not far from the Lever factory which deposited snowdrifts of Lux soapflakes on windshields each Wednesday morning. At the end of the backyard there stood a disused and dank chookhouse, a memento of Balmain BG – before gentrification. It was also nestled in what was once a rainforest gully. Our backyard caught the sun like a butterfly net and I spent many hours there, lying recumbent in the sun on bean bags like a pasha, moisturising my face with Oil of Ulan and discussing such weighty topics as the NSW Summary Offences Act and Patti Smith's latest album, *Easter*.

Philip came over one afternoon. He too had recently returned from London and hoped to survive as an artist in Sydney. But he spent most of his time at a Martin Place macrobiotic eatery, making lumpy pie-flans for sour-faced vegetarians. He was petulant and broke and it seemed our separation would continue. For a time I was quite content to just share with Annie, in a kind of queer marriage of convenience.

During the trendy seventies our neighbours were starting to replant tree ferns, macadamias and Bangalow palms, hoping to lift their quotidian lives with Rousseauist flashes of colour. They wanted to improve upon the old Australian staples of banana and frangipani. There were dogs and kids in the street just as in Asia, but to me the cul-de-sac seemed like a theatre set. Our house was opposite Thelma's, a deserted wife who left her front door open to the street and gossiped all day. Two doors up Sutton Street lived a taxi driver and next to him a drag queen. At the time, I thought of it as a joyous island, a subtropical paradise, as vibrant and as Oz as *The Summer of the Seventeenth Doll* and many miles from the pinched proprieties of Mont Albert Road or the snarling fascisms of London's East End.

We were close to the Unity Hall Hotel and near enough to Balmain's 'local', the sandstone London Hotel. The London was jam packed with schooner-clasping, rollie-smoking workers, students, drop-outs, writers and unmarried mothers, laughing and swearing with lubricious familiarity. It was both exciting and intimidating. With their rollicking blasphemies and threadbare clothes, they looked as though they might have tumbled off the *Lady Penryn* in 1788. As the sun slanted above the Harbour Bridge, men in stubbies and thongs and women in Indian garb reeking of sandalwood unguents spilled onto the footpath overlooking Darling Street. These sunny bohemians could hardly know how soon the good times would be over. Within five years as the eighties unrolled, most would become midlife losers, disgruntled loners or dope-smoking alcoholics, prematurely pensioned off and locked into a state of penury and paranoia. The few who made it out of the ghetto became artists or performers, got themselves onto the public payroll or worked for Rupert Murdoch. I ought to know.

I began writing profiles for Sydney's gay monthly magazine *Campaign*, then owned by businessman Rod Stringer and edited by Lee Franklyn. By working on a gay magazine I had made a declaration of sexual identity in Australia. Fired by the electrical energy that coming out gives one, I scurried like a keen possum all over Sydney on my mission to cover every gay event. I was present at zaps at the University of New South Wales and interviewed visiting celebrities: the publisher of the international *Spartacus Guide*, a gay male couple in Glebe or a lesbian *ménage à trois* in Leichhardt. Yet for all the activity, there was no money in it.

I soon extended to the straight press, getting a job on the *Nation Review*. Begun in October 1970 as the *Sunday Review*, '*NR*' (nicknamed 'the ferret') was the most intelligent and sex-radical mainstream paper ever published in Australia. Along with Whitlam's government, it helped revolutionise what had once been a very sleepy, timorous, marsupial South Pacific country. As *NR*'s editor Richard Walsh recollected in

1993, 'We wanted to make a more stimulating, more complex, more sophisticated and more passionate Australia.'

Under the hilarious Prime Ministership of McMahon, *NR* had been a subversive sensation, selling up to 50,000 copies a week. Paradoxically, *NR* was to be undone not so much by Gough being sacked as much as by him getting into power in 1972. Once he was Prime Minister, the ferret got less feral and became more apologetic. It tottered on, like a haemophiliac losing blood, until the cataclysm of 1975. Yet despite his meanness which everyone hated, Walsh was actually an editor of genius.

After Walsh resigned as editor, the paper fell apart. All the glittering writers and artists of *NR*'s glory days started looking for their own boltholes. For several years the masthead was available to anyone silly enough to buy it. Finally in 1977 it was purchased by Geoffrey Gold, a wealthy, football-loving Monash-educated Maoist who turned out to be a very liberal publisher. The price was reputedly $50,000 and both sides thought they'd done well. My friend David Wilson had lined me up to become a Sydney correspondent. I contacted Gold and was put on a modest retainer. But by the late seventies with its squalor and stagflation, the oomph had gone out of idealism and the new editor Chris Forsyth's blatant sensationalism did not impress Australia's angry radicals. Though none of us believed it at the time, the paper was on its last legs. The writers were duller, the tone sadder. It was pregnant with disillusion, a manifestation of the 'what's the point?' mood which had paralysed Australia's left after Whitlam's dismissal. Malcolm Fraser had said he wanted politics off the front pages and so it happened.

My restored colonial humpy in Balmain became the Sydney office for Gold's offbeat, ratbag publication. This suited me, since they were keen to publish stories about the Sydney gay scene. Sydney suddenly became the centre of a new type of activism over sexual politics, which was now called identity politics. For years Sydney had been the magnet for homosexuals and lesbians from all over Australia. There was a flourishing commercial scene and several 'lavender' suburbs headed by Darlinghurst, Potts Point, Paddington and tending beachwards to Bondi and Tamarama, a phenomenon well described in Garry Wotherspoon's classic history of gay Sydney, *City of the Plain*. For seventy years gay men and women had been attracted by the beaches, the anonymity and the cultural density of Sydney. And yet myriads were now chafing under the schizophrenia caused by seventies sexual liberation and a wowserish state government. In those days the New South Wales police force, never noted for its finesse, was atrociously homophobic and, ironically, therein lay the seeds of our eventual liberation.

A GOLDEN SUMMER OF SUMMARY OFFENCES

Under the Summary Offences Act police could arrest not only streetwalkers but also gay males who were deemed to be 'loitering' or indulging in 'offensive behaviour'. It was a sort of catch-all law that gave police carte blanche to do as they pleased, and to the burgeoning gay movement the repeal of this act was even more pressing than repealing the anti-sodomy provisions of the NSW Crimes Act.

At the time, the gay movement was spearheaded by Camp Inc., NSW, which comprised everything from cautious 'reformers' to activist student bodies and the Marxist new left including the Trotskyite Gay Solidarity Group (GSG). Though the innately fissiparous Trots have always been easy to deride. Having come from London I was impressed by their dedication to sexual politics and to direct action, both on the street and in their similarly named inflammatory newspaper.

In September 1973 a Gay Pride Week attracted only three hundred people, but by 1978 things had become larger and more purposeful. In Sydney, student activists Ken Davis and Anne Talve received a letter from the San Francisco Gay Freedom Committee calling on radicals around the world to commemorate the ninth anniversary of the Stonewall riots.

In the Trotskyist manner, there was a flurry of activity and many meetings. As coordinator of the GSG, I put together a press release with Max Pearce, the group's president, advising a 'first ever' day of international gay solidarity on 24 June. We promised a morning rally to lift the spirits, an afternoon forum to incite the march, to be capped off with a satisfying march in the evening. Somewhat hyperbolically, we said similar marches had attracted

375,000 in San Francisco and 100,000 in Barcelona. This exaggeration was atoned for in the second part of the press release (which hindsight now suggests was an understatement): *10.00 p.m. A Mardi Gras at Taylor Square to march down Oxford Street. This will involve a band, singers and people in fancy dress 'the more outrageous the better'*. The press release featured slogans such as 'How about a Close Encounter with your Own Kind?' and 'Better Blatant than Latent'. We were locked in now for what was to be a large gay celebration and police confrontation which turned into a historic homosexual riot.

At a meeting chaired by Margaret McMann at the Stanley Palmer Hall in Darlinghurst, we canvassed the issue of gaining a licence for a public demonstration, which the round trip march required. This was crucial since the police had only given us permission for a one-way march to Hyde Park. But this was a start, because a failure by the police even to respond to your request, in law, was deemed a refusal. The point was frequently made that the Summary Offences Act had been last amended by Premier Askin in 1970 to improve public order. In other words, to undermine the Vietnam moratorium demonstrations. Before that it was possible to march without police consent. The Kings Cross riots eventually achieved the restoration of this right.

I went to Les Hollings, Editor-in-Chief of the *Australian*, and persuaded him to run a four-page liftout called 'Homosexuality in Australia' in the *Weekend Australian*. In the middle of the bisexual seventies I thought this was a very marketable subject for an adventurous editor. A tall, gangling man with bushy eyebrows and a grey cardigan, Hollings hardly presented as the editor of a national daily. He spoke in the slow sepulchral voice of a north country undertaker and quite indiscriminately called everyone 'Ma-ate' in a diphthong.

One of the reasons for the success of Hollings' editorship was his daily communings with 'God' who lived in Manhattan and had recently bought the *New York Post*. This vantage point gave Lord Rupert an unrivalled inside look at the then burgeoning gay culture of New York, the fashions, the decor, the huge discos, the moneyed lifestyles, Studio 54 and all that. Always quick to pick a trend, Murdoch decided that catering to the gay market could well give one an edge over a competitor. Out of New York a slightly Americanised voice said, 'This gay thing is very big here, Les. It's exciting. We're finding terrific marketing possibilities on the *Post*.' As a result, his Australian apostles had jumped to attention at what could be regarded as the ultimate Murdoch aphrodisiac: something new and sexy from which money could be made.

Having brought it into the world some twelve years before, the *Australian* was the apple of Rupert's eye. Within News Limited, it was proudly called 'the flagship of the fleet', but it was actually the figleaf, a canopy over a seedy batch of tabloids headed by the Sydney *Daily Mirror*. From 1978 the circulation of the *Weekend Australian* increased dramatically. Agent of this success was Tim 'Crazy Horse' Hewat, a Geelong Grammar-educated journalist-larrikin in the tradition of Max Newton and Murdoch himself. But in those days, the *Weekend Australian* had strong competition, principally from the Fairfax press whose wowserism made it impossible to allow the word 'homosexual' in print.

Always trying to get up the sniffy Fairfax nose, both Hollings and Hewat were easily persuaded. They were interested – up to a point – in my suggested gay story, as long as I gave them *names*, especially politicians, actors, sportspeople. A tentative list was compiled which included Russell Fairfax (certainly a camp rumour), a champion Olympic swimmer and novelist Patrick White as well as several actors who, because they merchandise fantasy, are more unlikely to come out than any other profession. As Hewat graciously explained to me, 'We want people of substance to come out, not shabby people like Peter Blazey.'

I was given all the editorial help I required: photographers, journalists, researchers, secretaries, expenses. I spent a few weeks making a nuisance of myself but collecting no names. When the articles did appear, they were more radical than Hollings had anticipated. The supplement came out on 24–25 June 1978, to coincide with the forum and march already organised. Murdoch would be horrified, but I believe the fact that the *Australian*'s banners that morning read 'Homosexuals in Our Society' attracted many more thousands to the activities, guaranteeing it became a national event, not least of all for the media.

Though I say it myself, the supplement was punchy

and provocative. In his otherwise worthwhile book *A History of the Sydney Gay and Lesbian Mardi Gras*, Graham Carbery fails to reveal that the articles were integral to the size of the march and its subsequent success. Nor does he point out that the *Australian* reported first and solely on the gay riots.

The front page of the *Australian*, headed 'Mardi Gras is an Act of Defiance', invited everyone interested to join the march, and the butterfly 'logo' of the Gay Solidarity Group appeared to give the paper's approval to the march. The back page was headed 'A Potential for Revolution' and featured a long piece by novelist Jill Neville who had covered a lesbian conference and spent a night with a lesbian, although finding the experience not to her taste. There was a small box, 'The Case Against', inserted for 'balance', and a large article arguing 'The Case for Coming Out'. In this polemical piece I argued that 'a majority of homosexuals are forced to live lives of deception, deceit and fear. The exception are those fortunate few who are wealthy or artistically gifted and not subject to the usual occupational, social or marital pressures.' Perhaps I was writing about myself.

Some of the points raised in this article were

incorporated in a letter requesting an interview which I sent to Patrick White at this time. Eventually I received a reply:

Dear Peter Blazey,

Sorry not to have replied sooner, but your letter disappeared into a mountain of others.

I thought everybody knew by now that I don't give interviews. It's not a rule I made for any perverse reason, only because they consume time and energy which should be going into what I'm writing. Certainly my private life is the last thing I'd want to be interviewed about, it would no longer be private. I'd expect this to be the reaction of any normal homosexual male or female, even any hetero who valued a relationship. But of course there are plenty of exhibitionists ready to flaunt themselves to the press.

I read your article in yesterday's Australian *and was not altogether convinced by it. I've known so many homosexuals who've led homosexual lives and been accepted. They were not necessarily 'rich or artistically gifted' but they didn't scream their heads off and wave their handbags in people's faces; they behaved in a civilised way and were respected for it.*

Sorry not to oblige you. I can only be as I am.

Yours sincerely,

Patrick White

White revealed in his published *Letters* that he was prompted to start his important 1991 autobiography *Flaws in The Glass* before anyone else should write about him and Manoly. I always like to think the events of this time got him going.

The first Mardi Gras was in essence a full day of gay solidarity and included a morning rally ironically under police protection from Paddington to Martin Plaza, a forum at Paddington Town Hall in the afternoon and another march down Oxford Street to Hyde Park that evening. A group of three hundred people on the morning rally finished up around Martin Plaza singing 'Every woman can be a lesbian'; 'Sing if you're glad to be gay'; 'Lesbians are luverly', the rather fingerwagging 'Learn to love your homosexuality' and 'Bi-bi-sexual', sung to the tune of 'Bye Bye Blackbird'. This rally garnered favourable TV coverage. The afternoon forum was also a sedate and well-received affair. It featured Dennis Altman talking on gay riots in Europe, Ken

Davis giving a history of the modern gay movement, Lance Gowland on Chile, Brian McGahan on Cuba, Margaret McMann on lesbianism in Australia and me on the *Gay News* blasphemy trial in London. At the forum one of the speakers disclosed to an unbelieving audience that homosexuality had recently been legalised between consenting white adults over twenty-one in South Africa, of all places.

During the forum there occurred a symbolic moment reminding us yet again of the male-versus-female separatism which bedevilled gay politics in the seventies and which must seem anomalous in these days of coalitionist politics. A leatherman stood up saying that a group of his friends had had 'shit' put on them when they assembled in the morning under a banner which read 'S&M, the sport for men'. A woman organiser had told them that this slogan was sexist and that it couldn't be used because it created a negative image for the TV cameras. They dropped the banner, but complained at the forum that this was discrimination of 'exactly the same sort that was meted out to lesbians' in the early women's movement marches in the United States. To defuse things, Altman warned there was an obligation to carry banners that didn't offend others on the march. Thus men might object to a women's banner that read 'Castrate all men'.

When time came for the evening rally, some five hundred people, fired up with gay pride and solidarity, gathered at Taylor Square. I had arranged to meet Philip there for at this stage we both warily sought to rekindle our relationship. We walked down Oxford Street together. I saw many familiar faces, some earnest, some insouciant, many joyous, suddenly realising the enormity of what they were doing. There was Dennis Altman, Sasha Soldatow, Terry Batterham, Garry Wotherspoon, Gary Dunne, artists Peter Tully and David McDiarmid, Craig Johnson, Brian McGahan, Max Pearce and hundreds of others. There was Margaret McMann, Betty Houndslow, Kimberly O'Sullivan and Sue Wills, as well as lesbian lovers holding hands for the first time in public, excitedly calling, 'Out of the bars and onto the street!'

Almost as if responding to that command gays and lesbians tumbled down from furtively hidden upstairs bars that had previously marked the Darlinghurst 'scene'. From Ruby Reds in Crown Street or the gay bars in Oxford Street – Capriccio's, Flo's Palace and Patch's – gay men and women, drag queens and other sex radicals joined the throng. Down Oxford Street emotions ran high: after years of shame, it was a huge relief, as if the great stone we lived under had been lifted from our lives. Many marchers decided that day they would never dissemble about being gay or lesbian again.

But trouble began before the rally reached Hyde Park. It had been assumed people would gather in the park and sing songs, but the police had been hurrying us throughout the route. They told the driver of the truck leading the march (the Mardi Gras' first ever float!), 'If you don't drive faster, we'll break up your procession.' His subsequent disobedience was a response to police contempt. Cops were used to harassing or gaoling poofters and dykes, not escorting them.

The truck was the focus since it had all the PA systems on it. Now we were parked at Hyde Park as people crowded round the vehicle. When Lance Gowland started to read telegrams of solidarity from other gay groups around the world, the police suddenly cut off the PA system, ordering the truck to move north down College Street, dragging a shouting Gowland off. They were provoking a riot.

The crowd became angry and confused. I approached a cop trying to drive the truck away and said if they continued doing this things would get out of hand completely. He was scared, pale and sweating. He said, 'We don't want a riot. Jump on and tell people.' I did, but the mike had been disconnected and the shout now went up: 'Fuck the police. Let's go to the Cross.' Not being a hero, I jumped off the truck and asked the officer why he didn't leave it in College Street instead of taking it across the road into Stanley Street. He said, 'If we did that it would be double-parked.'

We started walking up William Street towards the Cross. We were illegal and for once thriving on it, singing songs and shouting slogans. The cops radioed for reinforcements. Some vehicles tooted support, other hoons in cars tried to run over us shouting 'Fucking poofters!' Bedraggled but elated, the throng began moving on towards the El Alamein fountain, the designated meeting place. At this stage everyone was in a good mood. I remember another first, proudly holding Philip's hand in public.

As we turned past Tina's Bar at the top of William Street we noticed two police trucks ominously parked at the entrance to Darlinghurst Road. A make-do barricade. Still we kept on chanting: 'Stop Police Attacks on gays, women and blacks,' and breathed a sigh of relief to be in the Cross, the one zone in Sydney friendly to sex radicals. Walking down Darlinghurst Road, we found many Cross denizens were screaming encouragement: hookers, bouncers, punters, fun seekers, street people, riff raff and drunks were cheering us on, shouting out of windows and from the footpaths, 'Good on ya!', 'Fuck the cops', and 'We love camps!' It was a marvellous moment, a bit like walking up Oxford Street during a Mardi Gras.

Then several paddy wagons from the 21 Division appeared and drove right up to us. Out of the vans poured police in what resembled South African paramilitary-style khakis and face visors, tearing off their insignia and laying into the crowd, punching and hitting indiscriminately. They were crazed – they had wanted to get stuck into us all day. People were panicking and getting abusive. The arrests began. Garbage, shoes, bottles were thrown. Men and women were flung into paddy wagons like sacks of spuds. There was no possibility of crowd control since nobody had a megaphone.

By 12.30 am, fifty-three people had been arrested and the paddy wagons were driving back to Darlinghurst Police Station. There were twenty-seven women and twenty-six men thrown into one large cell with two blankets between them. A communist, Peter Murphy, was released 'with a large swelling on his leg that was like a plastic bag full of water', as a hospital orderly later reported. He had been bashed in the police station and had to be virtually carried to hospital.

Many people recall that horrendous night, whether they were arrested or bashed or ran away. Some remember it from hiding places where they watched with disbelief. Several hundred began an all-night vigil at Darlinghurst Police Station. The keening went on until morning. On the hour, the plaintive cry could be heard: 'All we are saying is leave gays alone.'

Weeks of frenetic activity followed: meetings, money-raising, petitions to then Premier of NSW Neville Wran, enlisting the help of sympathetic lawyers, and more vigils outside the Darlinghurst Police Station. The gay community and its friends went into overdrive: for the first time, it was a community. Rage at the injustice mobilised people all over Australia. Our own Stonewall had happened.

It was ironic that Rupert Murdoch, who had a hand in this significant event, subsequently ordered the gay coverage in the *Australian* to be toned down. But it was too late: the genie was out of the bottle. The pompous *Sydney Morning Herald* refused to acknowledge what had happened at all. On Monday morning there was no mention of the riots. In one hundred and fifty years, the paper had never used the word 'gay'. Now, suddenly, on the morning of Tuesday 27 June 1978, after the hearings of the fifty-three arrested at the Central Court of Petty Sessions, the *Herald* reported charges arose from 'the homosexual rights protest march in Darlinghurst' the previous Saturday night. But that was not all. The names and occupations of fifty of the arrested, who were now freed, were deliberately printed. This inconsiderate mass outing caused a great deal of pain.

*

The eloquent, Merlin-like Premier was also the Police Minister. Wran's new Labor government, the only one in office on mainland Australia, was a very cautious Labor government indeed. After the Promethean excesses of Whitlam, Wran was hostile to new left ideology, yet, in his successful 1976 election campaign he had promised homosexual law reform. Perhaps he initially stalled because for two years he had only a one-seat majority, yet after his landslide victory in 1978 he *still* did nothing.

After the 1978 riots, however, the Summary Offences Act was repealed within a year, making it possible to march without police permission. This was the start of the procession we now know as the Sydney Gay and Lesbian Mardi Gras.

Throughout these struggles Wran played a contemptibly hypocritical game. He posed as a civil libertarian yet his administration kept on enacting viciously anti-gay activities, like having the Vice Squad raid and close down the popular gay men's club Club 80. Wran's stance infuriated many activists. Lex Watson and other queens responded by parking a caravan called 'The Gay Rights Embassy' outside his house in Woollahra in 1983. It was just a mobile reminder of the promise he had made in 1976. The queens irritated neighbours like radio pundit John Laws by dressing in drag or leather and running around as fairies with wands. They danced, had pyjama parties, cake-baking competitions and got lots of publicity.

Decriminalisation only occurred in 1984 when the four articles covering sodomy in the NSW Crimes Act were deleted, eight years after being promised. It was finally done by Wran through the introduction of a private member's bill, and presented as a fait accompli to Cabinet and caucus: the whole thing was over in a week. There was no backlash; a courageous premier would have done it years earlier.

IN WHICH I FEEL IMPELLED TO NOMINATE FOR PARLIAMENT

Exploiting the newfound energy caused by the riots, an important Fourth National Homosexual Conference was held in August 1978 at the Paddington Town Hall. Opened by Senator Susan Ryan, the theme was 'Homosexuals at Work'. State Attorney-General Frank Walker made vague and mollifying sounds about gay rights but some of the audience hissed him. The conference was significant for me because I had decided to stand as the GSG candidate in the coming Earlwood by-election, which was caused by the resignation of Liberal politician Sir Eric Willis.

In those days it was easy to stand for a by-election. One simply left a deposit of one hundred dollars cash with the returning officer, plus a nomination form signed by six local voters, and one was declared a candidate. When the list was published I found to my delight that the Labor candidate, Ken Gabb, was an unmarried man living with his mother and the Liberal candidate was Alan Jones, the right-wing media commentator who subsequently became the subject of an incident outside a London bog. Labor was thought highly likely to get the 4.6 per cent swing needed to win.

Philip became my campaign manager. Like Don Quixote and Sancho Panza, Philip and I trudged around the mean and unromantic streets of Earlwood, letterboxing, putting up posters and talking to people in supermarkets. We used the catchy slogan, 'Put a Poofter into Parliament', and I gathered together about twelve local queens who were keen to help.

Other members of the left such as former Whitlam staffer Richard Hall greatly assisted. The problem was to run a credible campaign in an ageing, conservative electorate with an increasing influx of Greek and Italian migrants. I saw it as a good way to get TV and radio coverage for gay rights in New South Wales, which it was.

In my luckiest TV appearance, Mike Willesee's crew followed me while I was soliciting votes in the main street. There were diverse opinions expressed, but one little old lady dazzled the audience when she said she would vote for a gay candidate and that she approved of homosexuals. 'We've got two of them living in our apartment block. They're much nicer than men,' she said. Strangely, I was unable to persuade the two major candidates to debate gay rights. They avoided me like poison.

Not all homosexuals approved of my campaign. Some did not want the issue discussed. Others said, 'Oh, isn't she common!' Philip and I stood outside Sir Eric Willis's place with a photographer accompanying us. We said we were seeking the previous candidate's blessing for our campaign and gaily waved to Sir Eric and Lady Willis who were watching us from the picture window. At first they smiled but when Philip and I engaged in a long kiss, the venetian blinds crashed down with a savage snap.

The Earlwood episode hardly helped my career. George Negus had finally got me a job on Channel Nine's new show '60 Minutes' in which he was one of the four stars. The job was worth fifty thousand dollars a year. On the morning of the publication of the names of the candidates, the show's producer, Gerald Stone, rang me and said the job was not available as I was 'no longer an independent observer but a political participant'. I could imagine his tanned face and pearly teeth on the other end of the phone. 'What if I'd stood for the Liberal Party, Gerald?' I asked. He said it didn't matter, any candidate of any political party rendered me invalid as an independent journalist. I knew deep down he was correct and that was that.

But the most spectacular reaction came when I rang Doone to tell her. I said, 'Mum, I've decided to run for Parliament.'

'Oh good, Pete,' she said. 'Which party?'

'The Gay Solidarity Group,' I replied.

There was a long pause. Finally she said, 'You're

trying to destroy the family. This will kill your father. He's an old man and you mustn't tell him.' I replied that he was only sixty-nine and he had known for years. She said that he may have known subconsciously, but that he must not be told. 'He will suicide if he finds out – though he's not really the suicidal type,' she added. 'Your father has always hated homosexuals.'

'Does that mean he hates me?' I asked.

'He doesn't hate you, because you haven't told him. But he will. I am doing my utmost to see that he doesn't hear about it. If he does find out he will probably die. I'll do anything, absolutely anything, if you withdraw your nomination now. Please do it for the sake of the family,' she pleaded. I said I couldn't withdraw now, as my name was printed on the ballot paper and I had an obligation to finish the campaign.

With tremulous hands I rang Alan at Hortico. I said, 'Dad, there's something about me you ought to know.'

'Yes, son?' He sounded pleased to hear from me.

'I'm homosexual.'

'That's all right,' he replied. 'I've suspected it for years.'

‘But Mother said the knowledge would kill you.’

‘Well, I’m still alive. You mustn’t worry, son. You’re old enough to know what you want to do.’

We had a long and friendly talk, the first in ages. He said he would try to placate Doone, that she had been getting upset very easily of late. After thirty-eight years the great taboo had finally been broached with him and the sky hadn’t fallen in. I felt relieved and hoped it pointed to a less distant relationship in the future.

Labor won Earlwood and I got 108 votes, a fairly respectable showing, though I lost my deposit. I still believe that every act of gay visibility is good in itself and that my running in Earlwood helped promote the issue in the public arena. Gay liberation is about personal resistance and public affirmation. It is one of the only ways we can beat the many forces which still want to keep us isolated, fearful and silent.

INTERNATIONA
MR. LEATHER
CONTEST

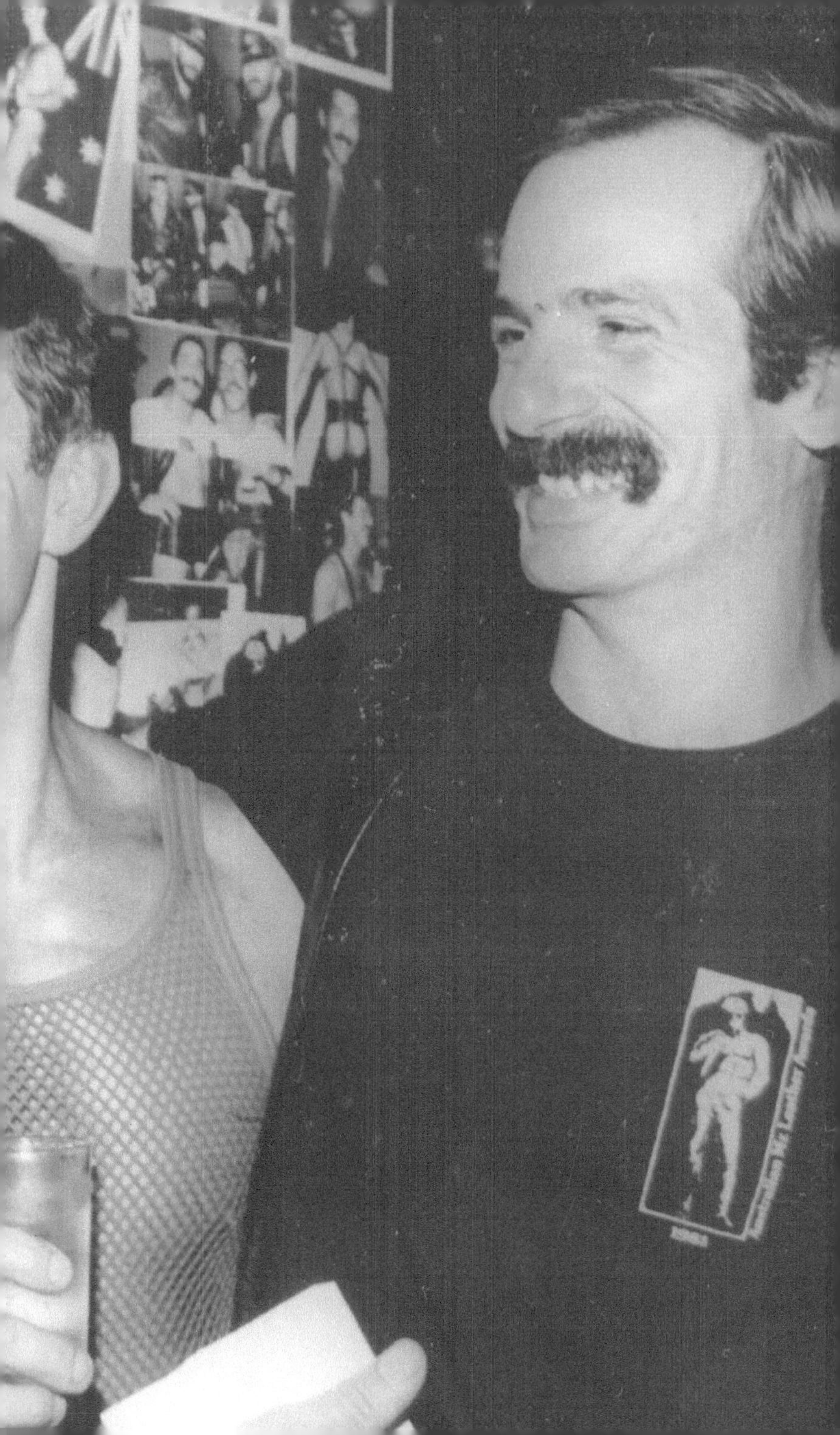

Manhattan Transfer and Beyond

The clone speaks in monosyllables. He dances alone in the discotheque, pinching his own nipples. The clone is self-sufficient. The clone is hot sex. He never stays over for the night.

DAVID B. FEINBERG, *EIGHTY-SIXED*

Every New Yorker harbours the smug delusion that a good job and a good apartment on Manhattan is the summation of what life can offer. It is the widely held opinion of those who live or work on this rocky island twenty miles by five, that they are at the exact centre of the known universe. This was probably true in the late seventies when 'Gotham City' was the capital of the world in so many areas, before it slid into a nightmare of violence, homelessness and AIDS in the eighties (the first cases of which were reported in the *New York Times* in 1981).

After London in 1964 it was the second time I had hit an imperial city at its decadent apogee, on the turn as it were. Maybe this was why I was standing with a friend outside a nightclub on 54th Street screaming, 'Steve! Steve! Let me in!'

Yes, journalist Susie Anthony and I were among

the scores of people clamouring to get into Studio 54, the hottest disco in the world. Steve Rubell, one of the club's owners, stared at us with amusement, his capped teeth glistening, an insane glint in his eyes. Occasionally, if he liked the look of someone, he would point to them, and they were IN. This only increased the frenzy of those who had been left out. The more desperate people were, the more they were treated with contempt. One woman arrived with great éclat in a hired limousine. The crowd, thinking she was a star, fell back like the Red Sea as she made her way to the velvet cordons that protected Steve and his good-looking minions from the throng. She told Steve she had come all the way from LA and gave her name. Steve had never heard of her. She wasn't a star at all! With a disdainful nod Steve looked elsewhere and, humbled, she stumbled back to her limo.

The first time Susie and I went there we had a letter of introduction from a News Limited source. Steve scanned it and rejected us. Next time, we were better organised. Through one of his bouncers, an Australian called Howie, we got onto his 'comp list'. We told him our names, Steve scanned his check sheet and beckoned us in with a scowl.

Rubell might have been gay or bi but he didn't keep very wholesome company. His attorney and business partner was the seedy, powerful closet queen Roy Cohn, Senator Joe McCarthy's one-time assistant and hatchet man. Cohn was the attorney who sent the Rosenbergs to the electric chair. He was also a notorious persecutor of gays, who finally died of AIDS.

In the late seventies disco-mania had taken off and, among other things, it was a code for gay liberation. It had its own divas such as Donna Summer, Gloria Gaynor and Grace Jones. The style of dance was totally unlike straight dancing, less inhibited, more 'lewdly' sensual, more drug inspired. The crowd inside Studio 54 was about seventy per cent gay and thirty per cent straight. The media hyped the celebrities who went there: Woody Allen, Margaret Trudeau, Mick Jagger and Andy Warhol; but when I finally got in I discovered these people disported themselves in a little VIP rockery below and away from the hoi polloi.

Steve wore an incandescent grin. Perhaps the clue to its origin lay in the fact that Studio 54 collapsed after he was discovered in possession of five ounces of unusually pure cocaine. Even though we had cracked it, we still had to pay $12 a head to enter, the drinks were exorbitant but we felt almost heroic to have finally made it to this fabled pleasure dome, basically a converted cinema done out in black glass. The disco stage was scintillating. Revolving coloured lights on six booms were raised and lowered from the flies above the stage. Down below on the dance floor were gyrating queens, some wearing jockstraps, some on roller skates, with brassy egos and eyes in constant cruising mode.

Upstairs in a bar I was accosted by a foppish young man tapping cocaine from a silver spoon onto the back of his hand. He suggested we move to a cubicle in the 'smoking room', but all four were filled with people already doing what we had in mind. Eventually we went to the 'dress circle' section of the disco where a series of six-foot-long 'cuddle seats' were being used as beds by about twenty undulating couples. My effete friend and I lay down in one and had coke and sex in that order. I must admit we didn't see Liza Minnelli on a swing snorting coke nor Truman Capote downing daiquiris. In fact, when Susie and I later danced we agreed the place reminded us a bit of the Bondi Lifesaver. I won't say we were disappointed but the place didn't live up to expectations – but then with all that hype how could it have?

I was in New York because I had been offered a job on the left-leaning *National Times*, then the most exciting paper in Australia. To celebrate, I took six weeks off to go to Manhattan. I was thirty-nine and wanted to see it before turning forty. I went alone, dressed in what I thought was the height of fashion – a white ice-cream suit *à la* John Travolta in *Saturday Night Fever*, with western boots. Unfortunately this ensemble marked me out as a crass provincial and sadly I felt rather more like Jon Voigt in *Midnight Cowboy*. By good fortune I stayed at the Chelsea Hotel on West 23rd Street, the seediest, most bohemian hotel in Manhattan, home at various times to many celebrities: Andy Warhol's Chelsea Girls, Joni Mitchell, the Sex Pistols' Sid Vicious (who met his end there), and our very own Sidney Nolan and Brett Whiteley.

I arrived in the dog days of a July heatwave. My first few weeks walking around New York were rapturous, driven on the manic energy and danger lust of the street. Uptown I cruised Central Park where potential tricks beckoned from the thickets or beside gothic follies built by nineteenth-century philanthropists. Afterwards I checked out the scene downtown, especially the derelict piers along the Hudson River where casual sexcapades were even more flaunting.

The huge homosexual population, living mostly around Greenwich Village, used to go to the tubs or the piers all day and dance like automatons until dawn. Many Australian gay artists like Peter Tully, David McDiarmid and drag performer Miss 3D had already taken part in this exile, declaring New York a paradise which they would never leave. During this period one famous transsexual, Jan Morris, wrote: 'Manhattan is the only city I know permanently on the brink of a nervous breakdown.' Miss Morris also saw Manhattan as manifesting 'the utter self-absorption of the schizophrenic'.

Maybe an oversupply of drugs had something to

do with it. Central Park reeked of the marijuana the locals smoked every lunchtime. I remember going to a free James Taylor concert which attracted a quarter of a million people; again with more grass in the air than oxygen. Down in Times Square, every third hustler asked whether one wanted pot, coke or mescaline. In the Village it was a touch more sophisticated with tastes running to MDA (Methalyne Dioxyamphetamine) whose salesmen promoted as a smooth, non-speedy hallucinogen essential for the disco. There was also PCP or Angel Dust, originally an animal tranquilliser which in humans combines acid's tripping properties together with delusions of power. It is unpredictable and volatile and widely suspect amongst drug aficionados. My first experience of it was a major mistake when offered some by a couple of would-be hustlers.

I had taken them back to a ritzy apartment on East 39th Street. It was owned by a prissy New York queen and had been loaned to me for a week by his tenant, Ms Pera Wells, an Australian diplomat then having a close friendship with the *National Times*' Paul Kelly. Her great favour in giving me a respite from the Chelsea was done not knowing that I would betray her.

The apartment had gilded mirrors, crimson flock wallpaper, a Steinway piano, and it was packed with rare artefacts and bibelots. It was no place to bring two hick Southern fag bashers. These young men told me that their Angel Dust would blow my head off. As soon as we arrived we snorted it, which I found as acrid as Ajax. We proceeded to drop our pants and commence a mutual jerkoff. This went on for several minutes until I moved closer to the blond one, gently rubbing him. Seeing this, his friend freaked out.

'You can't do that,' he said.

'Why not?' I asked. 'That's what I brought you back for.'

'You're nothing but a fucking faggot!' he screamed.

'Well, how come I picked you two up on Christopher Street?' I replied.

He became violent. Determined to imprint his rage on the apartment, he rushed to the fridge grabbing a dozen eggs and started pitching them at the walls and the piano. I tried to stop him and he fell against the kidney table which disintegrated. It was now only him and me; his friend was totally immobilised by the Angel Dust. With a sweep of his hand, he wiped a collection of thirty miniature liquor bottles all over the floor. We wrestled in the bathroom where he smashed an ormolu table. No doubt the Herculean energy rush from being high on PCP enabled me to drag both of these creeps out the door.

The apartment was a shocker. For the next week I brushed egg off the wallpaper and hired 'Maids Unlimited' to minimise the damage. Pera came and helped, for she hadn't told the owner she was sub-letting and was sure to lose her thousand-dollar security deposit. I thought we had done a reasonable job but when the owner returned he went ballistic, presenting me with an inventory of twenty-one damaged items, shrieking that his lawyer was onto me and that he would stop me leaving the country. I finally extricated myself by paying 1500 dollars and returned gratefully to the chaotic Chelsea Hotel.

IN WHICH I MEET MY DESTINY

At a disco, I met a black man from South Carolina called Li, who was so enchanted by my Travolta suit he took me home to his apartment in the village and fucked me several times in one night without a condom. I believe I caught the virus from Li, but he was such a good lover, so passionate, so playful and so large, that I have never regretted spending the night with him, even though it has changed my world.

Within a week I caught a short, severe flu which meant I was sero-converting though, obviously, I didn't know it at the time. We shared the virus and the memory of our desire.

I often think about him. Of course, I cannot be sure it was Li, but having been more of a voyeur in New York than a promiscuous participant, Li remains the most likely candidate. He might well be dead by now.

My best disco experiences occurred on another of my trips to Manhattan at Paradise Garage, a genuinely funky gay disco untainted by heavy drugs, criminals or *faux* hetero sexuality. Part of this funkiness and 'sincerity' was the fact that its customers were either black or gay Puerto Ricans escaping the horrors of Spanish Catholicism back home. Of course there were other places like the Ice Palace in Midtown, trendy Village venues like the Mudd Club and, best known of all, the Saint, a disco central to Manhattan's gay culture which survived through the eighties. Oddly, the real gay discos (like the Saint) were dry, specialising largely in fruit juices. Whatever patrons took was generally ingested before arrival.

Never a good dancer and totally out of it on chemical enhancements, my memory of Paradise Garage is hazy, though I do recall waiting for hours on an ascending ramp leading to the vast upstairs space and being frisked for weapons at the top. By four in the morning Philip and I (now at the fag end of another separation) were thrilled when Grace Jones mounted the stage and sang some of the numbers from her *Nightclubbing* album. Clad in black with a 'pillbox' haircut, she used an effeminate gay man as a prop. The crowd started roaring when she sang her funky streetwalker's song 'Walking in the Rain', but it was when she purred the lines from the following number that she really sent the fans into orbit: 'Pull up to my bumper baby with your long black limousine . . .' She then slid up to her submissive prop and pretended to be seriously fucking him while he began to buck fore and aft. Every dinge queen in that barn was in ecstasy. It was a sensational spectacle.

Soon after, I moved out of the Chelsea Hotel

and in with Philip, our separation at an end. He had been in New York longer than me, nearly a year in fact, supposedly furthering his art career but largely subsisting on cleaning apartments. Since Manhattan had 400,000 'artists', mostly *soi disant*, it was a fairly tough life. Philip originally lived on Prince Street with a gaggle of Australians in a vast loft, but when they dissipated he rented a flat near Alphabet City, close to the Bowery. In this Cuban-Chinese quarter, dealers badgered you every night as you went home.

We spent two bitter-sweet weeks together, in which I admitted the two people I preferred to him had both rejected me, while he revealed he had been unable to find anyone else. It looked like we were stuck with each other. We decided to recommence our life together in Sydney. We had become habituated, and Philip had certain qualities I admired: his devotion, his lateral mind, and his culinary brilliance.

THE GOLDEN YEARS

Several months later we returned to Sydney, moving into a large grey concrete art deco bunker in Elizabeth Bay Road that was also known as Gotham City. From

1978 and on through the early years of the following decade gay life in Sin City was at its most exuberant. Our building was brimming with arty queens, and even Peter Tully (also back from New York) was living in a flat above us. We hosted some debauched parties in our flat including one that featured a blue Mandrax punch. Everyone finished up on all fours, if not lower.

Gay Sydney had entered a kind of golden era at this time where the unlocking of energies through gay liberation had flourished and infused the life of the sub-culture. There was a series of original art shows including the subversive 'Poofters and Faggots, Dykes and Whores' held at Paddington Town Hall. Once again Peter Tully and David McDiarmid exhibited along with other artists such as Philip, Bill Morley (better known as a DJ), David Martin and Miss 3D, who showed her plaster of Paris cupcakes. At this event McDiarmid had a huge perspex drape featuring graphic images of male genitalia. An irate dyke rushed up to the art object with a carving knife and emasculated it. This was a period of separatism when many lesbians were hostile to pornography; indeed, at one demonstration outside the Parliament they found themselves demanding censorship along with Fred Nile and his fellows from the Festival of Light.

Despite evangelical resistance and police harassment, gay male venues kept on expanding. The Purple Onion turned into the KKK Sauna with sumptuous drag shows by the swimming pool, while Oxford Street became the epicentre of male action, with pubs like the Unicorn and the Albury cultivating the new ghetto mentality. There remained the grand drag venues such as Capriccio's, Tropicana and my personal favourite, Patch's (now DCM). More than a decade before *The Adventures of Priscilla, Queen of the Desert*, this part of the 'Golden Mile' was bedevilled with busloads of suburbanites gawking at the drag queens.

Upstairs at Patch's one could watch the tall, terrifying Trixie Lamont who had a tongue like a broken bottle. She modelled herself on Shirley Bassey and was completely fixated on TV gossip, especially rumours about Mike Walsh of Channel Nine's 'Midday Show' and an attractive blond singer he was grooming. It was reported that Trixie would smash beer glasses in the dressing room to keep her performers in line.

Some of the stars of Patch's included Miss 3D, Teresa Green, and Cindy Pastel whose rendition of 'Stand By Your Man' always got heaps of stamping applause. An occasional visitor was drag diva Sonia McMahon, who was as big as a jumbo jet with a dress like a huge wind sock. She used to bring the house down doing 'LA International Airport'. Perhaps Sonia was the first self-consciously tragic drag artist.

Drugs and alcohol were fundamental to the lifestyle. In the Midnight Shift dancers would 'HiNRG', jive non-stop for several hours, inhaling amyl and butylnitrite from a tiny bottle which protocol insisted be shared by a ring of friends. Many of these inhalers are now dead. It is reasonably believed that the rare skin cancer, Kaposi's sarcoma, when combined with HIV, blossomed as a result of such ingestion. Even in the late nineties it remains taboo to criticise this drug and it is still advertised in the gay press. The party must go on.

Later I teamed up with photographer William Yang and we started a gossip column for *Campaign* magazine called 'Out and Out'. For more than a year we party-hopped the social circuits, both gay and straight, with William snapping the shots for my satirical text. We went to the Mardi Gras, Sleaze Ball, warehouse parties, art openings and book launches. William's photographs recorded a cachinnation of Eastern Suburbs glitterati as well as capturing a unique gay saturnalia. We attended the Barracks, Flo's Palace and the Signal Bar before moving on to the fortieth birthday party of Hedley, a costume designer with the Australian Opera who arrived clad in a bizarre assemblage of giant phalluses and testicles the size of lawn bowls. Connected by chains, Hedley could barely stand as he thrust his phallic Medusa into his birthday cake while his friends sang 'For She's a Jolly Good Fellow'.

'Out and Out' was a widely read and popular column. But in October of 1981 the new editor of *Campaign*, Barry Lowe (whom we had never mentioned in our column), decided he wanted space for his social column and the pornographic short stories he wrote. So he reduced our salaries. We resigned instantly. It was getting tiring going out four nights a week and I was beginning to develop a drinking problem.

But the chronicler of those years was William,

who captured the best of it in his book *Sydney Diary*, which caused a sensation when it was published, and most recently in his 1997 record, *Friends of Dorothy*, which documents this time and the era beyond.

The Only Game in Town

Journalists follow authority like sharks follow a liner.
MALCOLM MUGGERIDGE

It is a truth often told that attaining what one most desires immediately renders it invalid: so it happened with me and the *National Times*. Paul Kelly, then deputy editor, liked my work on the *Nation Review* and promised me a gig on the *National Times* saying, 'We'll make a star of you.'

The *National Times* was the trendy paper par excellence, a sort of *Nation Review* specialising in Chardonnay and Bollinger socialism. Radical articles were interspersed between Volvo and Dom Perignon ads. Its founder was Max Suich, a volatile, carroty-haired newspaper executive of great originality. Sadly, I never worked under him when he set up the paper, instead I marched into the centre of a power struggle between three would-be editors: Melbourne editor John Jost, Paul Kelly, and the more conservative Evan Whitton who eventually won the job. The fatuous

Fairfax board was scared of the two 'radicals' and felt Whitton could tone the weekly down.

Whitton was a fine crime reporter, but as an editor I found him hopelessly paranoid. Most of the staff, from David Marr and Patrick Cook to Marion Wilkinson, were appalled by the choice. It got worse when he demoted reliable Fairfax staffers – business editor Peter Robinson and foreign affairs editor Yvonne Preston – and there was real alarm after he appointed an unknown ex-Melbourne Truth journo friend to be his deputy. He simply didn't trust any of the regulars. His nominal deputy, Paul Kelly, was sent 'on the road' to Canberra. The place was now called Chateau Despair.

Although I loved being at the *Times* and did good work there, I admit my comportment was not always exemplary. Arriving at a truly gala wedding between journalist John Edwards and Pam Watson at the Royal Sydney Golf Club, I immediately took three Mandrax tablets. Now tragically banned, Mandrax is the parent of today's 'eckies' or XTC. These hypnotic sleeping pills were ideal on the disco floor because they made you tingle all over. At the Edwards' wedding, however, the pills had a decidedly soporific effect. While others imbibed champagne and chatted gaily, I found it extraordinarily difficult to actually keep upright as I kept swaying and buckling at the knees, so I gently manoeuvred myself towards the stage and lay down under a Christmas tree for a rest. I was sound asleep while Whitlam's former minister Clyde Cameron was giving a speech on behalf of John and Pam about the rights of man, the dignity of labour and what a perfect contract the marriage tie was. As he reached a rhetorical height and paused for effect, I happened to turn over under the Christmas tree and emit a long, unmistakable snore. Cameron looked down with some amazement at the fallen Travolta by his feet, his speech now totally derailed. The wedding audience was vastly amused by my uncalled-for interruption, and it took Clyde a few champagnes to get back into his stride.

On another occasion, at a Christmas party at Nathan Waks's house at Balmain, I arrived having taken only two Mandrax. I thought I had learned a lesson. But even two was too much. It had the effect of allowing me to stand but making me want to piss. While swaying with Whitton on a parapet overlooking the Harbour I decided to do the latter.

Opening my fly to shouts of derision, I micturated on his leg. I would like to think that the quality of my work was the only criterion for my continued employment at the *Times*, but with a Queensland Catholic former schoolteacher like Whitton running the paper, one never knew. Maybe my flamboyance around the office was what finally got to him when I was sacked several months later. In what I felt was a cowardly gesture, Whitton left a signed sheet of copy paper in my typewriter saying my desk would be needed in the future. Whitton or no Whitton, drugs and alcohol had sullied my star potential.

IN WHICH I DISCOVER 'THE ONLY GAME IN TOWN'

My next job was a distinct departure from journalism. I teamed up with maverick UK documentarian Bill Bemister, sinking the last of my savings into a production company called Program Development. Bill was one of the great unsung 'characters' of the eighties. He had been a spy for the British in Rhodesia, and I suspect had worked for MI5 in London under cover of being a journalist. New projects were his forté.

We set up offices in Edgecliff and lobbied politicians in Canberra to make sure the foreshadowed 10BA film scheme, being offered by Fraser in the 1980 election campaign, included not just feature films but documentaries. Although it took many years and much fiddly financial work, Bill was extremely astute with figures and we finally raised nearly two million dollars through a stock broker to make three films: *Petrov and Philby*, *Warriors of the Deep* (a recreation of the night Jap subs entered Sydney Harbour in 1942), and a sixty-minute corporate video about the journey of a Qantas plane to London. This documentary was supposedly based on John Grierson's original 1936 film *The Night Mail*, but the comparison was far fetched. Our film was mainly a vehicle whereby we could obtain an endless supply of Miscellaneous Charge Orders (MCOs) and Promotional Exchange Orders (PEOs), which translated into absurdly cheap air tickets.

The first, a ninety-minute docudrama initially called *The Hedgehog and the Fox*, dealing with the Kim Philby story which still obsessed Britain in those days, was the project we cared most about. The name came from the Greek poet Archilochus who said, 'The fox knows many things, but the hedgehog knows one big thing.' Philby was the clever fox while Petrov was the stolid hedgehog who knew the 'one big thing' which is defence, ie, survival. It was a rather obscure quote that didn't really fit the concept but it worked well on the thousands of brochures we sent out to clients of our stockbrokers.

The trouble was that our accountants, Coopers and Lybrand, began getting nervous about the ever-inflating budgets, the first one for *Philby* coming in at about $700,000. They objected particularly to the setting aside of $20,000 for 'inducements' (really bribes) to various people to be either interviewed or filmed. Although the money had been collected from clients, they held us up for more than a year, Bill and I finally storming down to their boardroom and threatening to leap out of their ten-floor Bridge Street building unless feed money *at least* was made available. In the end they allowed us half a million through an imprest account with the State Bank, and the next day we were on the plane.

Within a fortnight we had two camera units, and researchers in Washington and London. Bill stayed with relatives, but in his ineffable British snobbishness he insisted that I book into the Curzon Hotel, Mayfair. The cost of this extravagance alone would have made at least one sixty-minute documentary, but we were both in another world. In making the film we met *Sunday Times* 'Journalist of the Year' Phillip Knightley, who was very friendly with John Philby, Kim's son who lived in Kentish Town. John, who looked the dead spit of his father, was hired to play Kim during the thirties. Our great coup was getting John to fly to Moscow with a clandestine video-8 camera and film his father walking around the Arbat. Philby, now a Colonel in the KGB, would allow no audio interviews, but he let his son videotape him. The footage was unique at the time, since it showed Philby shy, in a big felt hat, playfully wagging his finger, hiding from one tree to another: one minute pretending he was somebody, the next, nobody.

My six months in Mayfair were delirious. I decided to revisit the trot squat where I'd spent six totally broke months in 1978. When I entered the kitchen of the dingy, smoke-stained commune, and saw the same eager, hopeless faces, it seemed like nothing had changed. I was somewhat overdressed and looked the essence of a capitalist pig. Bundled up against the cold, I was wearing a Savile Row suit and a huge Bonwit Teller overcoat with a collar made of raccoon fur. The boys gathered in the kitchen, eager to hear about my transformation. Some snuck away, finding the news of my accommodations with capitalism simply too disgusting, but most were impressed with the totality of my sellout. One of the South Africans, young Robert, even asked me to help set up a 10BA scheme in Britain.

The rest of the time consisted of PEOs all over Europe, including a Concorde trip to New York for an interview with Sir Issac Deutscher that was never used. The Philby story involved disguise, subterfuge and 'drops'. Our task was to re-enact many of these events and pseudo-events. The film was incredibly if not overly academic. Swathes of Cambridge academics were interviewed sitting in view of King's College or the Cambridge 'backs' and opining on the severe, scientific, ruthless, mathematical – even Cromwellian – traditions of Cambridge, compared to the more lax and libertarian mores of Oxford. (One of them wittily referred to Oxford as the 'Latin Quarter of Cowley'.) We got footage of Cambridge rowing crews from 1937, '38 and '39; we got people talking about 'The Apostles', the club to which most of the traitors belonged; indeed, our search for archival footage was worldwide. This was going to be the finest spy film ever made.

The best parts of my stay in London were the dinner parties at the Knightleys' in Paddington. Yvonne Knightley, an ebullient Catholic from Mangalore, was a superb Indian cook. When I first walked in the door in my Bonwit Teller coat, they all shrieked, 'We know who you are. You're Burgess!' At one dinner party Germaine Greer was present with a lot of Australo-UK people. Germaine dominated conversation with an endless barrage of facts from the wheat silo of her mind about an article she was writing on Amazon women. Bill tried to sell her the idea of fronting a show on matriarchs. She liked the concept and started talking about her mother, as well as Indira Gandhi and many others.

Later I drove her home. She remembered me from Melbourne University. I reminded her of the clash she had had with Knopfelmacher in 1959. She paused, wrinkled her face and replied, 'It could be right, but it doesn't ring true because I've never been that mad about sucking men off.' I told her I was gay and she replied, 'How tiresome, everyone is gay these days.' Still, she asked for my phone number.

One morning she rang up and sought the assistance of Program Development to research the espionage situation in wartime Malta for the book she was writing about her father. Later, though they had signed a heads of agreement, she fell out with Bemister – as everybody did – screaming at him on the phone that he was the most negative, neurotic man she had ever met.

MEANWHILE, THE FURIES DESCEND

The size of the bills coming in from all over the world were sending Coopers and Lybrand into a spin. We promised to be more frugal. But Bill was hypermanic. It may have been my Presbyterian background but I simply hated his boom and bust attitude to money which was to spend it all while you had it. Finally Coopers pulled the plug, and we returned home to an editing suite in Darling Harbour for six weeks of day-and-night work to finish.

We had to make some sort of a cut to the film by the end of the financial year to justify the 10BA concession. The editor, Max Lemmon, was able to stay up all night just by smoking heavily, but the rest of us had to resort to cocaine. The building, containing fifteen editing suites, was packed with 'financier producers' who had never seen a Steenbeck; accountants who thought a script was something you gave to a chemist; and lawyers who thought 'treatments' were procedures carried out by medicos.

In these frantic months, the people who owned the hardware made the money. As the last weeks approached, wages soared. Editors who had been worth four hundred dollars a day suddenly demanded a thousand. They knew the Directors of Photography had already had their snouts in the trough, and they wanted some too. Our own DOP, Tony Wilson, not only bought a house from his earnings, but married production assistant Lucinda Strauss, whom Bemister was unsuccessfully chasing around the globe.

Eventually the re-enactments, the archival material, the 'exteriors' and the interviews were pulled into vague shape. Bemister, as writer, director and producer, had holed himself up in Paddington with a newly bought sports car. He was with one of the blonde English bimbos who loved to serve him but who were less keen on staying after dinner. Naturally Bill was stalling on the narration script. Max had no idea where to go or what to cut. Days turned into weeks and hysteria mounted. Coopers insisted the film, about three hours long, be reduced to an hour to make it easier to sell.

Finally with one day to go, the Ansaprint was ready for showing to the brokers, investors' representatives and the bureaucrats. By this stage we were terrified of investors since the phones rang day and night from them requesting repayment of the ten and twenty thousand dollars they put in several years ago, or at least a dividend from a film sale. The film, now renamed *Petrov and Philby* (the 'Petrov' supposedly appealing to the ABC), was actually an original and high-class piece of work. There was no questioning the depth of the research and the knowledge. For many years it was the most authoritative film about Philby. It was Bemister's masterpiece.

But there was far too much information in the script. The narrator had to race like an Olympian on speed to make it fit. There was an overload of both audio and visual material and some of the plotlines got confused. Later, to my surprise, I got back my financial stake, since I claimed the Australian rights, and eventually sold the film to the ABC, with permission to air it twice. It was now titled *Spytrap* and ran for ninety minutes.

The ABC buyer had been utterly uninterested in *Petrov and Philby* and 'spygames' for weeks and months, but when I told him it had already been bought by the BBC, he wrote out a cheque on the spot. It seems that many Australian films made for the ABC still follow the lead given by the Beeb.

TWO WEEKS IN THE BEAR PIT

During the time with Bemister I did a lot of extra journalism, partially in order to disengage from a man with an even more unstable reputation than my own. I wondered why I had been so biddable to such a scammer and whether I could blame it on low self-esteem – the bane of many gay men of my generation. But I managed to disentangle myself from my Bemesis, and returned to the *Weekend Australian* in 1983, this time as the lead feature writer. It is hardly surprising that journalists with access are flattered, cajoled, duchessed, wined and dined by society figures such as politicians, writers, artists and industrialists to write a piece on them. They eventually feel like whores and if they do it long enough they write like it.

I was hired by Editor-in-Chief Les Hollings and enjoyed working in an elite enclosure, complete with orchids, enviously called by other Murdoch journalists 'The California Suite'. This suite was the only part of the entire building which was inhabited by self-respecting human beings. The rest was as a darkened cave, with gnome-like creatures bent over buzzing machines desperately awaiting the next break. The building was filled with lifelong Murdoch vassals, people who were crushed with failure, overworked and alcoholic, capable only of expressing servility and their blokey, sexist, sensationalist tabloid anger – Murdoch's great gift to world journalism.

My boss was the ACP-trained Pat Dasey who liked bright, off-beat, colourful magazine stories. What I found marvellous about working for the *Weekend Australian*, a part-time job anyway, was that one could dictate one's copy to a row of twenty female copytakers.

In the course of a series of political profiles I offered Dasey, she decided to put Rosemary Foot at the head of the list. Frensham-educated and independently wealthy, Rosemary had recently launched a coup in the Liberal Party whereby Nick Greiner became Leader of the Opposition and she his deputy. I first met her in May 1983, which was an important rendezvous. In her spacious office overlooking the Domain she threw her staff out of the room and made the most of it. The *Weekend Australian*'s conservative A-B market was perfect for her. I was stunned by Rosemary's style, her designer clothes (Louis Ferraud) and her fast wit. Her blue blood background was well known – the polo-playing Ashton family. She tipped a bucket on the silver-tongued Wran for his subtle misogyny. While many of her friends were rich eastern suburbs bachelors like James Fairfax and Charles Lloyd Jones, what most fascinated me was her gay-friendliness. Her two special friends were the late Peter Kuring and his American gym queen boyfriend Gerry Vest.

Rosemary and I got along famously during the interview but while I was writing up the article a few days later she rang me from Wollongong and pleaded with me to drop the references she had made inadvertently about the 'dowdiness' of her North Shore parliamentary colleagues. I consented, and our unusual friendship blossomed. In camp lingo, I became her handbag. She took me to functions at the Royal Sydney Golf Club and to a weekend with Sir Warwick and Lady Mary Fairfax at Harrington Park in Camden. At this weekend I was judged a success since I could discuss philosophy with the senile Sir Warwick, who had written books about the subject. Indeed I even seemed to know the difference between Nietzsche and Hume. His glaucous eyes tried to settle on me as we sat in the gazebo, but really they were fixed on happier times when he influenced Menzies' cabinets and shipped his Rolls-Royce to Europe for his annual tour. Sir Warwick had been ousted by his son James in a boardroom coup in 1978 and he was bitter.

Later on after dinner Lady Mary busily claimed she was a Polish Jew and nothing made her more furious than to be mistaken for a Hungarian. 'Yes,' Sir Warwick chimed in, 'they are utter gypsies, thieving with money and vulgar to boot. Look at the way they behave on the hill,' making slighting references to a well-known knight and others. Yet after dinner a certain Magyar opulence was displayed as a vast map of the intending subdivision of most of their estate, Harrington Park, was unrolled before us. Now Sir Warwick became more animated. He said it was outrageous the Wran government's zoning policies would not give permission to access this bonanza. His eyes lit up. 'Thousands and thousands of happy couples could live around here,' he croaked. I casually asked how much the subdivision, which is at the back of Campbelltown, would net the Fairfax family. He just as casually replied, 'Oh, about $275 million.'

As the Member for Vaucluse, Rosemary had discovered through Woollahra Council sources that the Hermitage Reserve had been slyly gazetted away from public use and into the hands of entrepreneur Warren Anderson, who owned a property adjoining it. It was done over Christmas and Anderson was virtually gifted a total area of approximately 2,270 square harbourside metres which presumably greatly enhanced his property at 15 and 17 Queens Avenue, Vaucluse. In an urgency motion to the House on 23 February 1984 which she presented with great difficulty, Rosemary pointed out that the six hundred metres that had been offered to Anderson at $145,000 was in fact worth $700,000. She concluded that the state Labor government was performing favours for

Anderson. This speech caused uproar since it went to the heart of the corruption implicit in the NSW Labor Right.

Rosemary was a queen among the Paddy's Pigs of the NSW Parliament. I have worked in three parliaments, the stately Victorian, the self-important federal – but never have I worked in a Parliament House that is so raucous and crudely male. The NSW Legislative Assembly, the oldest in Australia, is truly the place where Australia's 'convict stain' seeps out. It is a small, narrow Georgian building often admiringly referred to as 'the bear pit'. When I was there louts from both sides of the House would shout schoolboy abuse that would be ruled out of order anywhere else. The Labor backbench in particular loathed Rosemary – her class, her money, her assurance, her Joyce Grenfell diction. They shrieked with delight whenever she entered the chamber and, urged on by Wran, mercilessly ragged her.

Because of her astigmatism, she required reading glasses for speeches and therefore a lectern. One day as she was fiddling short-sightedly with the stand the then National Party leader, Leon Punch, in a rare moment of gallantry, moved to raise the lectern but also fumbled. After a few seconds a Labor backbencher shouted, 'Look, Leo can't get it up for Rosie.' Rosemary blushed and went on with her speech, although the laughter took many minutes to die down.

In a moment of folly, while still working on the *Weekend Australian*, I had taken two weeks off to research more about Warren Anderson and his connections. This led me to an interview with Tom Domican, a 'trainer' who was believed to be responsible for bashing some Labor MPs attached to inner-city branches. Domican was a scary man who was probably on steroids and very volatile. When I rang him he agreed to see me, saying he had fallen out with Anderson. I arrived at his home with a bottle of Johnnie Walker whisky. Domican decided to use my presence in his house to screw more money out of Anderson by calling him at his palatial home in Fern Hill, as for several years he had been in receipt of fifty thousand dollars a year from Anderson's company Owsten Nominees Number Two. But Anderson was not going to be so easily blackmailed. He refused Domican anymore, so Domican then proceeded to spill his guts. He confirmed that for years Anderson had paid him and disclosed how a prominent Labor figure had set up the deal whereby Anderson paid Domican in order to increase the strength of the right wing of the ALP. Domican said that Anderson had established a 'web of influence', controlling Labor councils in order to facilitate his purchase of land for New World supermarkets for whom he was working.

When I typed this out in a statutory declaration on his rickety Remington, he stood behind me banging a baseball bat on the lino kitchen floor saying, 'You're a much slower typist than David Halpin' (an investigative journalist who has since died). This was undoubtedly true and as he stood there brandishing his bat I was getting slower. I told him to put the bat in another room, which he did. When I emerged with that statutory declaration and showed it to Rosemary, we knew we had hit the mother lode. The crucial information in her urgency speech to the House was devastating. Always tending towards choler, an apoplectic Wran arose and rubbished her furiously.

This coup against the NSW Right became national news, but Rosemary and I (nicknamed

'Rosemary's Baby' by the press gallery) were foolhardy in our determination to have the full story revealed. Rosemary was well aware of the dangers in speaking outside the House, but acquiesced to numerous media requests for a press conference the next day. Repeating the allegations in this way made Rosemary subject to libel, and it was not too long before the writs started rolling in. The Liberal Party offered Foot no backing whatsoever, either legal or financial, a situation without precedent. After threats of claims for millions, in the end, inclusive of legal costs, she was forced to settle for $153,000 and had to sell up a country property and leave politics. It had been a very gutsy run by a politician who is still remembered for her courage.

Of Bad Timing and Bad Seeds

Parents are the bones on which children sharpen their teeth.
PETER USTINOV

One of Doone's more memorable admonitions to my waywardness was the line, 'When are you going to get a time sense and a money sense?' For her, these classic middle-class virtues collapsed on the death of her husband in 1983. At seventy-four, Alan Blazey had been experiencing stomach cramps for some time. He was wrongly persuaded to see a surgeon at the Freemasons Hospital for an exploratory operation in which his pancreas was found to be riddled with cancer. They sealed him up again, hoping nothing would happen; but the incisions had released the cancer and within a week he was dead.

Doone was devastated. I was in Sydney and she rang up saying, 'He's dead, he's dead, I can't believe it.' I went to Melbourne immediately. Clive and I visited the Freemasons' morgue. Clive believed that if Doone saw his body she would accept the finality of his death. This rather hippyesque notion was quite inappropriate for our mother's mental state, which had been on the decline anyway. She stared at his naked doubled-up corpse in a refrigerated morgue drawer and broke down sobbing.

I didn't cry and rarely do, but I was affected. The ache and the grief lasted for more than two years. He upset me more in his death than he had in life. Perhaps this was due to remorse about lost opportunities. Alan and I rarely met more than once a year at brandy-sodden Christmases down at Whimsy. Several times he had invited me up to stay with him at the 'birdwatch cabin' as he quaintly called it, his retirement house on a bend of the Goulburn River. I accepted his invitations but never went, for I realised that the two of us in that tiny two-bedroom kit home would induce awkwardness. We may have liked each other but there was no real intimacy. Those demonstrative SNAG-gy dads who hugged their sons and spent 'quality time' together were still a long way off. The only real bonding that I can recall was attending the Father and Sons Day at Melbourne Rotary in Collins Street in the sixties, where Alan was a proud representative of the chemical industry. Together with a tribe of mostly overweight businessmen and their offspring we sang:

I love to go awandering along a mountain track,
And as I go I love to sing, a knapsack on my back
Val der ee, Val der eye, a knapsack on my back!

The thought of Alan and me in lederhosen was quite diverting.

When my Bolte biography was published Alan proved to be one of its greatest fans, to my surprise. I was thirty-one and it was the first time I was aware that he actively approved of anything I had done. When the book was being serialised in the *Age* he came home one night from a party saying that he had just been asked if he were Peter Blazey's father. That gave us both a laugh. I asked what he thought of the book and he replied drily, 'It was a worthwhile addition to the Gross National Product.' I was ecstatic.

Alan mellowed as he grew older, and even seemed to approve of Philip. A poignant episode occurred when my parents visited Philip and me at our flat in Gotham City a year before Alan died. Staying at the Rushcutters Bay Motel, they walked across the park for morning tea and we all sat around an extravagant art deco table. Philip, Alan and I all had whiskies from a Johnnie Walker bottle on the sideboard. Alan was jovial but Doone was on edge. On being introduced to Philip she snapped, 'We've met,' when they actually had not. During small talk she paced the room, saying, 'Who else lives here? What do people do in this building?' Philip showed Doone our flatmate Bill Morley's magnificent collection of Clarice Cliff Spode china. Back at the table she replied she had never heard of Clarice Cliff and added how strange it was for men to be collecting porcelain. Father was amiably talking about Philip's artwork when Doone jumped up and exclaimed, 'Alan, it's time to go. We want to get a coffee in Kings Cross.' Alan replied benignly, 'But my dear, Philip is making coffee right now.' They left soon after. This was one of the last times I saw him.

Back in Melbourne, Alan became caught up in more serious family concerns. The fact he had been pressured from the board of the company by one of his own sons was a cause of anguish to him. He occasionally said, 'Nothing can cause the pain that children can cause,' and we knew to whom he was referring. Antony, now successful as managing director of Hortico, had got rid of his brother Clive in 1978 as Hortico's home garden manager. On being threatened with demotion, Clive resigned not because he was incompetent (far from it), but because he was a rival. It was a messy business. Clive was not aided by his father, since Alan's military cast of mind supported the superior officer. Shortly before Alan died, Antony said to me, 'I've arseholed the old man from the board.' 'Why?' I asked in some amazement. 'He's served his usefulness and besides I've got my own people,' he replied.

Alan's retirement involved spending three days at Portsea and the rest of the week at the birdwatching cabin, where he grew all manner of vegetables, watched swans nesting through binoculars and listened to endless tapes of his musical hero, Paul Robeson (another Depression boy). In a way, he was entering the Australian equivalent of a Sanyassin stage: disencumbering himself of past, family and possessions – the only thing he lacked was a begging bowl. He owned a mere 260,000 Hortico shares – fewer than his wife or any of his three sons. His tax return for the year 1983 showed a taxable income of about $33,000 – again, less than any of his family. In his lifetime he had helped create great wealth for Hortico shareholders and his family but he kept little for himself.

It was a measure of Alan's modesty and quiet good works that four hundred people turned up to his funeral in Camberwell. I had always imagined him to be an isolated person, but here at Le Pines Funeral Directors the hall overflowed with acquaintances, friends and admirers I had never before encountered. As Alan's eldest son, I was mobbed by ex-Hortico employees from the forties and fifties whose families he had helped out in some way or other, usually by giving them discounted shares. He strongly believed in staff share ownership. It all made me realise there was a side to him I had never seen, and indeed had wilfully avoided. I felt humbled.

Clive, Doone and I went to Springvale crematorium and later took his ashes back in a casket to the birdwatch cabin. Three weeks after his death Doone was still in shock. Clive and I buried the ashes under a huge red gum by the lagoon where the black swans nested. With a chain-saw we inscribed on the tree his initials 'ACB', nothing more. It was ceremony simple yet apt, for his life had been devoted to growing and the environment, and I was proud to see that, to the end, this rationalist resolutely rejected the rites of Christian burial.

Though I had declined a job in Hortico in favour of a position on the *Australian*, my go-getter brother Antony was determined to rise to the top of the family firm. He had joined the company at the lowest level, learning his trade in the rendering business, one of the toughest. Antony modelled himself on Kerry Packer and the brazen character 'J.R.' out of the TV series 'Dallas'. He even wore a Stetson while driving his car.

He was ambitious and acquisitive. He accumulated shares while Alan was still alive, causing much unease about his intentions. Soon after Alan's death Antony launched a hostile takeover bid for the firm in October 1984 at $4.40 a share, which valued Hortico at $16.5 million. Hortico was a private unlisted company. If the bid were to be successful it would cost Antony $12 million, money which he had borrowed at a high interest rate from Citicorp Bank. The bid was conditional upon ninety per cent acceptance – which was challenging since Antony owned only about twenty-five per cent of the shares. Despite his urgings a large majority of Hortico's board rejected his offer.

Doone, Clive and most of the directors owned a large proportion of the shares through a family company called Samarkand. Doone's financial adviser was Tom O'Brien of Ernst and Young. Tom was a Hortico director. He soon realised that Antony's bid could not succeed. When his offer was first made it was given consideration, for even Doone had once said to me, 'You're only in business to make money, really.' But by November Antony had very few acceptances, the general complaint being that the offer price was too low. Doone was adamant that he was not going to get control of her dead husband's company. This was Doone's last great act of defiance.

In a totally unexpected move Cheetham Salt, keen to diversify their company, put up an offer of five dollars a share for Hortico, outbidding Antony by sixty cents. This was sufficient for Doone, her advisers and a majority of shareholders. They sold out to Cheetham forthwith, thereby denying Antony control. But Antony was desperate and engaged in a form of 'greenmail'. He upped his offer to $5.20. Surrounded by a phalanx of lawyers and financiers, he took Doone and the other Hortico directors to the Victorian Supreme Court, challenging the legality of their share ownership.

Antony's action outraged the family, especially Doone who was still *compos*. She received an interlocutory injunction while she was visiting the Manaus Opera House in Brazil. She was mortified by her son's legal action. Doone was still addicted to travelling the world on package tours but this time she shared a cabin with a rather deranged woman who chalked a white line between their bunks, warning Doone not to cross it. Without Alan, this trip upset her even more.

One month later, in December 1984, Antony himself sold out to Cheetham Salt, walking away with $4.5 million. He used this money to buy Defender, the snail-killing company, but was unable to service his huge bank loans and some years later wound up broke, forced to sell off all the property he owned. Since that time, Antony has been an outcast from the Blazey family though he has occasionally visited Doone when she was living at her Balwyn home or, later, in nursing homes. He wanted a reconciliation but Doone never forgave him. He was also seeking her blessing for his two new daughters by his second wife Catherine, to whom he is happily married. The last time I saw Doone with Antony she looked at him blankly, saying nothing.

*

The death of Alan improved my relationship with Doone. Perhaps because she was no longer prey to her Presbyterian hang-ups about being a 'wife', she became daffier, more carefree, even happy. Her vulnerability had turned her into a sweet old lady who would say 'Yes, dear', 'No dear' and 'That would be nice, dear'. Philip and I took her on a holiday to Mexico which she loved, and she became quite fond of Philip.

Of course Doone's newfound pliability could be linked to her being a little unhinged. Although not formally diagnosed with Alzheimer's disease until 1989, it was obvious to the family that something was amiss long before that. The saddest thing about dementia is the rapidity with which old friends discard the sufferer almost as if it were contagious. I made frequent visits to the family home in Balwyn.

When it came time to leave she cried repeatedly, 'I have no friends, I have no friends, except for you.' She became devoted to a series of dogs, one a labrador named Coffee whom she kept feeding until it had a heart attack.

She went to the bank frequently to withdraw large sums which were later distributed gaily around the local Balwyn park to the delight of the Camberwell Grammar boys whose school was adjacent. We put a limit on her banking activities but domestically things were worsening. After I found the iron in the Kelvinator freezer and, more alarmingly, caught her employing the dog as a dishwasher, slurping up the dirty plates before stacking them in the cupboards, it was obvious she needed professional live-in help. A family friend, Wendy McInness, became her home carer for several years, after which we decided to place her in a nursing home. The first of these was frightful and Doone became more agitated, grabbing other patients' food and even punching some of the staff. Predictably, she was fed strong pacifying drugs such as Stellazine and Melaril, which often made her more fractious.

Some of the nursing homes were airless dumps

that stank of urine. I nearly wept seeing her there with other demented geriatrics doing mad things. She had once been such a powerful presence and now she was reduced to this. After many attempts we found a really civilised and less drug-dependent home called Sorrento House, where the last time I visited she stared at my face for several minutes before pronouncing, in a friendly way, 'I know you.'

A SHORT STINT IN THE HOUSE OF KP

After the death of my father I was keen to get back into journalism. I rang up my friend Andrew Clark, then editor of *Australian Business*, the Packer finance weekly. I told him I would like to work on the *Bulletin*, so he went to the feline and powerful Editor-in-Chief, Trevor Kennedy, who put me on staff as an A-grader. To use a journalistic cliché, this job turned out to be a 'poisoned chalice'. Lacking the feline hypocrisy of Fairfax and the larrikin energy of Murdoch, Packer's magazine stable reflected the ruthless, acquisitive, overworked style of its owner. In this tight, morbid magazine, under the editorship of David Armstrong, I found the feat of writing stories advocating the reduction of sales tax on imported Volvos to be personally taxing. The wealthy were to be mollycoddled while the poor were to be either ignored or treated as a burden on the rich. Although I was given a column called 'The Intelligencer' (a title borrowed from *New York* magazine) and greatly enjoyed the power and access it entailed, I was unhappy.

One night, working late on another story in praise of the corporate cowboys then running our lives, I decided to take some files home. So it was that, at eight o'clock at night, with a cluster of folders under my arms, I was standing in the descending lift when who should enter but my very own chairman, Kerry Packer, and ex-cricketer Tony Grieg, with whom 'KP' had been carousing for some hours.

KP is an immense, not quite human presence. His looks and his height always invite saurian analogies: to me he was like a gigantic, well-dressed komodo dragon. Between sneering and towering, Kerry decided to use me for a little sport. Since he personally owns the entire building it was reasonable to assume that I, a mere member of staff, was taking his files out of his building, thus committing a minor felony. He asked me what I was doing with them. What was I writing about? Who was I? Where did the files come from? I silently pointed to the imprint of the *Bulletin* on their covers and stood rigid, staring straight ahead clutching my books like a virginal librarian. When we eventually reached the ground floor I tottered out chastely into the night to continue my work on his behalf.

This incident alienated me somewhat. One of the most unpleasant aspects of my job was having a desk in an open plan office next to journalist and entrepreneur Bruce Stannard, a humourless man who believed he was the finest correspondent in Australia. It seemed to me that Bruce was in the throes of a platonic love affair with Alan Bond. When Bond's zeppelin was moored over Sydney Harbour Bridge it was Bruce who first spoke to him by radio telephone; it was Bruce who endlessly quoted his most trivial thoughts; it was Bruce who boosted his prowess as a yachtsman, as a businessman, as a great Australian nationalist; it was Bruce who wrote glowing, oleaginous stories about Bond and immediately faxed them off for him to read. Eighteen months spent listening to Bruce made me a very cynical little budgie.

In order to write my features and my column I had started to drink from small flasks of Johnnie Walker's whisky, which lay in my bottom drawer instead of the legendary half-written novel. Fast trips to the toilet resulted not only in the imbibing of Red Label but also the inhalation of small lines of cocaine. I had to have several lines before writing a profile of Channel Nine's Ray Martin which appeared as 'Television's Hard Hitting Mr Nice Guy', a piece of in-house PR that was repulsive on all counts. When I interviewed Martin at the Midday Show cottages at Willoughby he went to extraordinary lengths to talk about his new wife and daughter and how these two people totally consumed the hours when he was not working for Mr Packer. I think the Channel Nine PR had warned him I was some sort of homosexual monster. I was getting close to the bottom of the barrel.

My morale at work hit a new low because of Barry Humphries, who has always exercised a peculiar influence over me. Humphries was in the process of making his flagrantly bad movie, *Les Paterson Saves the World.* I spent the day on the set at Alexandria in a disused factory that had been brilliantly transformed by an inspired art department into an Arab Casbah.

I was flattered when Humphries stopped the production, involving a thousand people, to talk to me. For a very expensive ten minutes we chatted amiably about Melbourne, about members of the Packer court such as David McNicoll as well as the meaning of this film. He suspected the film would be a disaster, but his fat executive producer's fee helped allay his anxiety. His then wife, Dianne Milstead, a Melbourne surrealist artist, had part-written the script. She was also acting as his production manager.

The few paragraphs in my column about the film were dismissive of it and panned its chances of success. Humphries flew into a vindictive rage. He got Milstead to courier me a bottle of Black Label Johnnie Walker, saying by all accounts I was extremely fond of the substance and she hoped it would help my artistic judgements. The sentiments obviously came straight from the Master, who had done his stint with AA (as I was to do a few years later). I returned the Black Label instantly, graciously thanking them, saying I only drank Red Label; but the incident stung.

A further complication at the *Bulletin* arose when, instead of reporting to editor Armstrong, I was told that except for hard news I was to report to James Hall, whom Armstrong had recently hired. Before long Hall's imperious personality began to grate. Submission of my expansive copy to someone so finger-wagging was infuriating.

I did not have to put up with this for long, however. About two years after my father's death the proceeds of the breakup of Samarkand came through. Because the Cheetham takeover left Samarkand worth nearly four million dollars, it had been directed by Alan Blazey's estate that the money be distributed equally amongst his three sons. (It was a mark of Alan's Roman fairness that he didn't disinherit Antony.) I could see no further point in working at KP's Grub Street. I resigned so fast, one friend accused me of lacking decorum. 'You're behaving like someone who's just won Tattslotto,' he said – but who could blame me?

Hammer Horror

I am the universe tonite
riding in all my Power riding
chauffeured thru my self by a long haired saint with eyeglasses
ALLEN GINSBERG, *WITCHITA VORTEX SUTRA*

Being a millionaire does not guarantee human happiness, but it permits a simulation of this state for a few years. In late 1985 we three sons each received $1.3 million. I began to fly around the world investing in gold mines, buying property in Hollywood, plunging deep into the fine art market, and making documentary films about aborigines that were never screened, not even on SBS.

One of the first things I did was visit my friend John Halpin in Thailand. He was about ten years younger than me and in the thick of the Vietnam generation when David Wilson introduced us thirteen years earlier; he was a romantic figure and draft resister always on the run from government agents. That was how we met – he needed a place to lie low and I wanted a caretaker for my Carlton house.

After being in Chieng Mai for a week I became part of the weirdest scene you could imagine. There was a full moon, and the bar in northern Thailand was packed with *farangs* (foreigners). It was one of those hyper-kinetic nights when everyone was flying and demons were being set loose. At the centre of the bar, lionised as usual, was John Halpin. He was rubbishing and bullying his fans and as drunk as a skunk on Mekong whisky. There were imprecations everywhere. He could have been in the Albion or Stewart hotel in Carlton, except the liquor was stronger, he was surrounded by Asia trippers and adoring Vietnam vets and all the women were Thai. They were being manhandled and abused in a way Carlton women would never have tolerated.

I came to Chieng Mai to visit Halpin who had been living there for four years with his 'Thai wife' Nit and his son Marty from former girlfriend and Carlton identity Mary Duggan. He had hit a dead end in Melbourne: no job, no career, and a minimal desire to work except for wildcat forays into underground journalism. John returned from northern Thailand several times in the late seventies. He came back to see semi-criminal friends in Melbourne who fascinated him, and to pick up maintenance money for Marty from his parents. He was also trying to place stories in Australia about CIA involvement in heroin trafficking from the Golden Triangle, and about Khun Sa, a heroin warlord who controlled an army of mercenaries in the Thai border areas. By exploiting the nationalistic ambitions of local ethnic tribes, Khun Sa was able to grow and market huge quantities of heroin to the Western world.

His base was a heavily guarded compound in a suburb of Chieng Mai close to where John lived. The white concrete walls were fifteen feet high and there was barbed wire on top. Khun Sa's house looked more like a gaol – or an army base, which it was. John, who could speak northern Thai, always got the gossip about whether Khun Sa was in town or not. He occasionally caught glimpses of his heavily armoured car going into the compound. Halpin was fascinated by Khun Sa – his power, his flair, the way he was protected by the Thai military, the fact that he made money out of a product to which John claimed he was no longer addicted: high-grade heroin.

The ironic thing is that John had not touched heroin for six months, although he lived in the world capital of it. He was trying to go clean, to get the monkey off his back. Having been addicted several times before in Australia, knew the horrors of drying out; now he was thinking of Marty. He dreamed of being a foreign correspondent but, while sitting on top of some of the best stories of the eighties, he seemed incapable of writing them. When I was on the *Australian* I lined him up with all the necessary codes and connections for filing copy, but none was forthcoming. Now that he was fucked and far from home he hoped to write a thriller based in Chieng Mai.

Being the first old friend to visit him, I stayed in his old-style Thai home, made of teak logs, when he showed me the beginnings of his novel. It ran for about fifteen pages in an exercise book, and then petered out when the hero met a very young girl. And that was that. John had always been evasive about the fact that he liked visiting brothels which had young girls in them.

I first clapped eyes on Halpin in 1972. He had steel-rimmed glasses above his huge nose and his puppy dog ears gave him a sort of bounding, jocular animality. He was very matey, very ocker in the manner of the times and he wore then, as always, Reeboks and jeans. Apart from his Draft Resisters Union activities he was a journalist on the collective which published the radical monthly Digger.

I got to love Halpin's speciality, which was the great Australian chiack: 'Howya goin', you fascist bastard?' or, 'How much white lady have you sold for the pigs this week, you copper's nark?' When he called people running dogs, molls, junkies, fascists, imperialist pigs and charlatans, they adored him and he was sending himself up – comically alluding to what he had been. By a special alchemy, the more he belittled people the more they loved him. Halpin cared enough to deliver the exquisitely accurate insult. He had courtesy, a terrible passivity (which got worse) and a curiosity as huge as the nose with which he snorted the smack that eventually ended his life.

For several years he had been on the run as a draft dodger. He was quite a romantic figure, tall, blue-eyed with a loping gait; he moved between hideaways in the Dandenongs, South Yarra, Prahran and Carlton. In common with other draft resisters, he spent his time evading Commonwealth Police, ASIO spies and campus informers. But by December 1972, within a month of Whitlam's election, Halpin was suddenly 'legal' since all charges against draft resisters had been dropped while Australian troops were being pulled out of Vietnam. Halpin's war was ended but he never got over it.

We had drunk together through the seventies on Friday nights, joyous tribal revelries during which outrageous, unforgivable things were said under the influence of various drugs, to be forgotten the next day.

Even then John wasn't earning enough from his writing and it was obvious he was living on family money as he moved from one cheap Carlton dump to the next: on the run again. Just like the old days – except now he was a part-time junkie with a family. His girlfriend Mary didn't help matters by her own fondness for the drug and she later died of an overdose. As for John, there was too great a disparity between the influential radical he had hoped to be and the pub joker and buffoon he had become. He was a failed revolutionary – another victim of the Vietnam War. When in Sydney I'd call him in Melbourne and say, 'I'm not going to live in Carlton because it's a crash pad for failures.' 'Well at least we've admitted it,' he would say. 'We've faced up to it down here. We're not consumed with guilt about it.' He laughed at my priggishness.

IN WHICH I ENTER THE HEART OF DARKNESS

I had flown to Chieng Mai from Tokyo where I had been doing a Buddhist pilgrimage for a Japanese sect, Soka Gakkai, which practised the uncompromising fourteenth century teachings of Nichiren Shoshu, who believed all other forms of Buddhism were heretical. This entailed chanting *nam myo ho renge kyo*, a Japanese translation of the lotus sutra. I had been practising this in Sydney for several years and found it to be a powerful incantation. For Australians to be invited to the head temple on the slopes of Mount Fuji was an honour and, after chanting for a week, I was feeling high.

So John and I were overjoyed to meet at the airport. He was feeling paranoid and neglected and I was much richer than he was. Early on in the stay we decided to get some good-quality heroin to have a little nostalgic snort. I had been a weekend user but had never got hooked, unlike John.

It was a sultry night in the Thai–German Dairy, a backpacker's hotel in Chieng Mai. Halpin purchased for me three ounces of Number Four heroin, the world's purest, from a Chinese dealer for 500 baht. Not wanting to hide the cache in his own house, we selected neutral ground, burying our treasure in the herb garden at the back of the hostel. It sat there like a time bomb for the next few days, alternately beckoning and repelling us. We breakfasted daily at the hostel where Halpin, as usual, was too popular for his own good.

Thursday night was the regular *farang* boys' night out. On this night the full moon was heroin-white, so bright you could see the faces of people walking in the street past the evil-smelling *klongs*, and clearly see the silhouette of the surrounding mountains. Like a dream, everything that night was both absurdly skewed yet deadly lucid. Earlier in the evening I had picked up a Thai transvestite called Marilyn. I arrived at the Oasis Bar at about ten in the evening, very late and quite sober. My eyes took in the scene: cane cubicles, Vietnam photos on the wall, coconuts and elephant tusks hanging low. Everyone was drunk, buzzing and elated. At the bar there were four or five *farangs* who seemed to regard Halpin as the king. These included a few Western expats, some hard-bitten Vietnam veterans, and a soppy Canadian student who claimed that 'once Asia gets into your blood, you're smitten for life'.

That night under the full moon Halpin and I felt a disharmonious connection. Spiritually I was a mess. I was filled with a chrome-plated sanctimoniousness gained at Mount Fuji by chanting for a week, a sense of appalling invincibility, which appeared ill against John's obvious vulnerability. As soon as he saw me at the Oasis, he abused me. 'You weak cunt, Blazey. You're only in Chieng Mai for the dope, not for me.' I replied, 'They go together, don't they, darling?' He seemed peeved at the suggestion, claiming that he hadn't touched heroin since returning from Melbourne at Christmas.

I was amazed he was talking about heroin in front of all his drinking buddies. But he was hopelessly drunk. Since everyone was out of control the demons took over: free will had gone 'out the window', a favourite phrase of ours indicating total madness. But John was also on the ball, and his sixth sense had selected me to be his nemesis, a possible agent for his longed-for departure.

He suddenly swung around and said, 'I'm sick of your bullshit. It's about time you listened to some of my bullshit.' Then he said prophetically, 'People are going to do some stupid things tonight.' He grabbed another glass of Mekong. 'Even your best friend will shop you on a mad night like tonight.' He looked at me laughing as I denied the charge. The other drinkers seemed mystified and told him to shut up, but he continued to hold me in his glittering eye. 'When the crunch comes they'll lie and cheat and betray you. It's always been that way – and if you don't know it, you don't know what life is about,' he said. He actually thought that I, Peter, would betray him at the third crowing of the cock, casting himself as Jesus. I was astounded and ridiculed his suggestion, but it was almost exactly what happened.

By the time we staggered back by the stinking *klong* to the Thai–German Dairy, we both knew we were going to get that smack buried in the herb garden. It was so obvious we didn't even mention it, looking forward to flying higher than the Hindu Kush. Our strongest bond was that we were 'smack brothers'. When you know you've got some Number Four waiting for you at home, and you're drunk, there's more anticipation than there would be for the most brilliantly staged orgy you can think of.

From that point I can recall things happening with the precision of marionettes, or figures walking under water. As soon as we got there I strode out to the back yard. Unusually, Chan, the immensely civilised Chinese manager of the hostel, was not on duty. He too was inebriated and had gone to bed early. I went to the cache, reaching first for the tin of vegetable oil which concealed it. Below it I found newspaper, then a plastic-wrapped package as thick as your wrist. I triumphantly took it back to the bathroom where John was waiting.

'Jesus, thank God you've found it, mate,' he said. We were both salivating. This dope was ten times purer than you could obtain in Australia, even from an honest dealer, and we had enough to kill an elephant. I opened the white paper and poured out a thick line on top of the toilet. It was an *insane* amount of heroin.

I cut it in half with a knife we had got from the kitchen. John went first. He bent down over the toilet and hoovered up the heroin with his left nostril, in two or three snorts. 'Now that,' he added with great satisfaction, 'is some of my bullshit!' He laughed and laughed, punching me gently. His first smack in six months, beautiful, pure stuff, enough of it to take you to paradise. 'That was great, mate!' His flight had already commenced. He pushed my 'half' towards me.

I must have heard the angel of death rustling in that grimy bathroom stinking of the toilet, acrid coriander and five spice. 'Here, take some, mate,' he said affectionately. 'Have your half, you weak cunt.' But suddenly I wasn't weak. I said no, I wouldn't have any. Instead I took a few pinches and carefully poured it into a cigarette, which I smoked. I didn't want a huge snort. Was I being pious or priggish? Maybe if I'd been as drunk as him I would have snorted the same amount.

He pushed the heroin towards me again. 'Take some!' he implored. But I was stubborn. I should have packed it up and put it in my pocket. If I had really cared about him I would have. In that moment he bent down and hoovered up the rest of the finger-thick line with his right nostril, laughing maniacally,

'More of my bullshit!'

Like fugitive lovers we needed an empty room for this thrilling trip. Too smashed to go home we moved into the room next door where there was the same blond Canadian student named Bob sleeping with his Thai girlfriend. When Halpin keeled over a few minutes later, I said perhaps he should go to hospital, smelling an overdose. But Bob said, 'No, leave him. He's only drunk.'

I promised them another room and said I would pay for it tomorrow. So John and I were left alone. He was breathing deeply, and his skin was slowly changing colour. Anywhere in Australia one would have taken him for a strenuous walk, but I was paranoid about Thailand.

At three o'clock a *samlor* driver walking past the open door caught a glimpse of John's ashen face and no doubt suspected another *farang* OD. He must have seen the same thing happen to scores of others, and insisted that I take him to hospital – or he would take him there. He jumped, he danced, he grabbed at me. John's face was becoming more ghostly, his breathing more fitful. This was the time to go. Now. The early cocks were starting to crow.

But I was anchored by fear. I held an image of the Chieng Mai police in the sheerest terror. John had said a few days before, 'There was an Italian here last year. He was shackled to the floor for *six months*. He said he'd got gangrene and they had to take the shackles off, but they didn't. Instead they amputated both his legs!' John had told this tale with glee. It was one of his typically exaggerated stories, that contained his usual flair for grisly detail.

So the *samlor* driver's insistence that we take John to the hospital made me absolutely adamant that we would not. I was phobic that we'd finish up shackled also. The *samlor* driver gave me up as a crazy *farang*. I was left alone with John for a Thai Gethsemane. I sat by him. Sensing things were getting out of hand, I chanted *nam myo ho renge kyo* over his body, wasting another vital hour.

Then I started to break down. I cried out, 'Damn you, Halpin, you stupid bastard, you stupid, stupid cunt. You'll land us all in gaol. You've really done it this time.' When he didn't abuse me back it was obvious we were now in serious trouble. I was sobbing like a child. But I still resisted doing the only thing that could save him – getting him to the thoracic unit of the Chieng Mai hospital. His breathing was faltering and I was paralysed by panic. Being the custodian of John's life, it was only late in the piece when I finally came to my senses. At five o'clock, with the sun rising over the mountains and the cocks of Chieng Mai crowing in a deafening chorus, I rushed out to the *samlor* men who had waited all night by the klong, got them to ring the hospital and take him there.

The hospital had a heart-starting machine for such cases, and it was used often, though it took some time to secure the staff and activate the machine. They pumped and pumped but soon they realised he had given up the ghost several minutes after they strapped him in.

Later Chen, the normally serene manager of the hostel, berated me. He was also fond of John. He was angry because he'd gone to bed drunk and had been unable to help him. He was annoyed with himself for getting so drunk, since his friend's life had been left in my foolish hands. In cold anger he said to me, 'He could have been saved if he'd gone in at four o'clock. But you said no. You are a very stupid person.'

I could hardly disagree. I had gone to the hospital and seen his stiff blue body. Everyone had cried hysterically except me. Yet I was in a shocking state. I cursed everyone, saying it was all the fault of the Americans, the Viets, Thais, the Vietnam War, the white lady, John's deathwish and his big nose.

On the second day, my emotions finally erupted and I sobbed inconsolably. Failure was one of the great themes of our friendship. I had perfectly fulfilled his prophecies of the night before. I had betrayed him monumentally. And yet looking back on it now, I wonder whether he had been programming me to trigger his destruction – a thing he was unable to do himself.

The worst thing was taking the news from the hospital back to his home at nine in the morning after the bedside vigil. Then the real horror began. John's girlfriend Nit and Marty were in an agony of grief, especially Nit who now had to return to her hated parents in the Thai countryside. I took Steve Larssen, an American war veteran friend of John's, back to the hospital to identify the body. He kissed and hugged it, and put his fist through a plate glass window at the hospital in rage. He kept saying, 'Fuck it, fuck it, fuck it. They killed you, Johnny.'

On the day of his death I rang John's parents in

Shepparton. His father was in his seventies. 'It was a heart attack,' I lied. 'He drank too much Mekong whisky and he keeled over, had a fit and died.'

'Good God,' said his father, stunned, 'I've had three of them and I'm still alive.' Then he said, 'I've reared four kids, and now with Marty I'm starting on another one.'

I had to attend Thai Buddhist purification ceremonies and report John's death to local police (lying about my part in it), and to the Chief of Police who turned out to be another friend of John's. It had to be reported to the local bureaucrats, to the Australian Embassy, to Thai Airlines. I was compelled to keep it out of the papers. The awful thing was flying back to Australia with Marty.

A wake for John in Carlton a month later was another nightmare. Everyone knew he had died of an OD, and my lies to minimise my complicity sounded suspicious. Why didn't you take him to hospital? they asked. Because I arrived too late, I countered. But you said you were there all night. No, I was in another room. Oh, they said, disbelieving. I felt the contempt of some of his close friends, such as writer Bill Garner, who refused to look at me he was so upset.

After John's death I kept right away from heroin. Marty was brought up by his grandparents in Shepparton. A lawyer friend of John's became Marty's guardian and looked after him when he came to Melbourne. I ran into him again after Dinny O'Hearn's funeral at Stewart's Hotel, almost a decade later. We were introduced by his guardian. Marty was in his late teens, tall and thin, sensitive and boyish with John's lanky frame and his mother's face. He could hardly remember Thailand or his father. He had vaguely heard of me, but was unable to recall anything much. Trauma had obliterated his past. He was sweet and friendly and trusting. We talked desultorily about his job as a trainee at a major bank. Unlike most people at Dinny's wake, he wore a dark suit. He stood out from the khaki and denim rebels in their forties smoking dope and carousing around him. Though polite and willing, Marty was not interested in their old left rhetoric or their seventies protest songs. I wondered if John had lived, would Marty have been working in a bank?

Sorry, Wrong Number

You could eat off this floor, and you probably will.
DIVINE, *LUST IN THE DUST*

Though the pagan in me resisted the belief that money is the root of all evil, my Buddhist sympathies suggested differently. Already it seemed my inheritance had been tainted with bad karma. After all, I had spent a week's 'Tozan' or purificatory chanting on the slopes of Mount Fuji which was then followed by the disaster at Chieng Mai. Was there a connection?

Soon I would be locked into the great karmic wheel of all affluent Sydneysiders: property. I was keen to purchase a brick bungalow at Dover Heights, an almost derelict deceased estate of two bedrooms built on a rock ledge perched four hundred feet above the ocean. I was interstate but had instructed Philip to buy the house at auction and he did, with great *sang froid*, capping any other bidder by instantly upping the price.

After several years of buzzy off-beat apartment living in Gotham City, the move to Dover Heights was unsettling. It is a very peculiar place, more like a crematorium than a suburb. It is treeless with elegant houses (many in P&O style) and fantastic views, but no people. Every Friday the unmistakable tang of e. coli wafted up from the treatment plant and outfall where Eastern Suburbs raw sewage was then macerated.

It was not just the smallness of the house which made me feel isolated. Soon I felt constrained by the claustro claws of suburban coupledom. Philip adored the place since he could do his artwork there, as did the cat, Puss; but I found myself spending time away from this suburban idyll in such sex-on-premises bars as Club 80, as well as various saunas. After a decade, our sex life had become perfunctory, but at least we had an 'arrangement' to have sex outside the relationship provided it was never discussed. Many gay couples prefer this situation, which gives an illusion of freedom, even though they may infrequently act on it. Except in rare circumstances, lifelong sexual fidelity is unnatural, idiotic and oppressive, especially for men. As Quentin Crisp once sagely remarked:

'Gay men are always making love to people they actually like, whereas real men are always making love to people they're thoroughly tired of.'

Phillip's taste in art was quite particular. He was quite a serious contemporary art buff who encouraged me to expand my collection. He devoured art magazines ferociously, from Parkett's to *Art in Australia*, though preferring *Flash Art* and *Art/Text*. I'd had a number of Keith Looby paintings for years, but I soon added two large paintings by my favourite artist, Juan Davila ('Ned Kelly' as well as 'Gulf ', a superb piece of homoerotica), and a huge, moody James Gleeson, 'At the Propitious Moment', from his Queensland landscape series. From Ros Oxley's contemporary galleries I also bought several Maria Kozics and some works by Robert Campbell Jr, a self-taught Aboriginal painter.

Around this time Westpac started flinging money at me – $200,000 in bank bills which I didn't really want, but which they insisted on. During the eighties banks acted like heroin dealers, giving everyone a free taste to get them hooked. So, one boozy and momentous afternoon, I went to Sotheby's in Melbourne and bought about sixty thousand dollars' worth of pictures, the most remarkable of which was Arthur Streeton's 'Three Boys Bathing' for $36,000. In an outrageously inflated market I bid for a Sidney Long and two gorgeous small pictures of Bourke Street, Darlinghurst, in the 1840s by colonial artist George Peacock. I really went to town, imagining I was an eighties entrepreneur, whose catchcry even Juan Davila had employed on canvas to satirise: 'I don't know much about art but I know what appreciates.'

When Philip and I picked up my new purchases from Sotheby's in Sydney, he was horrified that I had bought so many pictures he didn't like that he refused to help load up the Toyota. The two Peacocks were still on the roof of the van when we drove off. The two beautiful pictures worth ten thousand dollars each fell off somewhere in the gutters of Glenmore Road, Paddington. After an appeal through the *Sydney Morning Herald*, I got one of them back, but the other had been ground into the bitumen or, more likely, picked up and flogged to a shady 'secondary' dealer. These acts of hypomania and hubris were what the Alcoholics Anonymous texts call 'Big Shottism', as I discovered when I started reading them.

When the Taylor Square Clinic confirmed in 1983 my expectation that I had been infected with HIV, I was both shattered and gratified, since I thought it gave me licence to do whatever I liked. Many acts after that time were directly attributable to the 'eat, drink and be merry' response that being HIV-positive prompts in some people.

Philip and most of his friends categorically refused to be tested for HIV, fearing a government plot. They were wiser than they knew. Not getting tested meant not panicking, not being conned into taking the toxic array of deadly anti-virals which killed many positive men of their generation. In the case of HIV testing, ignorance truly is bliss, although there is a case for warding off PCP (the AIDS pneumonia) by taking Bactrim as a prophylaxis.

The wan excuse used by the AIDS Council of New South Wales and most HIV doctors, that testing helps predict the onset of AIDS-defining illnesses is simply untrue. T4-cell testing is notoriously volatile and unreliable, scores change hourly, and, most important, it cannot predict the only thing that matters with HIV-AIDS; that is, survivability.

My first antidote – not to the virus, but to this life of suburban strangulation – was a world trip, during which I stopped off in Hollywood and met my old school friend Barry Sloane. Barry, a fellow ex-Scotch Collegian, founded and presented the ABC's groovy pop show 'GTK' in the early seventies. He made many TV specials and finished up as Hector Crawford's representative on the west coast.

Dressed in black, sporting a slick moustache and a black turbo Saab, Barry had indeed found a niche in Lala Land. He had segued out of TV production and into real estate broking in the Hollywood Hills. Because of his gift of the gab and his knowledge of stars, he was doing extremely well.

I stayed with him in his apartment, which was once owned by William Randolph Hearst. It delighted him to pour scorn on the Australian film industry. His favourite saying was, 'Let them do the wanking, I'll do the banking.' Each week he picked up, dropped off or avoided Qantas planeloads of besuited Australian producers, directors and stars all bedazzled by Hollywood.

I joined him on a 'caravan' which involved ten shark-like brokers in their black Mercedes and BMWs investigating the properties in the LA multi-listing directory that had come on the market that week. It was through a 'caravan' that we happened upon my first Hollywood property, a triplex in an older suburb called Whitley Heights. This strange little enclave, designed in Mediterranean fashion, had once housed all the early silent screen stars of Tinseltown. We stared at Rudolph Valentino's house with its erect cupola, and marvelled over the former homes of Charlie Chaplin and Barbara La Marr (an early Hollywood junkie). We salivated over Jean Harlow's pink mansion and Gloria Swanson's beautiful Italian villa, where people like Somerset Maugham, Dame Judith Andersen, Ethel Barrymore and Greta Garbo had stayed. But Whitley Heights only lasted ten years until the talkies dawned; then, in the early thirties, all the stars suddenly upped and went westwards to Beverly Hills. This was an early manifestation of the first law of LA demographics (also known as 'White Flight'): whites always move to the west, even unto Malibu, to keep away from the blacks and Latinos.

Barry and I cased the triplex which had charming agave and other cacti in the gardens. No star had lived there, but to my eyes, bloated by the excesses of the Sydney property market, it seemed astonishingly cheap at $230,000. I told Barry I had the cash and bought it forthwith. I hired a landscape gardener from Mexico called Jesus Sanchez and his team of seven who re-did the whole terraced garden and laid terracotta tiles. I kept two of the tenants and used the third apartment as my foothold in Hollywood. Through the good landscaping of Jesus, I managed to sell the place for $400,000 on a rising market. This became the seed money for a deeper plunge into Hollywood's golden past.

One Tuesday morning Barry Sloane and I discovered that the amazing Barbara Stanwyck house, Villa Hillcrest, was for sale. Perched on the Whitley Heights plateau facing west, and with grounds tumbling down several hundred feet towards Highland Avenue, it overlooked the Hollywood Bowl. This mansion had three floors, twelve bedrooms, a swimming pool and a three-storey guesthouse attached. To my amazement the place was being offered for only $750,000; further, there was already a loan on it with the CALFED Bank which meant I could secure possession for a mere $135,000 (plus mortgage repayments of five thousand dollars US a month).

Bazza might have been my friend, but he was also a real estate broker and Siren-sang the praises of the deal. Although grand, Villa Hillcrest was quite dilapidated and required hundreds of thousands of dollars and many, many Jesuses to save it. I identified with this run-down house since I believed every year would be my last. I saw resurrecting the house of Stanwyck as a worthwhile mission. Naturally I didn't look at the fine print too closely when I signed the contract and assumed the loan. I went about rehiring Jesus and his bunch of young Mexicans and a series of tradesmen to renovate my new mansion.

Soon after a young aspiring French actor called Manuel de la Rochefoucald whom I had met in Sydney turned up in Los Angeles and I commenced a sporadic affair with him. Manuel was short, wiry, mentally alert and a fantasist of magnificent proportions. He was sure he was going to make it as a Hollywood star, although his talents on a couple of Australian television soaps had required his rapid, unintelligible spoken English to be dubbed over.

'It is nothing, mon cherie. When I am at the Lee Strasberg School of Dramatic Acting, they will teach me how to speak English slowly.' He was a shameless flatterer who lauded me for my few third-rate documentaries, saying, 'A great producer like yourself can have me as star in your first picture, yes?'

Manuel finally landed himself a tall, long-limbed straight-seeming sailor from Marseilles called Guy. Naively I made them caretakers of Villa Hillcrest before swanning off to meet Philip at the '89 Bicentennial Celebrations in Paris, where we had sub-let an apartment in Le Marais. Even more foolishly, I left a signed blank Bank of America cheque for Manuel to fill in to cover any contingencies. One morning Philip and I were lying in our Paris bed when I got a collect call from Hawaii. It was Manuel. I said in some amazement, 'Manuel, why are you in Hawaii?' He said, 'Guy has always wanted to see Honolulu.' Sadly the penny did not drop until I returned to LA and found out that the very day I wrote the open cheque to Manuel, he presented it to the Sunset Ogden Branch and withdrew sixteen thousand American dollars in one hit. More than irritated, I also found out that Manuel had forged my signature eight times, taking a total of $23,000.

On my return I confronted him and he sobbed, saying Guy had left him and that he had used the money to invest in his film career. I told him that the Bank of America had already been alerted to his forgeries, admitted negligence and repaid me the full sum (which was true). I said they had also placed Manuel on the US immigration black list which meant he could never return via any US port (this was untrue). On being told this, Manuel's brown eyes welled up with tears and he started shivering all over, saying his film career was finished. I agreed and took him down to LA International airport.

On the way, I told him he was being silly about a film career: he had not reached first base, which was making a porn video – the foundation upon which practically all great film careers are based. He then confided that he had tried to get in a porn video, having ventured with Guy out to 'the factory' in North Hollywood where gay porn movies were made by three old queens called the Three Stooges. Since Manuel was small and rabbit-like, the three queens showed no interest in him at all, even though he told them he had been trained at the Lee Strasberg school. 'We get ten a week,' one of them snapped. However, they showed interest in Guy and persuaded him to undress. When they saw the size of his *marchandise* swinging gently from one thigh to another, fully nine inches long, they fell about and offered him a script to start filming immediately. Manuel had already complained to me about the difficulties he was having accommodating Guy's schlong; it was almost tearing their relationship apart. Guy didn't mind being admired, but being a bisexual Frenchman, he did not want to act in a porn movie. So he got dressed again, gave a Gallic shrug and said he'd decided against a film career as he wanted to go home to his girlfriend in Marseilles.

As we waited at LAX's Air France terminal for Manuel to board, I said, 'Darling, you don't have to make it big in Hollywood. You are French, be proud of it. You must make it big in France and *then* you can go international like –' I scrambled for a name, 'Gerard Depardieu.' Manuel kissed me gratefully as he went to the plane. 'Ah yes,' he said, 'you are so right. I shall be Gerard Depardieu!'

It should not be thought the eighteen million people of Los Angeles are star-struck, 'in the industry', or have just finished the most brilliant script which Spielberg 'really liked'. Most Angelenos have totally mundane family lives doing normal American jobs and living in the two valleys or the huge conurbation around LA. The part I am talking about is Lala Land, of which Whitley Heights was the epicentre. Here between the Hollywood Hills and the Pacific live several million astroidal people who are either present stars, past stars, wannabes or dreamers, whose entire identity revolves around a career in film. Since most people who pull petrol have written several scripts – it goes without saying eighty per cent of the people of Lala Land have never made it and never will – but they still have stars in their eyes that no amount of rebuffs or lack of talent will extinguish.

Although not aligned to the industry I was part of Lala Land's never-ending search for glamour. Philip and I drenched ourselves in LA Style: we took in its palms, deserts, Santa Fe bars and freeways, along with the movies, the modern art and the fabulous LA people, so cool, so warm, so generous, and so divinely deluded.

In addition to being seen in new restaurants and at art openings on and off Melrose Avenue, I amassed a network of art-mad ex-New Yorkers through my friend Paul Taylor, the Melbourne-born art critic. The most appealing was Sean Caley, black-clad art writer and fan of Baudrillard who spoke fluent French and arrived in Hollywood at Paul's behest to rent out a room at Whitley Terrace.

Because Sean knew John Boscovitch and other avantgarde film people, she soon commenced a raging affair with performer Sandra Bernhard. Although Sandra is principally lesbian, Sean was really bisexual. She was star-fucking Sandra who didn't seem to mind. For one year they had assignations all over the states. They never made it at the Villa Hillcrest, always at Sandra's North Hollywood home. I came to adore Sandra's bitter-sweet humour and her accuracy in portraying the blue-collar badlands of American life. But Sean jilted Sandra and went off with a rich gallerist called Stuart Regan, who survived cancer and became the co-producer of the surprise hit movie Leaving Las Vegas. Sean had made it in Hollywood going through all the usual steps.

When Philip arrived from Australia he was impressed: the Villa Hillcrest was infinitely more palatial than anything he had ever lived in. I was unable to do large renovations without Philip and he proved a splendid companion. Together we searched most of Los Angeles for the essential accoutrements, even ransacking stonemasons' yards in El Monte to get sandstone banisters, finials and Greco Roman cupids for the garden. We were revamping the house in a major way and Jesus now had at least ten followers arriving every morning as he supervised a massive stone colonnade from the street to the lower floor to allow a grand Tara-style entrance to my new mansion. (The building of the balustrade went on for nine months and cost forty thousand dollars.)

The day I sold the house to Australian director Phil Noyce and his producer wife Jan Sharp in 1990, they decided they wanted a discreet entrance to the house and that the stone colonnade would have to go. When I told him about it, Jesus wept.

Jan, whom I had known for years in Australia, saw a Chinese herbalist to assess the Feng Shui of the house. He looked at its northerly aspect tumbling down the hill and assessed that it was really a funnel for large amounts of money. I had spent about $300,000 on it. But Noyce and Sharp spent much more, I suspect, proving the herbalist right.

It seemed appearances could often be deceptive at Villa Hillcrest. While Philip was painting his naive abstract canvases in the studio of the guesthouse, I was concocting more fleshly schemes. Although we still slept in a double bed in the master bedroom with the Hollywood sign waking us up every morning, our love life was on the skids. Lack of exercise, too much cocaine and the cheapness of American booze had us sozzling quarts of gin and vodka and packing on the kilograms. I had become repulsive to him and he only tolerated my advances out of memory. For me, sexual desire was always on the boil ever since I had given up writing.

A Southern scriptwriting friend, Beaty Reynolds, had told me about a strange gym called the Flex where everyone worked out naked, near Koreatown, just past the Paramount Studios at 5555 Melrose Avenue. When I first walked into this members-only club and saw five or six well-muscled men pumping weights totally nude, I knew that I would give up the Sports Connection in West Hollywood, where self-absorbed lycra-shorted twinks primped in front of mirrors.

At the unfashionable Flex, there were two pools dotted with scrawny paw-paw trees and peopled with naked queens idly eyeing others off, not looking for Mr Right but Mr Big! This whole gay Babylon was in full view, I feared at first, of cars coming off the Hollywood Freeway, US Highway 101, which went to San Francisco. But no motorists noticed the Flex; or if they did, they didn't care. That was one of the good things about living in Los Angeles: people hated to be thought uncool.

I got obsessed with a Native American with long squaw-like black hair from Canoga Park and later, with a blond mechanic called Skip who lived in Glendale with his boyfriend. We were all cheating on our boyfriends, that was what the Flex was about; it provided a cover.

I would tell Philip that I had hired a personal trainer, the ultimate Los Angeles cliché, and that we had to 'work out' every other day. Maybe he believed it at the start, but he must have noticed that my physique didn't improve after several months on this new athletic routine.

I put quite a lot more energy into picking up hustlers on Santa Monica Boulevard and taking them up to the chaparral near Mount Hollywood where we had scratchy sex. I became fond of one: Adrian from Santa Cruz, who was blond, curly-haired and flexible. Like all the boys on the Boulevard, he dreamed of being picked up by a rich queen who owned a house in Beverly Hills and a condo in Palm Springs. He also dreamed of being in a porn movie but I fear he lacked the *équipage*. I gained an extra frisson from these activities – much like a naughty boy hoodwinking mother – because if Philip discovered what was going on he would be seething with jealousy.

In order to have some space I sent Philip to Hawaii for a fortnight and hit the 'Dial A Man' phone circuit, which offered four rough categories: S&M, B&D, Vanilla and Tutti Frutti. It was easy to arrange meetings on the phone for three or four keen orgiasts who were prepared to drive from as far away as Laguna and Manhattan beaches. It is a testimony to human insanity that someone will get into a car and drive for an hour in expectation of sex with someone who has only heard your voice, but it happened daily. Frantic young men with pixilated eyes straight off the freeway walked into the lounge room saying, 'Hey, man, where's the orgy?'

Sometimes these young men were unattractive and there was no orgy for them, but other times they were suitable and threesomes or foursomes took place spontaneously. Adrian was often present, having proved himself an adept orgy master, capable of dismissing the undesirable with dispatch. One participant, in need of a breather, walked down through the secret passages of the house (which had once been a prohibition still) and came out in the garden by the swimming pool. He was naked but for his Reeboks and somehow tripped a floodlight, immediately throwing himself into Greco Roman relief. He was a statue that moved. This was noticed by both the straight neighbours and the LAPD helicopter which hovered overhead several nights a week. They thought the floodlit hustler had something to do with drugs. They radioed base and soon the house and garden were swarming with pistol-packing LAPD officers searching for illicit substances and bringing the orgy to an unscheduled end. Perhaps in some small way, I was reliving

Kenneth Anger's *Hollywood Babylon*. After all, Rudi's purple erect tower was barely a hundred feet away as the gin bottle flies. The accidie of my life, of which sex and booze were only a manifestation, was that I had ceased writing ever since I had left the *Bulletin*. Because I hated writing for Kerry Packer I stupidly thought I need never have to again.

IN WHICH A PAPER MILLIONAIRE LOSES ALMOST EVERYTHING

Maybe Philip was right to slander me for being so ruled by my lower chakras but the only means of breaking the cycle was to fall in love with someone else.

I met Tim Herbert in 1987 on one of my brief return visits to Sydney. He was to be my fifth and final partner. We met inside the smoky lounge of 'Writers In The Park' at the Harold Park Hotel for the launch of Denis Gallagher's seminal anthology of AIDS fiction, *Love and Death*. It was a mad night. Academic Dennis Altman was chasing writer Gary Dunne and Dunne was chasing the tall, angular ectomorphic Tim Herbert who, being a bit of a gerontophile, was chasing Gallagher. But Dennis himself was after some rough trade that wasn't responding. What a crazy whirligig of unrequited desires.

Tim was introduced to me by filmmaker Richard Turner. I was with Philip, whose lizard eyes missed nothing. So although I was attracted to Tim I was uptight and dismissive. Tim asked me about writing freelance for the *Bulletin* and I gruffly replied if he showed me some of his work I'd see what I could do. I gave him my phone number. A week later we lunched at the Bayswater Brasserie. Over dessert I loosened up and told him he had gorgeous eyelashes, whereupon he immediately asked me home to his digs in Glebe where he showed me some poetry and fucked me.

Then about twenty-seven, he was slender, tall and good-looking, and an aesthete, my favourite type. I liked his intelligence, his talk, his gossip. He was a son figure, a non-drinking me at thirty. I admired his ambition, the fact that unlike many young gay men, he was not addicted to the bar scene, no longer smoked and rarely took drugs. I particularly liked the fact that he was totally 'out'; I didn't want to spend a few years giving courage to a timorous closet. Although

HIV-negative, he was modern about AIDS. We both insisted on safe sex.

We saw each other sporadically thereafter; he, studying for his final-year English exams at Sydney University, and keeping me at a queenly distance while using my car on his endless movings. I was now hooked. I had been waiting for someone as brilliantly sexual as he, who was also literate and sensitive, qualities totally lacking in the boys on Santa Monica Boulevard.

Tim also wrote fiction. The first time he read me some, I was too inebriated to appreciate it. I remember it being about his obsession with his then boyfriend, a heavy-drinking storeman and packer named Jack who lived in Erskineville. The story told me what it felt like going back to Jack's place, virtually a double bed behind a door off a street. One night we went there together, drunk after the Midnight Shift, and attempted a threesome, but Jack was horrified by my obesity, my drunkenness, and the enterprise was a fiasco.

Tim became even more appealing when I met his working-class parents in Caringbah, his father a retired Streets' ice-cream truck driver and mechanic, and his mother Nancy, who adored her baby, youngest of five, born when she was forty-six. Despite my faults, Nancy seemed to give her blessing to our relationship.

But, as always, I had to Go Too Far. I rang Tim. I plied him with letters. I even sent him five thousand dollars as a douceur to persuade him to come to the Adelaide Festival with me. I had specified that he either use the cheque or tear it up and that I would not tolerate its return, so fearful was I of his rejection. Wisely he took the money, but declined the trip. My ardour was making him back off. By the end of 1989 my determination to be with Tim had reached new levels of deception.

Telling Philip I was going to Europe to research another film documentary, I had a rendezvous with Tim who had headed for Spain after resigning from a successful one-year editorship of *Campaign*. Through a series of coded telegrams, we met in Barcelona, fittingly at five in the afternoon – *a las cinco de la tarde* – in a hotel off the Ramblas. We were to travel together on the Garcia Lorca Express to Granada. I was thrilled at this seeming honeymoon but I must say Tim had deep reservations about being escorted by a bombastic, boozy old poof wearing a battered Issey Miyake suit studded with cigarette holes.

The suit was made of parachute material though it looked as if I were wrapped in seaweed, or Japanese kelp. Much like my white ice-cream suit worn in New York, I thought it was the height of fashion, but I was alone in this judgement. My eccentricities included carrying around a one kilogram jar of Vegemite in order to combat the vitamin B-draining effects of my alcoholism, and knobs of raw garlic which I ate at every meal, much to Tim's horror.

We visited the birthplace of Lorca and noted the horrendous male/female strictures of Spanish Catholicism that later tortured the poet before Franco's men shot him. At his birthplace, Lorca's homoerotic interests flourished early. On his family shrine was a photograph of a nude Christ which the women in the family covered with a grass skirt. Amidst the glories of Moorish Spain, I found the rediscovery of mutual passion more inspiring than the Alhambra and the Cordoba Mosque. For Tim and me sex was often fervently theatrical. This was an experience unknown since the early days of Philip a decade before. We entered into some light S&M

scenes undoubtedly responding to the great Spanish Inquisition tradition. In fact we watched a holy parade in Seville, where pious ladies donned black mantillas to rub shoulders with the odd Spanish transvestite. Down it came, the Virgin bedecked in white and gold, carried forth by penitents on a candle-studded bier. We both thought the Virgin was the dead spit of Doris Fish leading the Mardi Gras parade.

But things were by no means hunky dory. As we went from the Pousadas of Spain to the Paradors of Portugal, it was obvious to Tim that I had not overcome my taste for drink, as I was picking at food and waiting for the fortified wines at the end. Occasional phone calls to Philip were rather strangled dealings since he now no longer believed my cover story and suspected that Another Woman was on the scene. After a particularly spectacular S&M tableau in a Parador in the town of Setubal I sped back through the ridiculous Queen Anne architecture of Lisbon to catch a plane to Los Angeles.

I finally decided to come clean with Philip, telling him what he already suspected. He was upset at the thought of losing me and the security I represented. Philip thought I had gone mad and that the drink and coke had finally overtaken a person he always regarded as a spoiled brat. Always tyrannical in his affections, he was astounded by my interest in the tall lantern-jawed Tim, whom he dragtagged 'Morticia'.

But I was determined to end the relationship with Philip. I had not written a book in the fifteen years I had known him and indeed had ceased writing altogether. Naturally one should not play the blame game with one's boyfriend, but his art too was hardly flourishing; something was wrong between us.

It took almost two years to disconnect from our 'marriage', but during the interim, other troubles were looming. When the post-87 crash credit boom ran out, Westpac Bank started to move on me. Owing more than a million on two heavily mortgaged houses in two countries (Oz and US), with no income apart from share trading, I was a broken bronco from the eighties, just one more of the many non-performing loans on that particular bank's books. Every day time was running out; I'd become a brontosaurus, history overtaking me. Having sold Villa Hillcrest at a modest profit, we returned to Dover Heights which the bank also forced me to sell.

The last six weeks at Dover Heights were a haunting

and horrible time for both of us. A little cravenly perhaps, I had kept the sale of the house from Philip for some weeks during which time he gave me an ultimatum that I must decide between him and Tim, otherwise I had to leave the double bed. I did, and slept on the floor. On the day I went to Double Bay to sign the contract of sale on the house, I found myself breaking down in a fit of weeping in the Cosmo coffee shop. I was mourning the loss of the love that Philip and I had shared; the comfort, the intelligence of it, our social élan and the delight of our daily dialogue on the human comedy.

But self-pity was also one of Philip's finest modes. He said, 'At least you can fall into someone's arms, I've got no one.' I was accused of taking him at twenty and dropping him nearly two decades later without a career and having lost his looks. During these lachrymose times I swore to give up Tim and said nothing should destroy our long relationship.

Because I tried to make up financially what I couldn't give emotionally, perhaps I had crippled Philip into dependency. Surely there was also a degree of contempt towards his benefactor, who had set him up in such a cocoon of material comfort.

Philip was furious when he found out about the sale of the house. After hurling a seven-pronged candelabra across the dining room at me (his aim deliberately askew), he banished me from Dover Heights saying in Garboesque tones, 'I want to be alone.'

I looked at renting a studio apartment in Forbes Street, Woolloomooloo, in a converted warehouse directly opposite Harry M. Miller's terrace but also extremely close to the Matthew Talbot Hostel. Harry had been unable to sell his house for years for that reason, and a juicy irony occurred while I was in the neighbourhood. When in Hollywood I had let out part of the Barbara Stanwyck guesthouse to Harry's son Simon, and Simon's American girlfriend. While I was in Paris I had offered Harry and his consort Deborah Hutton the master bedroom at Villa Hillcrest for a week, which they loved, and for which he repaid me with a copy of his autobiography. When Philip and I got back to Sydney, Harry and Deborah gave us a barbecue.

On the same afternoon as my apartment inspection, I was certainly not looking my best when I caught sight of Harry. I had just emerged from Nick's corner grog store carrying a bottle of $4.99 Kilkenny Cream. I shouted, 'Hello, Harry,' as I walked to my car. He stared at me, said, 'Ow are yer, mate,' turned around and literally ran all the way home. I guess he thought I was a derro about to mug him. Slowly all my delusions were being peeled away.

The flat in the 'Loo was not available for another fortnight and because I had been cast out of home I needed to find a hotel fast. I went from Jehovah Heights with its empty windswept streets, its treeless nature strips and the Hassidic cleanliness of the houses, into the Pelikan Hotel, in the heart of deepest Darlinghurst.

It may have been an atrocious come-down, but at least it was real. Miles away from a suburban lawn or a rotary clothes line, unsavoury and threadbare, it was a gay hotel. Since it advertised in the international gay press, it was crowded with male couples from Richmond, Virginia, or Manchester, England. Leather boys and their cockney daddies and southern belles in Hawaiian shirts crowded in for breakfast in the semitropical backyard twittering with caged lorikeets and studded with Bangalow palms. For something only fifty feet from Taylor

Square, the hotel's back yard was an oasis, but the building, managed by an acerbic old queen with a black toupee, was tagged 'cockroach towers'. The place stank of rectal mucus, amyl nitrite and moxa smoke from the acupuncturist operating from a front room.

To finish up with a thump in this dump signified the end of the good life. Antibody positive, I was now a negative millionaire, an heiress with plenty of nothing. We may protest like hell at the time, but in the end we are always grateful to be awakened from the bonds of illusion. To be disillusioned is ultimately a relief.

For Philip, coming to terms with the reality of loss would take more time. In May 1991 I had arranged to take him to the auction of the Dover Heights house. In the car he was relentless in demolishing Tim Herbert. He claimed that my attractiveness to people like Tim was based on the fact that we were a couple, glamorous, and unattainable to a 'Potts Point secretary girl sitting there waiting to trap a married man'. Though courageous and gifted, Philip was a terrible snob such as only an artistic queen can be. He always claimed that our marriage was special and that being in a relationship made me a good catch. According to Philip, now that I was leaving him I had been diminished, a fairly self-serving thesis, but at the time we were both distraught, clinically insane. We fought like tomcats in the car and I insisted he get out at Taylor Square.

The auction at Dover Heights went through without a hitch. Our clever renovations including the conversion of the garage into a bedroom/study with a sea window meant the bidding for the brick dump which had been bought for $235,000 five years before ended at $470,000. Sadly there was little real profit gained as most of the money went to both bank and taxman. The buyers were copyright barrister David Catterns and Sarah Ducker, whose relationship later broke up in the jinxed house. David moved out while Sarah moved in her lover, the writer Frank Moorhouse, whose writing studio is the garage we improved. Moorhouse tells me occasionally a strong gusty wind still blows up envelopes from the cliff with my name on them.

EVINRUDE

Belligerent Old Bugger

One must work, if not from inclination at least from despair, since, as I have fully proved, to work is less wearisome than to amuse oneself.

BAUDELAIRE, *INTIMATE JOURNALS*

It doesn't take a Buddhist sage to realise that an endless round of consumption and spending perfectly exemplifies the law of diminishing returns. By the early nineties, I was buried materially and spiritually in a black hole: without property or income, I had terminated with Philip and was going to intermittent AA meetings all over Sydney. Year Zero for me was 1991, as it was for most of Australia. During the previous decade I had flouted the trifecta of activities that is supposed to make for human happiness: love, work, money. My love had been hollow, my work nada, and my money was gone.

Earning a living was the only way to survive the mortgaged fairyland which had almost bankrupted me. The new decade had already offered an opportunity when Mandarin Australia decided to bring out a paperback reprint of my Bolte biography.

There was a rumble of media at the Imperial Hotel in Melbourne, as federal Opposition Leader Andrew Peacock launched the book. It was the middle of the election campaign which the Liberal Party had a strong chance of winning.

My brother Clive and his family were at the launch as well as Doone, who was having one of her more daffy days. Later we had a gathering of the clan down at Heronswood, Clive's mansion at Dromana where my niece Tessa at one stage complained vociferously, 'Why do the Blazeys always talk about money?' I was certainly keen to avoid any discussion of my own dire financial situation and I was grateful to Doone for taking the limelight.

On this afternoon, Doone contributed to conversation with a patter of middle-class niceties. But before too long the phrasebook went haywire, imploding with hilarious results. Sister-in-law Penny Blazey was discussing the recent funeral of her mother Pat and how Pat had always stated a preference for cremation over burial. 'Oh yes,' chimed in Doone, the widow of eight years, smiling smoothly, 'cremation's best. Alan was cremated and he loved it.'

A week later, in order to finalise the sale of Villa

Hillcrest, I left for Hollywood. I had let my publishers down by not promoting the Bolte paperback – it sold only 1500 copies and disappeared with the demise of the Liberals yet again. Tim, then living in Melbourne, was by this time well aware of my working history and on the phone sounded exasperated by my destructive impulses. 'I've always been more interested in love than power,' I countered, somewhat pompously.

While no longer owning houses in Los Angeles or Sydney, I still possessed a fibro cabin on the Hawkesbury River. I took Tim up there the day after Philip left for six months in south India, which happened to be Bastille Day. Tim was ecstatic about my bush hideaway with its six hectares of grass trees, casuarinas and angophoras accessible only by boat. It was also a bird sanctuary, bristling with king parrots, rosellas and, rarest of all, the glossy black cockatoo, a shy and discriminating bird (it only feeds on casuarina nuts) which Tim immediately adopted as his totem. Mine had always been the laughing kookaburra and I had even named the shack 'Kooka Lodge'.

Back in the city, however, things were not so edenic. Often when Tim came around to my flat in Woolloomooloo, we'd have a fight over my slovenly domestic habits. He said the place stank like a Bangkok *klong* from the huge, nine feet high Gymea lily rotting in its vase. He was also covered in bites from the fleas left behind by the previous owner's dog. It looked as if we could never live together unless I became a clean queen like him and not surprisingly he opted to remain sharing an Elizabeth Bay apartment with his best friend Kirstie, the beauty editor of *Vogue*.

More than four years after meeting Tim it was in this apartment that I finally broached the issue of my HIV status. The mystery and the horror of AIDS is that it affects one in the second chakra which is the seat of heart, family and love. So it enters the very centre of human existence. Countless people have been thrown out of home when they disclose their condition while many relationships have been terminated. Like most gay men, we had been practising safe sex and though I knew he was negative he had never asked me about my antibody status.

On this afternoon, I asked him for a shot of vodka from the bottle he always kept in the freezer. 'What do you want to tell me?' he asked. I nervously scanned the view across Rushcutters Bay before I replied, 'I've got some bad news. I took the test and I'm HIV-positive.' I felt a little fraudulent when he held me to him and said, 'Oh well, I suspected it anyway,' allaying my fears of rejection. Tim's immediate acceptance of what is now called a sero-discordant relation – ship cemented our love. It is a mark of AIDS hysteria that in those days such a relationship was rare.

Breaking the denial about my being HIV was a kind of second coming out. No more the blasé, cavalier attitude, the grasshopper singing his way through an endless summer. I cut down on the booze and began attending aerobics classes at the gym, while every day swimming laps at Boy Charlton pool. As I acknowledged the virus in my body I could sense a mental re-ordering akin to a mid-life crisis. Soon my addictions, from alcohol to amyl, cigarettes to sex, began to dissipate.

Liberation from my writer's block came with the submission of copy to the gay press. Tim had written several pieces over the years which had been published in *OutRage* magazine. He put me in touch with assistant editor Steven Carter, whose enthusiasm for my writing led to the establishment of my monthly column 'Out & Out', now in its sixth year.

With the help of my new agent Lyn Tranter, whom I had run into at one of Dick Hall's rowdy literary lunches, I soon began writing again for the mainstream media. An article, 'In Praise of Outing', which was rejected as too provocative by both *OutRage* and the *Australian* but finally picked up by the *Sydney Morning Herald* and Melbourne's *Sunday Age*, caused a mini storm. It argued that outing was a crude tactic for a brutal era but an effective weapon in breaking the homophobic silence that has pervaded society since the advent of AIDS. The catchcry defence of an individual's 'right to privacy' was regarded by me as nothing more than an apology for the closet, 'a pathological and schizoid condition . . . these days more dangerous than ever because furtive shame-filled encounters encourage unsafe sex, which does kill.' The hostility directed at me as a result of this piece, especially in gay circles, gave me my first taste of the missionary zeal in challenging group-think views about HIV/AIDS which would eventually become an obsession.

But initially, when it came to medically dealing with the virus, I adopted the party line. When my T-cells dipped below 350 in October 1991, my doctor,

Robert Finlayson, suggested I seriously consider taking AZT. This DNA chain terminator was designed for the treatment of leukaemia twenty years before but had since been discredited. In the desperate hunt for the magic bullet to eliminate AIDS, science was soon singing its praises again. Though it does attack HIV-infected lymphocytes in the body, AZT cannot distinguish between infected cells (about one in 1,000) and uninfected cells. Such a ruthless assault on the body can induce side effects more debilitating than having an AIDS-related disease.

While AZT had been shown to extend the lives of those in late-stage AIDS, a hectoring campaign had now begun to convince gay men who had HIV yet appeared healthy and asymptomatic also to take high doses of this anti-viral drug. AIDS councils throughout the country were soon launching their 'early intervention' and 'hit hard and hit early' PR campaigns which were funded in part by drug conglomerate Burroughs-Wellcome, the makers of AZT. The national health system was co-opted into this program at a cost of some $10,000 per patient per year.

I knew Paul Taylor had been taking AZT for

some time and I rang him in New York. While acknowledging that side effects such as lethargy and peripheral neuropathy could be a drag, Paul was adamant that his sense of wellbeing was on the improve. Tim was not convinced. He reminded me that the pro-AZT flyer put out by the Australian Federation of AIDS Organisations had been written by Dr Peter Steinheur, a friend and former housemate with an aversion to any holistic approach to the virus and who had recently died from AIDS-related lymphoma.

According to the AIDS Council dogma of the period, taking AZT was a means of making AIDS a manageable condition. Dr Finlayson reckoned it was akin to being a diabetic, shooting up insulin for the rest of your life. I agreed to try it out even though I was aware that popping another blue and white capsule every few hours was a constant reminder of one's precarious condition and a form of 'bone-pointing'.

It took a few weeks for the side effects to start hitting home. The draining insomnia, the pins and needles, the savage migraines with weird blue flashes. There was also the claw-like band of pain, a sort of 'ping' in the bloodstream behind the eyes as if someone had cast a fly on a glass calm pond. A black splash – but below the water – dragging you down, reminding you of death; the fly fisherman who ultimately lures us all, even those as fit as a trout. I took AZT for six months at 1000 milligrams a day. After all, every other smart queen I knew with the virus was doing the same.

JUST ANOTHER NIGHT IN LA

In April of 1992 there were some paintings and other paraphernalia to be cleared from Villa Hillcrest. I arrived back in Hollywood on the eve of the LA riots.

This was the fateful Friday when the cops freaked out with fear and were paralysed by guilt over the acquittal of those police linked to the bashing of Rodney King. They were nowhere to be seen when South Central Los Angeles exploded with around 1200 fires. Many thought that this Day of the Locust town was finally imitating Art – a bad disaster movie or maybe the deep cynicism of film noir, that uniquely LA screen invention.

I was staying in a basement apartment at the Magic Hotel in Hollywood. This proved to be extremely unnerving as according to the mapping out of the mayhem on my TV screen, the rioters were torching buildings only two blocks away. But I poured a whisky, tried to phone Tim in Sydney and began writing perhaps my best column for *OutRage*.

Suspecting the media were sensationalising things, I also refused to miss my dinner invitation at Villa Hillcrest from its new owners, Jan Sharp and Phil Noyce. Up on the Hollywood Hills we watched Koreatown and other parts of the city erupt. To see such a spectacle of arson, shootings and looting was more than Phil could stand and he wanted to drive down Western Avenue immediately to become part of the action.

By the following night there were reports that fifty people had been killed, leaving the National Guard to take over and impose a curfew – California's first ever. I went down to West Hollywood with my friend David Hay to the main gay disco, Mickey's, and watched in amazement as the queens negotiated a new set of conditions. The curfew meant that everyone was supposed to be home by seven-thirty so they were feverishly dancing the last hour which reminded me of Australia's old six o'clock closing. There was one hour to get pissed or in this case to get laid. In jampacked Mickey's I danced with Mark, a thin and phony New York clone. He was witty about his HIV status which he discovered in 1987, the year he left New York: 'I've tried everything. I've tried AZT, I've tried macrobiotics and even the Course of Miracles. It's the full LA story. But now I'm back into my old habits. I reckon there's something about alcohol and marijuana which knocks the virus out of the stadium,' he said. This was reassuring news. Not wishing to alert US customs goons (HIV-positive aliens were not allowed in America), I had left my AZT behind in Sydney.

We looked around the dance floor and saw a sea of Tom Cruise wannabes, twenty-five-year-old airheads with fabulous teeth who would never make it because they didn't realise they were too faggy. Hollywood had ironclad rules as to who it picks up in the age of AIDS and Outings, and when they finally realised it would be too late – they would be over thirty. Mark and I found these gorgeous young men looking right through us. We felt like two leathery old buzzards in a cage of tropical parrots.

Interestingly here in Boystown there were no armoured personnel carriers and no National Guards though they were crawling all over Hollywood and Koreatown. Did the generals think the queens would be docile, or did they think their boys would get either raped or AIDS? Perhaps this was another example of containment, precisely the thing the blacks were rioting against.

I suppose that whites had subliminally known for years that the black hole of South Central – its poverty and despair – was both a moral outrage and a powder keg. After the National Guard, the army was brought in and the riots were quelled. Beneath the hype, the myopia of whites would ensure that serious reconciliation will never happen. I said farewell to Phil and Jan, farewell to the Villa Hillcrest and breathed considerable relief as my Qantas plane flew over the burnt-out city.

A DADDY AND A BOY OF LETTERS

I came home with a beard and a new role as a 'Daddy'. The cult of the bear was gaining ground in

California, a means for hirsute, chubbier, older gay men to regain some sexual attention in a vacuous world of streamlined twinks. Tim was initially not too keen on being called 'Boy' as he had always been elf to my goblin, but he was amused by the camp perversity of such role playing.

A loving relationship between two writers is doomed if rivalry creeps into the equation. Tim had enough flexibility to make our working bond a success and he encouraged my writing as much I did his. His short story collection *Angel Tails* was launched at the Melbourne Writers' Festival by Dennis Altman in September 1992. Later, outside the Malthouse, impossibly packed with middle-aged ladies eating alfalfa and turkey sandwiches, I ran into a former girlfriend in Hilary McPhee and was entranced by her opening words which were, 'I loathe these events.' Of course as commissioning editor for Pan Macmillan she simply had to be there.

Out of this meeting came a contract to write a satirical work about the Victorian Premier, Jeffrey Kennett. *The Secret Diary of Jeffrey Kennett (aged 45 1/4)* was modelled on the Adrian Mole diaries and was completed over the summer at Whimsy.

My long-term friend David Wilson was furious when he heard about the book. David's wife, Tania Price, was then Kennett's press secretary, and David claimed I was being set up as a kind of swinging Liberal Trojan horse. Hilary's husband, Don Watson, was Paul Keating's speechwriter and desperate to besmirch the Kennett government as well as the imminent federal campaign of Liberal Leader John Hewson. David's tribal Carlton instincts might have been right but the end result was quite different. A peculiar phenomenon was that hardline ALP voters hated the book, feeling that it was affectionate in tone and humanised Kennett as a clumsy and endearing buffoon.

The paperback was a hit (almost ten thousand copies sold), albeit mostly confined to Victoria, where bumper stickers declaring 'I've had a Kennett of a Day' were a marketing coup for the publisher. Predictably, David Wilson rubbished the book in his review in Melbourne's Sunday *Herald Sun*. Another critic in the *Australian* considered the 'secret diary' the first postmodern political satire in the country and later made it one of her books of the year.

A savage review can sometimes work to one's

advantage. This was the case with my next literary project, *Love Cries*, an anthology of sexual transgression which I co-edited with Tim and Victoria Dawson. 'A vile book for mean and pitiful people' screamed the prurient headline in the *Sydney Morning Herald.* Soon this collection of 'cruel passions' and 'strange desires' was rocketing up the bestseller list. Tim had drafted up the concept for *Love Cries* in 1990 though it took five years and a string of publisher rejections before this explicitly erotic anthology was finally picked up by HarperCollins. It's partly true that the success of *Love Cries* inaugurated the grunge lit. mode in Australian fiction.

It was launched on Australia Day 1995 at the State Library as part of the Sydney Writers' Festival. There was a panel discussion presided by Linda Jaivin (alias Mistress Linda) with her six-foot slave on a leash and constrained in a rubber suit. Later, MC the Monsignor Porca Madonna appealed to the virtues of 'mortification of the flesh' before playing *Volare* on his piano accordion as more than two hundred people sang along. The hilarity was so infectious I was nearly out of my tree.

Love Cries may have been worth the wait but I was saddened that Paul Taylor had not been well enough to complete the promised introduction to the anthology. Paul had been moved by his family from New York after inoperable lymphoma had set in. I adored Paul and had not seen him since America. I had heard that he had shaved his head completely for chemotherapy and had bravely gone in this state to a Biennale in Germany six months previously. His chutzpah in Manhattan had been unbeatable – gate-crashing openings, approaching people like Madonna and Warhol, writing acidly about Sylvester Stallone's art collection for *Vanity Fair* – he was always brutally frank. Mercurial and witty, his most accomplished talent was in bringing disparate people together and his greatest legacy, the magazine *Art/Text*, remains influential.

When I first heard that Paul was dying in 1992, I was in Melbourne where I frantically rang the home of his mother, Pat Bartels. I found out later that Pat and Paul's other siblings were engaged in a bedside vigil at the hospital. After his death, Paul Foss told me he spent an afternoon ringing Blazeys in the Melbourne telephone book and he may well have spoken to Doone who, by this stage, could have said to me: 'Oh, so and so rang, I can't remember his name. It doesn't matter, does it?'

I felt a nagging sense of guilt and avoided Paul's funeral. On a typical Melbourne early spring day of Baltic winds and hail, Tim and I drove north to the desert country of the Pink Lakes in Victoria's north-western corner. It was a relief to be back in the sunshine of the mallee for this is an arid and starkly beautiful country of spinifex and salt paperbarks, of lonesome Murray Pines and mallee tea-trees with huge boles like baobabs to retain maximum water. The lakes themselves glow a bright pink because of the beta-carotene in the water's plankton. This discolours your fingers and stains the cotton fireweed around the rim of the lake, the lips of which are also whitened with dried salt. Flashing through the sky were mulga and blue-winged parrots, along with the odd rapid transit cloud of fiery finches. On the sand dunes surrounding the lake, some of them fifty feet high, it was easy to get lost.

What a strange and crystalline landscape this was. Hard and reflective for the eye, although not for the other senses. It is country of tough surfaces; of the ego, the linear, masculine mind – not the id nor any sense of interiority. European explorers were so arrogant in similar places by not digging for yams or grubs or edible vegetation. Only 'savages' knew how to live in this country they thought smugly, as they died of starvation.

At the lake, a most moving spectacle presented itself to us. There was the sun-scorched and salt-dried skeleton of an emu standing half-upright beside the shore. It had wandered in too far in a drought season so that its great clawed feet had left it stricken in the clotted mud. I looked at this and thought of Paul Taylor and began to cry. Such a gruesome emblem of death had me depressed and brooding on my own fate, wondering if there was any point in resisting.

OF YIN AND YANG, VIM AND VITRIOL

On returning to Sydney I took an Eastern and more holistic direction. Acupuncture, shiatsu and Chinese herbs were the first stage in boosting my immune system. The disposal of the rest of my AZT pills down the toilet seemed like a sensible move after the results of the Concorde trial in early 1993. This

Anglo–French study of some 1700 volunteers, some on the drug, the rest on placebo, found that treating asymptomatic HIV patients with AZT did not delay the development of AIDS during a three-year period of observation. As Burroughs-Wellcome shares plummeted, the spin doctors of the AIDS orthodoxy went into damage control.

Of course alternative therapies can have their own complications, bitter melon retention enemas being a case in point. For this I required an elongated knobbly green Chinese vegetable also known as koo gwa which was mooted to contain anti-viral properties with no toxicity. The word spreads fast in HIV land and supply could never match demand as desperate queens invaded Chinatown. I stocked up with each new arrival of this ugly cucumber which I thrust in a blender to produce a dayglo green goo. Next I filled a hot water bottle, connecting it to my rectum via a long rubber hose before lying in the bath like an odalisque for half an hour.

Though my enthusiasm for koo gwa waned quickly there was always another immune-boosting product to latch onto. I soon became an acolyte of Madam Liu, an all-purpose healer from Beijing who believed she could 'cure' AIDS. She twisted acupuncture needles, as thick as the bolts in Frankenstein's neck, into my chest, insisting that the flow of 'chi' was sluggish because of my weak lungs. She gave me an apron of potent herbs to pin about my waist and had me recruiting Tim first thing in the morning to point smouldering moxa sticks close to my belly, which sometimes scorched the skin. I was told never to drink cold water and to always wear socks at night, for staying warm burns out the 'gene' of HIV according to Madam Liu. The stove in my apartment was constantly hissing with saucepans of boiling red dates, black fungus and ginseng which soon had me farting like an old tractor.

My favourite of all these nostrums was dinitrochlorobenzene or DNCB, a solution normally applied in photographic darkrooms but which was now dabbed onto human skin. DNCB allegedly stimulates suppressor (CD8) T-cells and had some excellent trial results in the US, where those taking it remained healthy and never progressed to AIDS. I promoted its use in my new column 'Don't Treat Me This Way' in the gay newspaper *Capital Q* as well as having it discussed at a number of meetings at the

AIDS Council. Apart from it smelling a lot like amyl nitrite, DNCB's most brilliant quality was how little it cost and I arranged for it to be sold at Sharpe's Pharmacy at Taylor Square.

DNCB became the rage, but the AIDS priesthood was not impressed. Something so simple and inexpensive could make them irrelevant. The female head of the NSW Venereological Society wrote to the Department of Health, complaining that this 'unscientific' treatment had caused severe burns and further it was an S4 poison which should be administered by a doctor's prescription.

Extreme anxiety and vindictiveness had crept into both sides of the AIDS debate. I wrote vicious letters to the gay press. I said that eating Ratsak would confer the same benefits as AZT, which was being advocated yet again. In response I was classified as an 'angry AIDS victim', a person with possible HIV dementia, while a crony within the AIDS Council debunked me for having 'no qualifications'. I wrote back declaring 'the days of the omnipotent, omniscient Doctor went out with Aeroplane jelly, Oslo lunches and the tooth fairy'. I also blew the cover on qualifications at ACON – the chief executive officer trained as a librarian and the chief treatments officer was formerly a waiter!

I co-founded the activist group HEAL with two other long-term survivors, Stuart Bennett and Peter Jarrett. HEAL sought a more complementary approach to orthodox AIDS treatments including naturopathic remedies and even stressing a spiritual dimension in recovering from illness. Sadly, HEAL was not immune from conflicts of ego and disbanded after Stuart Bennett seriously questioned whether the HIV virus even existed.

It is hard to measure the real benefits gained from the many alternative treatments which I tried, though it did give me the advantage of rejecting the passivity involved in eating handfuls of cytotoxic pills. This psychic rejection of the HIV = Death voodoo, a central plank of the pharmaceutical/medical belief system, must be rejected if one is to survive being HIV-positive.

My T-cell scores may have been declining but I felt vibrant with health. Some of my straight friends seemed astounded that I was looking my best in years, as if somehow I should have been a walking cadaver. My former partner Philip took a different tack and railed at me over the phone: 'Everyone's getting a bit sick of the number of cures you've found to HIV. Why don't you just back off and shut up. It's obvious that you've got a benign form and you're not going to get AIDS.' I was thrilled by his verdict and felt even more invincible and messianic.

Towards the end of 1994 I had arranged to meet Rosemary Foot at an opulent dinner and fundraiser for the AIDS Trust but decided to visit the Taylor Square Clinic on the way. Dr John Byrne looked at the small, raised purplish lumps on my right arm and confirmed that this was my first opportunistic infection – Kaposi's sarcoma. I was coldly accepting, almost relieved to be a fully-fledged person with AIDS. At last the phony war was over.

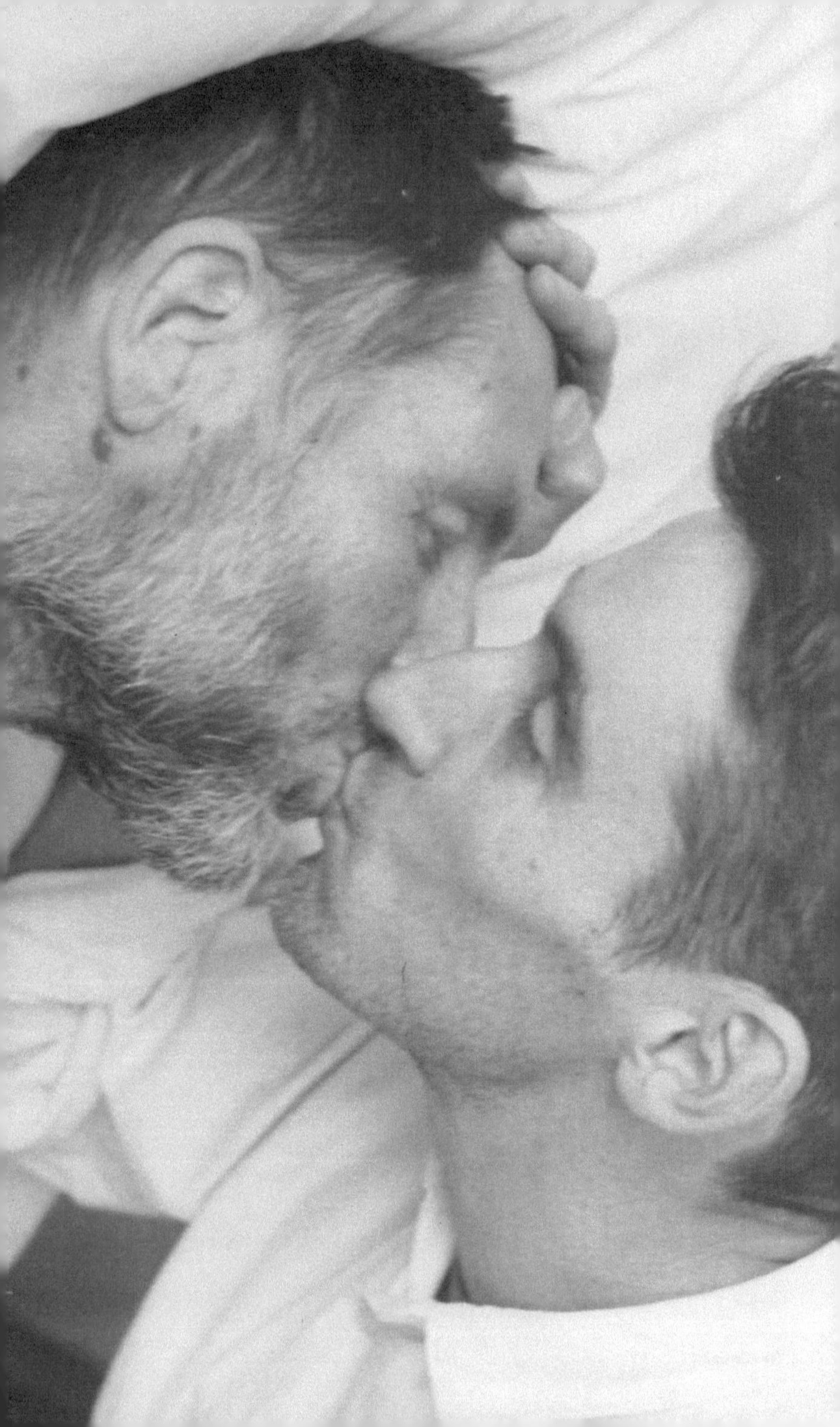

The Last Hurrah

It is a characteristic feature of the history of healing that people often prefer a cure that kills to no cure at all.
THOMAS SZASZ, *THE THERAPEUTIC STATE*

Sunday, 21 April 1996
Have just had my whole lemon drink and I feel terrific. I always do when I drink this thing. My whole body sparkles, whereas before it was heavy-laden. I was panicking about the Kaposi's sarcoma lesion I have discovered on the roof of my mouth. It's like a raised bubble and when I showed it to Tim he said yes it was purple and it was a big problem. It's the first time I've had KS inside me, having been a cosmetic thing until now. External KS was the reason why I qualified as AIDS Category 4 and have been on the DSS pension ever since May 1995. What a relief financially. Tim is worried about me getting sick. But I'll be able to survive the next six months for the completion of *Screw Loose*. We're very happy. It's like an unending honeymoon. Must be good for my T-cells.

Saturday, 13 July

The horrors have continued. Relentless diarrhoea, no appetite, soaking night sweats have me going through four or five T-shirts until morning – but things have abated. On Thursday I got a nasty fright as I crossed Macleay Street, having had an acupressure massage by David Petersen around my neck to 'open up the lungs' – as I crossed the street I spat phlegm and it was red. Bright, arterial blood. Arranged to see Dr John Byrne at eight next morning, got a chest X-ray and found I was A-OK: no PCP, no flu, nothing much. Greatly relieved, I went home and lay down beside the fire listening to Handel.

Tuesday, 30 July

Had an all-day blood transfusion at St Vincent's. Three packs of blood. I certainly feel stronger and more normal. I was anaemic. Was this due to the AZT I had stupidly taken all those years before (anaemia is one of the many side effects of AZT), or was it, as claimed, an 'HIV anaemia' – an inevitable progression of the disease? The explanation I prefer is the rather more romantic 'stress from the book'. It is certainly true that during the last two months I got an efflorescence of about ten Kaposi's sarcomas on my chest and neck which are still there – literary stigmata, no less.

Tuesday, 13 August

Yesterday I went to the launch of *Keating: the Inside Story* by John Edwards, huge gala event, K's first TV appearance since 2 March. All the mafia was there. Paul Kelly talking to Neville Wran and Jill Hickson. Many others. K began his speech. He's now so modest and humble! Suddenly I began swaying, I felt faint. I knew if I stayed there one minute more I would crash to the floor, so I turned turtle and walked unsteadily out. I think Hilary kissed me. Andrew Clark saw me, helped me down the steps and got a taxi for me to my car. Suddenly it was all right. Was it the one drink of white wine I had, which I haven't dared tell Tim about, or was it simply lack of oxygen?

Friday, 13 September

I've tried everything to beat these night sweats – WHO Oral rehydration solution (salt, bicarb soda, potassium and glucose) which they use in the Rwandan refugee camps, five cups of sage tea a day, sleeping in the afternoon – but still wake up drenched. Have a terror of even going to bed. Dr Mark Robertson gave me some steroids to boost my appetite and convinced me to go over to the other side and try out protease inhibitors. As I said to him, I might have to eat humble pie. He laughed and said make sure you have plenty of salt with it. There's three vicious letters in the *SSO [Sydney Star Observer]* attacking me: Get a life, Blazey! How dare you, Blazey! Who gave you the god-given right to decide what we should take? Scratch a queen and you'll find an autocrat. But I love this warrior mode, being a pamphleteer and infuriating people. Just wait till they hear that I've been converted to saquinivir!

Wednesday, 9 October

Community nurse just been. Thinks I'll be OK. Lying here with feet swelled up like Henry VIII, propped up on a pair of telephone books. Last night I felt I was going to die. Breathless. Chronic anaemia. Cannot move from room to room without gasping for air. Going into hospice next Monday for two weeks of respite care and to give Tim a break. I tell him he seems to love me all the more now I'm such an invalid, to which he laughs and admits to a 'Mother Teresa complex'.

Getting morbid too. Dreading tonight. If same despair/horrible night might send my obit to Gary Dunne at the *SSO*. Have already thought of its wording. Important they write the truth about me …

Wednesday, 16 October

Finally I'm here. A patient in Ward 17 South, more fondly known as 'Seventh Heaven', the AIDS ward of St Vincent's Hospital. Have been in here since last Friday when the flat was unbearable, 33° with a hot westerly coming in the window. I told Tim I'd never make it through the weekend.

I lay in the back of an ambulance being driven along the sleaze strip of Darlinghurst Road, bumpers, bells and red lights flashing. And then clattering past the latte belt in Victoria Street, wearing an oxygen mask (like Dennis Hopper in *Blue Velvet*). At long last I was the star of Bar Coluzzi.

The doctor in casualty informed me I've got chronic anaemia, severe dehydration and that my haemoglobin levels were down in the sixties (normal 110). This was not promising, though it explained my breathlessness and fatigue over the last couple of months. The doctor would attempt to replenish my sagging system with four packs of blood, three bags of saline solution plus other IV blood supplements such as platelets and albumen.

On Monday a battery of tests were ordered including some in the nuclear medical wing of the hospital. I was trolleyed into a huge orange electronic donut and CAT scanned for half an hour, then fed into a machine like a ginormous jaffle iron which followed me around zapping me with gamma rays from four sides.

Today I was given a single room and wore a nice floral nightie for a visit from Clive and Penny along with nieces Tessa and Matilda. Such boisterous, loving company. Tessa brought me a pink quartz crystal for luck and Penny, a posy of flowering tea-tree from Portsea back beach, not far from Whimsy where I spent a most idyllic summer last year.

Thursday, 17 October

Have hit the diagnosis jackpot. The biopsies on my liver, spleen and kidneys have come back and the doctor tells me I have large cell lymphoma – a cancer of the lymphatic system which could well be widespread and requires immediate chemotherapy. The oedema is already putting enormous strain on my heart and lungs. My spleen is like a vast sponge soaking up all the platelets and albumen they give me. After fifteen drips over four days I look like the Michelin Man, wider than Christopher Pearson and Paddy McGuinness put together. My scrotum is swelled up like a grapefruit and my dick had almost disappeared until a nurse mentioned that terrifying word catheter.

Am inspired by the nurses here. Specialised knowledge and a no-bullshit attitude. Judeth Materna is my favourite. A fellow Sagittarian of divine eccentricity, I tag her Brünnhilde from Bundeena because of her blonde beehive and sheer strength in getting me in and out of the bathroom (I think I now weigh more than eighteen stone). Am lying here like a pasha and listening to Gershwin's *An American in Paris*. Second time today. First time I wept with Tim and he looked so surprised. 'You never cry,' he sniffed, which made us both cry all the more. But this afternoon I'm feeling a lot more optimistic. Due for a big whack of lovely morph! The doctor comes soon to take a bone marrow sample, sticking a corkscrew into my hip to see how advanced the lymphoma is. Could be worse. Neil Barlow told me how one of these St Vinnies doctors wanted to drill a hole in his boyfriend's head to put in more AZT. And they reckoned *he* had dementia!

Monday, 21 October

Chemo begins tomorrow. My body's in a much better state than they first thought. My mind is firing too, determined to make it through despite Dr Milliken's warning that even if successful this time, there's a strong possibility the lymphoma will come back in six to twelve months.

Reading old diaries and dictating stuff for Tim. Recalling the last time I saw Doone in Frankston Hospital. She looked shrivelled, white-haired and was in a wheelchair. She had broken her hip falling out of bed – probably an attempted molestation from one of the ambulatory loons on the ward. Straight out of *Marat/Sade*. I was scared of seeing her as the nurses called her Lorna. I heard her shouting from the TV room, really loudly, 'Get away, stop it. No, no!' Quite alarming.

I sat next to her for half an hour massaging her neck and holding her hand. I noted her large nose which she inherited from Brad, her fierce determination and will. I fed her bits of chocolate frog, like breastfeeding I thought, with her purring and mooing. She gave me a toothy smile through the drug fog. 'I like you,' she said and I shed some tears. After all the years of hostility I felt a loving regard for her.

Monday, 28 October

The goon squad have just gone. Fourteen doctors and cohorts in my room including the registrar, the anaesthetist, haematologist, director of nursing, palliative care supervisor and Sam Milliken, the warm and chubby HIV specialist who is looking exceptionally pleased. After weeks of murderous pain, their most touch-and-go patient might just survive. It seems my blood is beginning to knit again and the oedema is seeping away. YIPPEE! My appetite's coming back too – am I the only one who can eat the food in here? Janet and Graeme have promised to bring in salmon roe and more Dutch herrings tomorrow but I prefer the shepherd's pie on the menu. You can't take Balwyn out of the boy.

Tuesday, 29 October

Am the envy of the ward. This morning I met Princess Diana outside the gymnasium. She shook my hand, we had a chat and I produced a posy of white roses from the back of my wheelchair. I even called her 'Ma'am'. The tabloids are right, she does have star quality.

Thursday, 7 November

Tomorrow I move to the Sacred Heart Hospice. Nothing grim, just respite care. Feeling much stronger now. No need for a wheelchair or a walking frame. Can make it down the corridor holding onto Hanna's or Tim's arm. Maybe we'll get to Portsea after all. Been dreaming about the ocean off the back beach and those long green rollers that make the heart race. The vicious chill of the Antarctic, Joyce's scrotum-tightening sea.

Friday, 8 November

Clive told Tim he has checked with Rosebud Hospital and that they can continue my chemo down there. He also said 'there's nobody with HIV on the Mornington Peninsula'. What a laugh. No wonder they call it the insular peninsula.

Few straights can really handle AIDS. I remember the last time I saw Andrew Peacock in late '94 when I called in at his Melbourne offices. He almost jumped away at my confession. It was quite obvious this subject was not discussed by billionaires such as Sir James Goldsmith – the circles in which he was moving. He readjusted his seating and said comfortingly, 'Shirley has some friends who are d– I mean, suffering from AIDS.'

Wednesday, 13 November

The hospice is overrun with Irish nurses called Mary. They stuck me in a dank room with three old men dying from cancer. So much for respite care. After the third sleepless night listening to their cries of pain and getting cups of morphine, I had to almost wrestle with the nurse for a valium because 'it could become addictive' for me. I asked the biggest Mary, Mother Mary, if I could transfer to another ward.

'Another ward?' she barked. 'What sort of other ward?'

‘Well, one with younger people, or at least those with a chance of getting better,’ I said.

‘Impossible,’ she said. ‘You’re lucky to be in here at all.’

Friday, 15 November

Going home for the weekend. Doing good physio in the gym and walking around the hospice garden every day. A paradox in that across the road is ‘The Wall’ on Darlinghurst Road where many young hustlers caught the virus. Father James Murray turned up yesterday. Had been in hospital too. Charming. Affectionate. Even said favourable things about gay marriage. My outing him caused much pain but also liberating, I think.

Sunday, 24 November

Leg playing up and barely made it up the stairs of the Lizard Lounge for a book launch. David Marr came rushing over to me. Thinks he’s fallen in love with someone half his age and is worried about it. Bright and self-deprecating. Not like the High Anglican teacup queen I interviewed for *OutRage* (*Patrick White: A Life* had just been released). Have always regarded David as a literary talisman: he has many positives – his curiosity, enthusiasm and his mental amplitude – but I must admit by the mid-nineties he took his role of Paddy White's earthly survivor far too seriously and the finality of some of his ex-cathedra judgements on the arts were outrageous. Australian arts is a very small pond.

Today I'm fifty-seven. Got about a dozen birthday calls. They all think it's going to be my last. Rosemary Foot, Clive and Penny, even Joanna O'Rorke. Bits of my beard are falling over the keyboard because of the chemo.

Saturday, 30 November

There's a hard lump in my leg and the oedema is coming on again. It's disappointing. Still taking all the pills but I don't like going outside 'cos of two sticks. Is it going to be like this from now on?

Tuesday, 10 December

Back in Seventh Heaven. Sam comes in with a long face. Lymphoma is back and much more virulent than they first thought. Gives me a one-in-three chance of survival. Second-line chemo begins tomorrow, but good news too – have rediscovered Tessa's crystal last seen three weeks ago at the hospice. A lucky omen I hope.

Wednesday, 11 December

Tina the English nurse is clad in a space blanket, orange visor and heavy gloves as if entering a nuclear plant. She carries packs of carboplatin and methotrexate – a gorgeous colour like yellow chartreuse – to be fed through the IV drip. Getting some ms contin – slow-release morphine so I can stretch my legs again. To stop blood clotting I am wearing white nylon stockings like a CWA lady.

Thursday, 19 December

Third day at home. Oedema down again and tumour in my leg has disappeared. But blood sugar still high and need insulin three times a day. Other things worsening. Thrush, and bloody KS has come back between my toes, I have herpes on my dick and my arsehole. Am thin as tin and weak as a kitten.

Wednesday, 25 December

A week in hell. Another emergency last Friday in an

ambulance to casualty. Tim said it was a bloodhouse. Drunken yobs knocked down by cars and just one doctor, who claimed it was the chemo that was out of control, that they'd given me too much methotrexate and my white cells had been wiped out. Don't remember a thing but we were stuck down there till sunrise trying to locate a vein to get some blood and saline through. Mucositis not much better. I cannot speak and can barely swallow. Morphine ruins your appetite as it is. Have ordered a symbolic plum pudding with brandy sauce from the Xmas menu. At least I'm getting a cocaine mouthwash.

Thursday, 26 December

Last night I wanted to die. Had a total break of fear. Didn't sleep, just stared out the window and dwelt on lines from a sonnet by Gerard Manley Hopkins:

> *O the mind, mind has mountains; cliffs of fall*
> *Frightful, sheer, no-man fathomed. Hold them cheap*
> *May who ne'er hung there. Nor does long our small*
> *Durance deal with that steep or deep. Here! creep*
> *Wretch, under a comfort serves in a whirlwind: all*
> *Life death does end and each day dies with sleep.*

Saturday, 28 December

Yesterday the Blazey clan came up. My ready-made family. Jolyon is now twenty-four with blond hair flaring like a sheep, massive bull neck and cornflower blue eyes. His dilated pupils testify to another generation X-er who has been through drugs but mastered them and decided to opt for life and a career. He builds rammed earth houses yet relates to his several girlfriends on a non-macho basis. Such people are the hope of the world.

His youngest sister Matilda is eighteen and has a more sceptical, observant personality, a bit of a polymath and is certainly the academically gifted one. Between them is Tessa, the most artistic and rebellious of Clive's children. I have a special bond with her because of her lewd female sculptures which once outraged her parents, and because she is making a career as a clever designer. Last year she strolled through the Namibian desert in a kimono with her parasol held high, being photographed with the Kalahari bush people. Maybe she too has a screw loose.

Wednesday, 1 January 1997

Thank god it's over, the 'greatest fireworks display in Australia's history'. No way. I had a hit of morphine and tried to forget it. What a long night it was. The governance by hoopla is repulsive and it's gonna get worse.

Friday, 3 January

Proofing, fact checking, redrafting of the book continues. I elaborate, Tim condenses. We are such a complementary couple. A big goblin, he used to call me and even 'Mount fattie' (as Alice B. used to call Gertrude Stein), especially after the '94 Mardi Gras parade when I dressed as dirty Gertie in brown calico with a fox stole. Now I'm down to ten stone – I flinch when I see my face in the mirror. Tim gets cross because I'm not eating. I used to get such a thrill hearing the clacking wheels of the food trolley. Only four glasses of cranberry soda today. Have to hang onto my hope.

Tuesday, 7 January

In the long reaches of another sleepless night I realise the endlessness of time itself. There are always sounds: the rustling of nurses' uniforms, the banging of a window, the stabbing of torchlight as a nurse arrives with yet another urine bottle to be filled, the hiss of oxygen, an involuntary cry of pain . . .

Afternoon. From the room next door a dog growls and then starts barking. I said to Judeth, 'I didn't think pets were permitted.' Turns out to be the coughing of a human being. Judeth explains that after many tests they still don't know which one from the HIV chamber of horrors he's got. Toxoplasmosis, PCP, meningitis, MAC, cryptosporidium – they keep on testing me for all these things and the results always come back negative.

Thursday, 16 January

Another fiasco. A mistake to discharge me. They delivered an oxygen concentrator to the flat but after two days it was obvious I was dehydrating and anaemic. The lymphoma has returned.

Friday, 17 January

Now in Room 9. Should I believe Con's ghoulish claim that the worse you get the closer you get to the morgue lift at the end of the corridor? This is the last room on the way. Apparently Stuart Bennett died in here. Still, Christopher reckons the number nine has brilliant cosmic implications. They've stuck a food tube down my nose. Quite tasty. My situation in limbo. Basically it all gets down to a question of will.

Monday, 20 January

Ironic that I've now been left in the tender supervising care of Professor David Cooper, Australia's leading immunologist. The professor and I know each other from a unilateral spat in which I referred to him in disparaging terms because he continued to recommend high doses of AZT which had the effect of poisoning many healthy gay men. This morning he sat by my bed and we debated the pros and cons of early intervention. I told him that in AIDS politics unforgivable things are said by each side, though I still maintained my position. I was touched when he got up to leave and clasped my cannula-free hand in both of his.

Tuesday, 21 January

Tim cannot read the scrawl in my notebooks.

Dictating and even doing some taping of entries to finish the book. Lump in my leg so swollen candid Tina, the gun-moll nurse, says it might even burst.

Monday, 27 January

Terrific letter from Beatrice Faust. She says: 'Are you confident that morphine and cytotoxics is the best way for you? Is it time to make life easier for yourself? The way I see it, no one recovers from cytotoxics but they do sometimes recover holistically. If you don't take control, you will feel awfully depressed (I'm big into learned helplessness and the helplessness theory of depression just now). You might give up poisons, enjoy some good tucker and maybe live. Or you could give up everything and die quickly and peacefully. The blessing I would give you now is the strength to make your own decision.'

Tuesday, 28 January

Steroids have reduced the tumour and increased my appetite. Tim brought me egg roll sushi and my favourite, Japanese green tea ice-cream. Australia Day holiday yesterday and Tim, Alex and Victoria drove me down to La Perouse with a wheelchair in the back. Botany Bay so calm, briny and blue.

Wednesday, 29 January

Sam Milliken gloomy. Prognosis of only a few weeks. Any more chemo has a one per cent chance of success but more likely to make things worse. Antony turns up at the same time reeking of whisky, with tears welling up. 'Ah, come on Peter, you're a Blazey, you can't give up now. Take the chemo!' Such testosterone posturing, but later I was moved by his declaration to being a 'failed megalomaniac out to start again'.

Friday, 31 January

Suddenly realise that the primary quest posed in the first chapter has failed. I shall never again hear the thump, thump, thump of the breakers at night on the back beach.

Saturday, 1 February

Have made an outline of my obituary and given it to Ben Hills. I remember the obit in the *Australian* for Michael Dickinson which celebrated his talents as an urban architect but was sullied by its last line: 'Michael is survived by his parents and his sister.'

Who, I wondered, was the 'sister' – could it have been Pierre, perchance? Pierre who was with him day and night for the last eight years, the man who got Michael's career firing, who went into business with him, who was the love of his life and did not crack a mention. It made me so angry. I'm assured it won't happen to Tim.

Sunday, 2 February

I no longer fear death – as much – as is well known to AIDS sufferers. It is a fact of life with AIDS that every day is different, that one day you might be euphoric because the previous day you were in agony. The greatest lesson of nearly facing death is the humility it engenders and the suffering it entails.

In a sense, after the second dose of chemotherapy, there was a period of about four days when I felt I *was* dead. And now I have to deal with the long, long hours of sleeplessness, since steroids keep you awake. I stare at the wall and the two Buddhist mementos stuck on the window in a transfer that had been left by a young Thai called Si who died in this room last year. The transfixing of my eye upon the lotus just breaking through the still pond has me recalling my earliest and simplest lessons about Buddhism, that human desire is infinite and doomed to constant disappointment; Buddhism, alone of all religions, acknowledges there can be no appointment, so there is only disappointment.

Monday, 3 February

Sam says at the end I'll probably drift into a coma. It might take days or weeks. Maybe I can get a hit of something. Be like David Hegelton, who as a naturopathic healer and a good Buddhist, went out on a full moon.

At 11.00 pm he asked his lover Chris to come over to his flat. He'd secured some morphine from somewhere and they lay on the bed in each other's arms talking a load of old rubbish all night. At one stage, Chris asked David if he'd like some tap water. My God, unfiltered water, I might die! They laughed like banshees.

He had twenty-five capsules of Normison but before he swallowed them, Chris went to the freezer and got out a Magnum ice-cream, one of David's rare indulgences in junk food. He fell asleep, Chris arranging his body in such a way that he could feel

David's expirations on the back of his neck. He felt the movement of his breath slowly subsiding and in an hour or more he sensed David shiver and cease breathing, his face waxy, smooth, composed, beautiful. Chris said he looked so rested and later Kate his sister said he looked so dead.

What is it like to cross over? I like to imagine floating up into a blue labyrinth like Buddha in his realm of joy. A surge of love pouring onto everything like the sun's rays. Once you decide you are going to go then everything is easy.

EPILOGUE

Sunrise on the first day of Chinese New Year. I hadn't heard a kookaburra outside my window for months. Such raucous rolling bursts of laughter. My mother believes that birds carry the spirits of the dead. Even before the telephone rang I sensed that Peter had died.

Less than twelve hours earlier, on the Thursday evening, Clive had come up from Melbourne. 'There's not much time,' I'd told him over the phone, despite my own inklings that Peter would make it through another week and upset the doctors' predictions yet again.

Clive slept beside his brother on a fold-up bed, the nurse waking him at six to feel Peter's pulse fading out. Clive was perturbed that he'd been there rather than me, but I didn't mention the laughing jackass, nor did he reveal until later that he was on the receiving end of Peter's last words: 'Bugger off,' said big brother as Clive stood dutifully behind the rail of the bed.

Peter had kept his larrikin spirit to the end. Aside from a few morphine hazes in the last weeks nearly everyone who saw him was amazed that he had lost none of his chiacking and bluster or impish sense of fun. His mental brilliance was still apparent as well, and miraculously it seemed to grow strong as his body grew weak. Despite the agony of seeing his grand figure of flesh now a sag of grey skin and Belsen bones, there was a quality of calm and radiance about him also.

On the Friday morning when I pressed his hand to mine and kissed his cold lips, he looked peaceful, almost beatific with El Greco eyes cast up to the ceiling (the nurse had tried and failed to close them) and his still-supple hands unclenched, no pain, no fight, like a sadhu who had accepted that his time had come.

I could be guilty of finding too much meaning in the death of a loved one. Yearning for dramatic signifiers, synchronicities and such. But Peter so adored the limelight that it seems only natural that his death might come across as slightly overblown.

Yet he called himself a Buddhist and quite clearly finetuned the moment. The process of dying as important as completing the book of his life. His spiritual dimension surprised many people. I wonder if he became an ardent practitioner upon wearing a sandalwood bead bracelet that had been blessed by a monk in Bangkok and which his nephew Jolyon had sent him in December. Then again, Peter was too sceptical and irreverent to be a complete convert to anything. He was interested in Taoism, Hinduism and even Jesus Christ, whom he regarded as a fabulous gay flower child who despised authority.

On Thursday afternoon I realised we had done as much of his autobiography as was practicable and that he could no longer manage his daily diary. There were books scattered on the dresser which he asked me to read him excerpts from: Sylvia Plath's *Ariel*, Cyril Connolly's *The Unquiet Grave*, *The Tibetan Book of Living and Dying*, poems of Gerard Manley Hopkins. In retrospect it's clear he was preparing himself for death. Last rites – though never too earnest. When he asked for some music, he bypassed Hildegard of Bingen for the Ronettes' 'And Then He Kissed Me'. And I did.

In the morning Clive pronounced that 'the Blazeys are not a sentimental family'. All I could suggest was that a loving brother had a right to grieve. But as I sat there, stroking the tufts of new hair grown back after the chemo was abandoned, I understood we were both coming to terms with our sense of loss.

A social worker dropped by. Platitudes abounded. Then came Hanna, the physio who adored him. She was crying, but gave me a sustained and muscular hug. 'He was such a divine man,' she said, which was all the comfort I needed.

Of course a death can make people insensitive too. A man from Peter's past turned up, 'Blaze's best mate', the fellow liked to boast, though Peter had let the friendship drift. He rushed to blu-tack Auden's solemn 'Funeral Blues' onto the bedhead and later wrote a newspaper obituary claiming that Peter was born heterosexual and later 'converted' to homosexuality. An unexpected gloss on a man who had deviated for more than thirty years: 'I send blessings and love to every truly out gay man and lesbian in Australia', Peter wrote in his virtual swansong column for *OutRage*.

Peter experienced great joy in sexual love, though he knew the risks involved, once remarking on the 'blowtorch of love and lust'. A man in his fifties with an adolescent's sex drive, even in his last months he never lost his sensual cupidity: 'I'm going to miss sex when I'm gone' he wrote in a diary after coming home for a weekend in November.

Peter believed in passion as well as a soul. He cared little about the empty shell left behind and was indifferent to a funeral service. Some people were unhappy at this. I heard that many an old lover had almost booked their place in the front pew. And so we had wakes. A flashy, exuberant one on a humid St Valentine's Day in Sydney, and another one two days later for Peter's Melbourne friends in the gardens of Heronswood. The Sydney wake was at a gallery exhibiting photographs from William Yang's book *Friends of Dorothy.* Peter had been despondent when his illness prevented him from making it to the opening a week before. With several shots of Peter already on the wall it was an apposite choice for remembering and celebrating his life.

Mother Abyss, from the Order of Perpetual Indulgence, was the MC. Peter's ashes were placed in an old meat safe which rested on a plinth. This meat safe had been found at Kooka Lodge and was much treasured by Peter. There were a couple of hundred people and speeches from Penny and Clive, Richard Ackland and Anne Summers. Instead of a minute's silence we played 'Oh Lawd, I'm On My Way', from Gershwin's *Porgy and Bess*, which Peter used to refer to as the 'greatest opera of the century'.

Jolyon read the faxes, beginning with one from Andrew Peacock – 'He is with me in Washington' – and another from Barry Sloane in LA, who claimed that Peter not only protected him from Scotch College bullies, but that 'his love for posing as the bad boy obscured the fact that he was really a good person and a very loving friend'.

At the wake in Melbourne, some friends read poetry, including Irving Reid who had written an 'Ode to Peter': 'To the unfettered fashioner of phrase, the uncontainable, unpredictable most lovable – Blaze'. Meanwhile Beatrice Faust surprised everyone with her view that Doone had always been tolerant of her son's sexual orientation. Peter's oldest friend Christopher compared the speeches made to the film *Rashomon*, where everyone's account was a distinctly subjective reality.

Yet Peter was a mythmaker too. He often turned personal history into anecdotes to minimise emotional pain. At other times he preferred to focus on the torments of others. In one of his diaries he recalled being persecuted when he was a nine-year-old schoolboy. Peter had worn calipers and suffered from polio. I wondered how he could dwell on having AIDS and never touch on this?

Peter could be as contradictory as he was complex, but when it came to burial he asked for something simple. We scattered his ashes at Heronswood beneath a Deodar or Himalayan cedar. I knew it was the right place for him when Penny told me that high up in its magnificent branches the local kookas gather in the late afternoon and laugh absurdly at the setting sun.

Tim Herbert, 1997

INDEX

www.ingramcontent.com/pod-product-compliance
Lightning Source LLC
LaVergne TN
LVHW041051080826
845145LV00007B/1538

* 9 7 8 0 9 8 7 6 1 9 1 0 5 *